P9-BYH-449

This Book Comes With Lots of
FREE Online Resources

Nolo's award-winning website has a page dedicated just to this book. Here you can:

KEEP UP TO DATE. When there are important changes to the information in this book, we'll post updates.

GET DISCOUNTS ON NOLO PRODUCTS. Get discounts on hundreds of books, forms, and software.

READ BLOGS. Get the latest info from Nolo authors' blogs.

LISTEN TO PODCASTS. Listen to authors discuss timely issues on topics that interest you.

WATCH VIDEOS. Get a quick introduction to a legal topic with our short videos.

And that's not all.
Nolo.com contains thousands of articles on everyday legal and business issues, plus a plain-English law dictionary, all written by Nolo experts and available for free. You'll also find more useful **books, software, online apps, downloadable forms,** plus a **lawyer directory.**

With
**Downloadable
FORMS**

 NOLO
LAW for ALL
Get forms and more at
www.nolo.com/back-of-book/LTK.html

⚖ NOLO   # The Trusted Name
(but don't take our word for it)

"In Nolo you can trust."
THE NEW YORK TIMES

"Nolo is always there in a jam as the nation's premier publisher of do-it-yourself legal books."
NEWSWEEK

"Nolo publications…guide people simply through the how, when, where and why of the law."
THE WASHINGTON POST

"[Nolo's]…material is developed by experienced attorneys who have a knack for making complicated material accessible."
LIBRARY JOURNAL

"When it comes to self-help legal stuff, nobody does a better job than Nolo…"
USA TODAY

"The most prominent U.S. publisher of self-help legal aids."
TIME MAGAZINE

"Nolo is a pioneer in both consumer and business self-help books and software."
LOS ANGELES TIMES

16th Edition

Living Together

A Legal Guide for Unmarried Couples

Attorneys Frederick Hertz and Lina Guillen

Sixteenth Edition	JULY 2017
Editor	LINA GUILLEN
Cover Design	SUSAN PUTNEY
Book Design	TERRI HEARSH
Proofreader	ROBERT WELLS
Index	ACCESS POINTS INDEXING
Printing	BANG PRINTING

Names: Hertz, Frederick, author. | Guillen, Lina, author.
Title: Living together : a legal guide for unmarried couples / Attorneys
    Frederick Hertz and Lina Guillen.
Description: 16th Edition | Berkeley, CA : Nolo, 2017. | Includes index.
Identifiers: LCCN 2017001960 (print) | LCCN 2017002182 (ebook) | ISBN
    9781413323795 (paperbook) | ISBN 9781413323801 (ebook)
Subjects: LCSH: Unmarried couples--Legal status, laws, etc.--United States. |
    Unmarried couples--Legal status, laws, etc.--United States--Forms.
Classification: LCC KF538 .I35 2017 (print) | LCC KF538 (ebook) | DDC
    346.7301/671--dc23
LC record available at https://lccn.loc.gov/2017001960

This book covers only United States law, unless it specifically states otherwise.

Copyright © 1978, 1979, 1984, 1988, 1990, 1994, 1997, 1999, 2000, 2001, 2004, 2006, 2008, 2013, and 2017. All rights reserved. The NOLO trademark is registered in the U.S. Patent and Trademark Office. Printed in the U.S.A.

No part of this publication may be reproduced, stored in a retrieval system, or transmitted in any form or by any means, electronic, mechanical, photocopying, recording, or otherwise without prior written permission. Reproduction prohibitions do not apply to the forms contained in this product when reproduced for personal use. For information on bulk purchases or corporate premium sales, please contact the Special Sales Department. Call 800-955-4775 or write to Nolo, 950 Parker Street, Berkeley, California 94710.

Please note

We believe accurate, plain-English legal information should help you solve many of your own legal problems. But this text is not a substitute for personalized advice from a knowledgeable lawyer. If you want the help of a trained professional—and we'll always point out situations in which we think that's a good idea—consult an attorney licensed to practice in your state.

Acknowledgments

Past editions of *Living Together* have benefited from the extraordinary legal research help of Ella Hirst and Alayna Schroeder and the exceptional editing and creative input of Marcia Stewart and Kathleen Michon. Thanks, too, to Amy Ihara for her hard work and creative contributions during the manuscript preparation stage.

About the Authors

Lina Guillen is a Nolo editor and trial attorney, with over 15 years of experience in family law and civil litigation. Lina edits Nolo's family law books and has written numerous articles on the financial aspects of divorce. In addition to being the coauthor of *Neighbor Law* and *Divorce & Money*, Lina has been quoted in several publications, including CNBC.com, *U.S. News*, *Real Simple* Magazine, and *How Stuff Works*.

Frederick Hertz is a practicing attorney and mediator and the author of *Legal Affairs: Essential Advice for Same-Sex Couples* (Owl Books) and coauthor of Nolo's *A Legal Guide for Lesbian & Gay Couples* and *Making It Legal: A Guide to Same-Sex Marriage, Domestic Partnerships and Civil Unions*. He lives in the San Francisco Bay Area.

Table of Contents

1 **Living Together:**
The Legal Companion for Unmarried Couples...................................1

2 **The Legal State of Living Together**...................................7

Sex and the Law...................................8

Domestic Partners...................................10

Common Law Marriage...................................13

Living Together Contracts...................................17

Why You Need to Put Your Living Together Agreement in Writing...................................25

What Happens to Your Written Living Together Agreement
If You Get Married?...................................28

Special Issues for Seniors...................................32

3 **Living Together Agreements: Why and How They Work**...................................35

Ten Tips for Writing a Living Together Agreement...................................39

Property Agreements...................................43

Agreement to Share Ownership of a Joint Purchase...................................57

Agreement Covering Joint Projects...................................65

Agreement Covering Homemaker Services...................................67

Agreement for Artists, Writers, and Inventors...................................71

Agreement for People in School...................................75

Agreement to Protect Person Who Moves a Long Distance
or Gives Up a Job...................................79

4 Debt, Credit, Taxes, and More: Practical Aspects of Living Together..81

Debt and Credit 83

How (and Why) to Check Your Credit Report 86

Buying and Investing Together 90

Discrimination 92

Sharing Your Last Name 97

Income Taxes 99

Social Security 103

Retirement Plans 105

Public Benefits 108

Insurance 109

Liability for Medical Care of a Partner 114

Making Medical and Financial Decisions for Your Partner 114

Wrongful Death and Loss of Consortium Lawsuits 119

5 Renting and Sharing a Home 121

Discrimination on the Basis of Marital Status 122

Leases and Rental Agreements 125

Moving In Together 126

Dealing With Objections When Moving Into the Rental Home
of One Partner 132

Getting Your Security Deposit Back 138

6 Buying a House Together 141

May Sellers Discriminate Against Unmarried Buyers? 144

How to Find and Work With a Real Estate Agent 145

Househunting Online 148

Home Financing and Mortgages 148

Proceeding With Your Purchase: Offers, Inspections, Escrow, and Closing 158

Taking Title to Your New Home 161

Contracts for Couples Owning a Home Together 170

Contracts for Equal Ownership of a House 172

Contract for Unequal Ownership of a House 187

Agreement for One Person to Move Into the Other's House
    and Become an Immediate Co-Owner 192

Agreement for One Person to Move Into the Other's House
    and Become a Co-Owner Gradually 199

7 Starting a Family 205

Having a Child: Legal Obligations of Unmarried Parents 206

Naming the Baby and Getting a Birth Certificate 207

Naming the Father: Paternity 208

Legitimacy of Children Born to Unmarried Parents 212

Adopting a Child 217

Public and Private Benefits for a Child of Unmarried Parents 221

Inheritance Rights of a Child of Unmarried Parents 222

8 You and Your Ex-Spouse and Children From a Prior Relationship 223

Getting a Divorce While Living With Someone Else 225

Living Together and Impact on Custody of Children From
    a Prior Marriage 231

Visitation With Children From a Prior Marriage 238

Child Support for Children From a Prior Marriage 239

The Effect of Living Together on Alimony and Child Support From
    a Prior Marriage 241

9   Wills and Estate Planning 245

What Happens If You Don't Do Any Estate Planning? 246

Typical Estate Plans 247

Figuring Out What You Own: Taking Inventory 249

An Introduction to Wills 252

Avoiding Probate 258

Estate and Gift Taxes 264

Balancing the Needs of Your Partner and Your Children 268

Funerals and Other Final Arrangements 272

10   Moving On—When Unmarried Couples Separate 275

Rules of the Unmarried Dissolution 278

The Process of Separation 280

Ten Steps to Resolving Your Conflicts 289

Mediation, Arbitration, and Other Ways to Resolve Disputes 293

Lawyers and Lawsuits: Going to Court 301

Solutions for Typical Property Division Problems 303

Tenants: Who Gets the Rental? 304

Homeowners: Dividing the House 305

Putting It All Together: Preparing a Settlement Agreement 316

Children: Custody, Visitation, and Support 316

11   Lawyers and Legal Research 329

When to Hire a Lawyer 331

How to Find a Good Lawyer 332

Appendix

How to Use the Downloadable Forms on the Nolo Website.... 339

Editing RTFs.. 340

List of Forms Available on the Nolo Website... 341

Index... 343

Living Together: The Legal Companion for Unmarried Couples

Living together has never been more popular. According to the 2016 Census data, over 8.07 million unmarried couples live together (which translates into roughly 16 million people). This is a 20% increase over the 2007 figures (6.4 million couples) and a 52% increase over the 2000 figures (3.8 million couples). Today, more than 62% of unmarried households have children.

Cohabitors also are an older crowd now, and the number of cohabiting seniors tripled since 1990 and is continuing to rise. The average American spends the majority of his or her life unmarried.

If you are part of an unmarried couple living together, it's probably comforting to know that you are far from alone. However, this doesn't mean that you can ignore how the law affects your relationship, especially if you are buying a house together.

This book will help. It explains the wide range of legal and practical rules that affect opposite-sex unmarried couples living together—from sharing money and property (contract law) to owning a house together (real estate law) or sharing an apartment (landlord-tenant law) to having a child with your partner (family law) to writing a will (estate planning).

RESOURCE

Same-sex couples. If you are part of a gay or lesbian couple living together, see the Nolo books *A Legal Guide for Lesbian & Gay Couples* and *Making It Legal: A Guide to Same-Sex Marriage, Domestic Partnerships and Civil Unions*, both by Frederick Hertz and Emily Doskow, available at www.nolo.com.

Legal rules that affect unmarried couples living together. When you understand the law, you and your partner can make informed decisions about how to structure your life, finances, property ownership, and family relationships to best meet your needs. Failing to learn about the law and take measures to protect yourself and your partner can have negative consequences. The special rules governing married couples (such as those relating to property ownership, divorce, and inheritance rights, to name a few) don't apply to unmarried couples. In order to compensate for this, you'll have to do some extra work. For example, you may want to write a will to ensure that your partner gets your property when you die, sign paternity statements to ensure that a father's parental rights are preserved, or create a "living together contract" to avoid protracted court battles over property if you split up. These burdens apply to couples who are cohabiting as a prelude to marriage, as well as to those who view their arrangement as a long-term alternative to marriage.

Important legal agreements and forms. To help you, we provide over a dozen written documents that unmarried couples can use to spell out their individual legal and financial arrangements, and detailed discussions of relevant legal forms, including:

- living together contracts regarding your money and property—whether you want to keep everything separate, pool all assets, or something in between (such as share ownership of a car)
- house ownership agreements—whether you're sharing costs and ownership equally or not
- basic wills and estate planning forms
- parenting agreements, paternity statements, and other documents relating to children you have together (or bring into your relationship from a previous marriage), and
- property settlement agreements for use in the event you separate.

Each form is easy to customize and has complete instructions, and there are filled-in samples in the text. You'll find downloadable copies of the forms on the companion page for this book on the Nolo website (see below for details).

What's in a Name?

One of the common issues faced by unmarried couples is how to introduce each other in a way that reflects the importance of your relationship—boyfriend/girlfriend, special friend, significant other, lover, or even POSSLQ (Person of the Opposite Sex Sharing Living Quarters, an earlier Census Bureau phrase for heterosexual couples who live together without getting married)—the choice is yours. Because "partner" is one of the most commonly used and neutral terms, we use it throughout this book to refer to one member of an unmarried couple.

We believe that most unmarried couples can safely and easily master the majority of legal rules that affect them. However, it's also true that an experienced lawyer's advice can be invaluable when it comes to dealing with more complicated situations. We'll point out how and when a lawyer's expertise can be helpful—for example, if one of you has children or substantial assets, or you're dealing with complicated estate planning.

Why live together and not get married? There are many reasons why people choose to live together without getting married. Some don't see the need for the state's approval of their commitment to each other. Many couples view it as a trial period before marriage. Some avoid marriage because they have gone through a messy divorce. Many people, especially in expensive urban areas with high unemployment rates, often live with partners in order to reduce housing costs.

Special concerns of seniors. The fast-increasing number of unmarried couples over age 45 that live together—over one-fifth of all unmarried couples fall into this category—often have financial and family concerns that come into play. For example, by not marrying they don't become legally obligated for their partner's medical treatment, and they reduce the risk of paying tax on Social Security benefits. And by not marrying, many avoid tricky inheritance issues if one or both partners have adult children from a previous marriage or own substantial assets.

One of the most common reasons older couples choose to live together instead of marrying is to avoid joint liability for debts, especially for long-term care or medical bills. Staying unmarried also enables each partner to qualify individually for public benefits, such as Medicaid, without draining the other partner's resources. There are detailed rules about how this must be structured to avoid inadvertent triggering of joint liability, so if you are considering such a strategy, consult with an attorney specializing in elder law before you make any big decisions.

And for some folks, staying unmarried allows them to live together without making a major legal or social commitment, which is psychologically preferable for one or both partners. As has been well documented, getting married doesn't mean the relationship will last forever, but that's how it feels to many partners—and it's a feeling that they don't feel entirely comfortable about. Older partners may be concerned about the reactions of their friends and children, and they may prefer to cohabit informally rather than suggest to anyone that their new relationship is as important as their former marriage was. And, not surprisingly, the reasons folks give for staying unmarried aren't often the full story.

Whatever your reasons for not marrying, this book arms you with information to tackle most of the legal issues that arise during unmarried partnerships, including managing your financial affairs better, protecting your assets, buying a house or other property together, having or coparenting children and addressing the concerns of your adult children, planning for your death, and dealing with a breakup.

RESOURCE
Check out the Alternatives to Marriage Project. This national organization provides resources, support, and advocacy for unmarried people living together. For more information, see the ATMP website at www.unmarried.org.

Get Updates, Forms, and More at This Book's Companion Page on Nolo.com

You can download any of the forms and agreements in this book at

www.nolo.com/back-of-book/LTK.html

When there are important changes to the information in this book, we'll post updates on this same dedicated page (what we call the book's companion page). You'll find other useful information on this page, too, such as author blogs, podcasts, and videos. See the appendix for a list of forms available on Nolo.com.

The Legal State of Living Together

Sex and the Law 8

Domestic Partners 10

   Statewide Domestic Partnership and Civil Union Programs 10

   What Are the Potential Secondary Legal Implications of Registering
     as Domestic Partners? 13

Common Law Marriage 13

   How to Tell Whether You Have a Common Law Marriage 14

   What If You Don't Wish to Have a Common Law Marriage 17

Living Together Contracts 17

   Living Together Contracts—What They Are and Why Unmarried
     Couples Need One 17

   The Law and Living Together Contracts 20

   Some General Legal Rules Regarding Living Together Contracts 22

Why You Need to Put Your Living Together Agreement in Writing 25

What Happens to Your Written Living Together Agreement If You
  Get Married? 28

   What's the Relationship Between a Living Together Contract and
     a Premarital Agreement? 29

   How to Convert a Living Together Contract Into a Premarital
     Agreement 31

Special Issues for Seniors 32

FORMS IN THIS CHAPTER

Chapter 2 includes instructions for and a sample of the Agreement of Joint Intent Not to Have a Common Law Marriage form. The Nolo website includes a downloadable copy of this form. See the appendix for the link to the forms in this book.

This chapter provides an overview of the key legal issues affecting unmarried couples—from the laws of living together (cohabiting) to making property and other financial agreements. This chapter also explains the rules regarding common law marriages and domestic partnerships.

Sex and the Law

The first edition of this book (published in 1974) devoted ten pages to a survey of each state's laws criminalizing adultery, fornication, and cohabitation. Many of these laws went off the books in the 1970s, but the United States Supreme Court finally entered the modern era in 2003. In *Lawrence v. Texas*, 123 S.Ct. 2472 (2003), the court struck down a Texas law prohibiting "deviate sexual intercourse" (in this case, sodomy) between two persons of the same sex. In that ruling, the Supreme Court overruled its own opinion in *Bowers v. Hardwick*, 486 U.S. 186 (1986), which had upheld a similar law in Georgia. The Supreme Court held that the Due Process Clause of the Fourteenth Amendment protects the decisions of individuals about intimate physical relationships from intrusion by the state, and that the protection extends to unmarried as well as married persons.

The legal effect of *Lawrence v. Texas* was to render all sodomy laws unconstitutional, including those directed at heterosexual couples. Of course, the laws of some of the states that continue to prohibit sodomy will stay on the books as a technical matter until they are challenged in court or repealed by the legislature. But if you live in one of those states and are ever prosecuted for sodomy or nonmarital sex (fornication), however, you should be able to get your case dismissed simply by raising a challenge under *Lawrence*.

Although it does not address such laws directly, *Lawrence* also implicitly invalidates all restrictions on consensual adult sexual activity, such as laws prohibiting cohabitation and fornication. (See "Historical Definitions of Prohibited Sex Acts," below.) If you and your partner are over 18 and neither of you is married to someone else, you can consider yourself fairly safe from criminal prosecution for your private, consensual sexual activity, even if your state still has laws on the books relating to cohabitation and fornication.

Adultery, however, is still illegal in many states, though such laws are rarely enforced. While it's unlikely that any of these laws will ever be enforced, they may not be invalidated by the *Lawrence v. Texas* decision, because of the special public policies involved in those laws (for example, support of marriage and protection of children). Adultery laws may still find their way into divorce, alimony, and custody proceedings, or in some rare instances, they may be invoked in cases involving property disputes. (See Chapter 8 for more on these issues.)

Historical Definitions of Prohibited Sex Acts

Fornication: Voluntary sexual intercourse between unmarried people of the opposite sex. If one of the partners is still married, this is generally considered to be adultery, not fornication. In many states, adultery is technically a crime, but rarely is anyone prosecuted for it.

Cohabitation: Two people living together in an intimate sexual relationship, without being married. Some courts, especially those in states where fornication was considered illegal, described a cohabitation relationship as meretricious, meaning "of an unlawful sexual nature."

Sodomy: Generally refers to oral or anal sex. Many states call it an unnatural act or a "crime against nature." Some states prohibit all sodomy, while others prohibit only specific acts.

RESOURCE

The National Gay and Lesbian Task Force (NGLTF) keeps track of sex laws affecting both heterosexuals and homosexuals. For more information, check their website at www.ngltf.org. The American Civil Liberties Union also monitors sex laws. For information, see www.aclu.org.

CAUTION

Speaking of sex—don't. It is critical that you omit any references to a sexual relationship or obligations for sexual conduct in any living together contract you write. If you do, and your contract is reviewed by an ultraconservative judge in a separate dispute or is entered into in one of the conservative states, the whole contract may be thrown out. (Chapter 3 discusses this issue in more detail.)

Domestic Partners

The term "domestic partnership" has come to mean a lot of different things, depending on the circumstances. In its most general sense, the phrase refers to two people who live together in a committed relationship intending to be emotionally and financially responsible for each other. But the legal meaning of the phrase can vary widely, with significantly different legal consequences.

Statewide Domestic Partnership and Civil Union Programs

Over the course of the past 20 years, mostly in response to demands for legalizing marriage (or marriage-equivalent rights) for lesbian and gay couples, several states have implemented domestic partnership statutes (called civil unions in some states) that extend all the state-imposed rights and duties of marriage to state-registered couples. It's a confusing situation, since many of these states use the same term (domestic partnership) that is popularly used for informal cohabitation and also is used for city or county, or even employer-based registration. Now that same-sex couples can legally marry in every state in the union, there isn't such a great need for the domestic partnership option, but several states still offer registration as an option.

Further complicating the situation, most of the states that offer domestic partnership or civil union registration limit their registration program to same-sex couples, since the gay community was pressing for these rights. Others extend benefits to any and all opposite-sex couples, and still others limit opposite-sex registration to couples where one partner is older than 62—in an effort to give benefits to older straight folks who prefer not to be legally married, or who might lose Social Security survivor benefits if they remarried.

At the moment, opposite-sex couples of any age in the District of Columbia, Hawaii, Illinois, and Nevada can register as domestic partners or civil union partners, and couples with one partner older than 62 can register in California, New Jersey, and Washington State. Because these registration programs extend all the state marital laws to registrants, we call those registrations "marriage equivalent." But you should check with local authorities, or do some updated legal research if you live in any of these states, as these laws are changing regularly, now that the marriage door has opened up for same-sex couples.

We expect that most of these marriage-equivalent registrations will be phased out over time, and of particular relevance to most couples, most employers are terminating their domestic partnership benefits programs now that same-sex couples can legally marry.

If you have state-registered in a marriage-equivalent registration (that is, in the District of Columbia or in one of the six states listed above), and you are living in a "recognition" state (that is, one of these states, or in a state that recognizes the marriage-equivalent registrations of another state), you will be treated just as if you were legally married under state law—and so the state-law rules laid out in this book won't apply to you for the most part. Instead, the marital rules of shared property, joint liability for debts, and financial obligations upon dissolution will apply, as will the requirement of getting a judicial divorce if you break up. However, if you relocate to another state that doesn't recognize your registration, or if you are looking for federally granted benefits (such as tax privileges, immigration rights, or Social Security benefits), the nonmarital rules as explained in this book still apply to you.

But you need to be careful: from time to time some states (most recently Pennsylvania) have ruled that a marriage-equivalent partnership should be treated as a marriage, thus subjecting the partners to all the marital law obligations.

We wish these rules weren't so complicated, but unfortunately we only are able to explain the law to you—we aren't able to rewrite the rules to make them simpler! If you find yourself having registered in a marriage-equivalent registration but are living in another state, you probably should consult with a local family law attorney to learn how the law in your home state handles this situation.

City, County, State Employee Programs

A number of cities and counties allow unmarried couples to register as domestic partners and many of these jurisdictions offer domestic partnership benefits for employees. Some only allow same-sex couples to register (because they can't marry in most states), whereas others allow any unmarried couple to sign up. Colleges and universities, plus some states, also provide domestic partner benefits to employees. And many private employers, including the majority of Fortune 500 companies, provide benefits to unmarried partners of employees. The Alternatives to Marriage Project website (at www.unmarried.org) has links to information regarding domestic partner benefits, including a guide to persuading your employer to offer domestic partner benefits. The benefits provided vary, but commonly include:

- health, dental, and vision insurance
- sick and bereavement leave
- accident and life insurance
- death benefits
- parental leave (for a child you coparent)
- housing rights and tuition reduction (at universities), and
- use of recreational facilities.

The complete list of potential benefits is extensive; the typical benefits offered, however, are not. In some cases, all that a company or city offers is bereavement or sick leave. In other situations, the benefits offered are extensive—and expensive. Often, either the employee foots the bill for his or her partner, or the company pays (if it also pays for spouses). However, regardless of who pays, the employee must pay taxes on the benefits. The IRS considers benefits awarded to an unmarried partner as taxable compensation.

Here are the questions you need to ask to see how and if domestic partner benefits apply to you:

- Who qualifies as a domestic partner—are heterosexual couples covered or only same-sex couples?
- How will an employer identify your domestic partner—by registration with a local registry (a public record of domestic partners)? Some companies may require you to have registered a domestic partnership before extending company health benefits to your partner. This is usually to ensure that mere "roommates" aren't taking advantage of the system.
- Must you and your partner be together for a minimum number of years?
- Must you live together and share expenses?
- Must you be financially responsible for each other? (Usually, you must live together in an exclusive relationship and share basic living expenses, such as food and shelter, with your partner.)

CAUTION

Now that legal marriage is available for same-sex couples, an increasing number of employers are phasing out their domestic partnership benefits programs. If you work for an employer that currently offers domestic partnership benefits, you should pay close attention to possible changes in the program. If your employer shuts down the domestic partnership program, you will have to decide whether to legally marry or lose your partner benefits.

What Are the Potential Secondary Legal Implications of Registering as Domestic Partners?

Depending on where you live, by registering as domestic partners or civil union partners, you and your partner may have created an implied contract for other purposes, such as sharing income and property. This is because the wording of most registrations includes a provision that each partner is going to take care of the other's basic needs and share financial obligations. While we haven't seen a lot of court cases in this area, this could come up if either partner dies without an estate plan and the surviving partner claims to own a part of the decedent's property based on an oral or implied contract. It can also arise in a dispute during a breakup.

If you are in a domestic partnership that contains such a provision, you should make a written property ownership contract clarifying your legal obligation, such as one of those included in Chapter 3. This is especially important if you do not wish to share savings, property, or income beyond your day-to-day expenses. A court might otherwise treat the fact that you registered as domestic partners as an indication that you had agreed to share ownership of your property.

Common Law Marriage

Marriage is the legal union of two people. Once they become married to each other, their responsibilities and rights toward one another concerning property and support are defined by the laws of the state in which they live. While a married couple may be able to use a written contract to modify some of the rules set up by their state, they can end their marriage only by a court granting a divorce or an annulment.

Many people believe that if you live with a person for a long time you're automatically married—that you have what is called a common law marriage—with the same rights and responsibilities of a couple that has been legally married. Many states enacted such laws in the 19th century when life on the frontier was rather informal, and legal technicalities were often ignored. In most states, this is no longer true. In these states, marriage requires a license and ceremony. Ten states, however, still recognize common law marriage. (See "States Recognizing Common Law Marriage," below.) But even living together in one of these states doesn't mean you are married. Your relationship will not be recognized as a common law marriage unless you intended to be married and "held yourselves out" to the world as married.

How to Tell Whether You Have a Common Law Marriage

There are no absolute rules, minimum years, or guidelines here; whether or not a common law marriage exists depends on the facts of each situation. However, a common law marriage can occur only when all of the following are true:

- You are a couple that lives together in a state that recognizes common law marriages. Now that same-sex couples can legally marry anywhere in the U.S., they can also enter into a common law marriage in those states that still recognize them
- You have lived together for a significant amount of time (not defined in any state). Despite much belief to the contrary, the length of time you live together does not by itself determine whether a common law marriage exists. No state law or court decision says seven years or ten years of cohabitation is all that's needed for a common law marriage. It's only one factor the court may consider.
- You hold yourselves out to the community (your neighbors, friends, and coworkers) as a married couple—typically, this means using the same last name, referring to the other as "my husband" or "my wife," and filing a joint tax return even if it is not legally authorized. The courts in states which recognize common law marriages have

been struggling in the past few years on how to apply these rules to same-sex couples, who previously weren't allowed to marry. (For more on the subject of names, see Chapter 4.)

Courts most often apply the rules of common law marriage in situations where one partner dies without a will and the other claims there was a common law marriage so as to inherit property under intestate succession laws. These intestacy laws automatically give a share of property to a spouse, but generally don't recognize an unmarried partner as an heir. (Chapter 9 provides an overview of intestate succession laws.)

If your state recognizes common law marriages and your relationship meets the requirements, you may need to end your relationship by divorcing if there are disputes between the two of you, just as you would if you had gotten married with a license and ceremony. And, one partner might be able to make a financial claim against his or her common law "spouse."

States Recognizing Common Law Marriage

Common law marriage is recognized only in the states listed below. If you live in any of these states and want to know the status of your relationship, you will need to read your state's law. Chapter 11 provides advice on doing legal research.

Alabama	Kansas	South Carolina
Colorado	Montana	Texas
District of Columbia	Oklahoma (but see below)	Utah
Iowa	Rhode Island	

In a few other states, common law marriages will be recognized if they were created before the date the practice was abolished. These are Georgia (created before 1997), Idaho (created before 1996), Ohio (created before 1991), and Pennsylvania (created before 2005). In Oklahoma, all common law marriages created before 1998 will be recognized by the state. If you entered into a common law marriage in Oklahoma after 1998, a court may or may not recognize your marriage. You should consult with an experienced family law attorney in your area for more information. Kentucky recognizes common law marriage only for purposes of awarding workers' compensation benefits, and New Hampshire (for inheritance purposes only).

Your Common Law Marriage in Colorado May Be Recognized in California

There's a little trick in the area of common law marriages. A state that doesn't provide for common law marriages will still recognize one if it was properly formed in a state that does provide for them. For example, if you have been living together in a common law marriage state for many years and then relocate to a non-common-law marriage state soon before one of you dies, the laws of common law marriage will apply to the division of the deceased partner's estate.

EXAMPLE: Colorado allows common law marriages; California does not. If Bob and Carol started living together in Los Angeles in 1980 and are still happily coupled today (but have never gone through a marriage ceremony), they are not legally married, even if they pretend they are. If, however, they started living together in Colorado in 1985 with the intention of forming a common law marriage and moved to California in 1995, both Colorado and California will recognize their common law marriage as valid.

Agreement of Joint Intent Not to Have a Common Law Marriage

Wanda Oglethorpe and _Rich Walters_ agree as follows:

We have been and plan to continue living together as an unmarried couple, and neither of us has ever intended to enter into any form of marriage, common law or otherwise.

Wanda Oglethorpe   3/24/xx
Signature   Date

Rich Walters   3/24/xx
Signature   Date

What If You Don't Wish to Have a Common Law Marriage

If you live together in a state that recognizes common law marriages and don't wish to be treated as if you are married, it's a good idea for you both to sign a statement making it clear that this is your joint intent. If you use the same last name and/or mix property together, it's essential that you do this, otherwise a common law marriage may later be found to exist.

We've included a sample of this type of agreement above. You may want to use this one on its own, or integrate it into one of the living together contracts in Chapter 3.

 FORMS

The Nolo website includes a downloadable copy of the Agreement of Joint Intent Not to Have a Common Law Marriage shown above. See the appendix for the link to this form.

Living Together Contracts

This section describes the basic legal rules of living together contracts and why they are so important for unmarried couples. Chapter 3 provides several different living together agreements you can tailor to your particular situation and directions for completing them. Be sure to read Chapter 10 for details on issues that may arise should you separate without having prepared a living together agreement.

Living Together Contracts—What They Are and Why Unmarried Couples Need One

A contract is no more than an agreement to do (or not to do) something. Marriage is, in a sense, a contractual relationship, even though the "terms" of the contract are written by the legislators, are rarely stated explicitly, and are not even fully known by the marrying couple. Saying

"I do" commits a couple to a well-established set of state laws and rules governing, among other things, the couple's property rights should one spouse die or should the couple split up.

Unmarried couples, on the other hand, do not automatically agree to any state-imposed contractual agreement when they start a relationship. The couple may have a joint obligation to a landlord or to a mortgage company if they rent or buy a place together, but that obligation is no different than if they were roommates. Living together, in and of itself, does not create a binding contractual relationship, nor does it entitle you to a property settlement (or inheritance) should you split up (or should one of you die).

A typical unmarried couple buys property, mixes assets, and invests together, often without discussing (let alone writing down) how they intend to divide their assets if they split up. Then, if problems about money and property come up later on, they usually try to reach an understanding or a compromise. Sometimes they visit a therapist or ask their friends to help. If they split up, most couples divide their possessions privately and go their separate ways, as they are not required to follow the legal rules that apply to marriage and divorce. For these couples, the "nonmarital" legal rules apply.

But some couples' relationships don't end so peacefully. They don't quietly divide the property and move on, but instead bring their battle to court. Courts in most states have responded to these claims by imposing general legal principles, mostly with the goal of trying to figure out what the couple had agreed to during the relationship and dividing their property accordingly. In doing so, most courts have ruled that unmarried couples generally have the right to create whatever kind of living together contracts they want relating to financial and property concerns.

As a result, if an unmarried couple chooses to sign a written contract or make an oral agreement together, or in some states if they act as though an agreement exists, that agreement will be considered an enforceable contract—a "nonmarital agreement" in legal terms, or what we call a living together agreement in this book.

These agreements do not usually cover personal aspects of your relationship, such as who does the cooking, feeds the dog, or cleans the house, or any sexual conduct terms. In fact, agreements on nonmonetary issues are unlikely to be enforced in court.

The most common use of living together contracts is in a break up dispute, to protect each partner in case the relationship ends. But in other instances, couples enter into them to communicate their needs and expectations, define their rights, and enhance one or both partners' peace of mind either at the start of the relationship or when the couple makes a major purchase.

Creating a well-crafted agreement not only helps you figure out how you really want to own your property, but also serves as a useful reminder if misunderstandings develop later or if one of you dies without a will. Another important benefit of a living together agreement is that if one partner is supporting the other, or if one partner has given up a career in order to take care of the home or raise children, the agreement will protect the dependent partner by ensuring that issues of support and compensation are stated in writing. Otherwise, the dependent partner can be left with nothing after having given up a lot. For older couples, a contract can help them formulate their estate plans (which are formalized in a will or trust), and also can protect the interests of their adult children. We find that the primary benefit of a living together agreement is that is inspires you to think and talk with each other about these issues, thus increasing the likelihood that you will organize your financial lives in a considerate and fair manner.

Even though some courts will enforce an oral agreement—or even an implied one—many courts won't, and so we believe that a written agreement is essential, though it's surely not a complete substitute for trust and effective communication. A contract won't enable an unmarried couple to continue loving one another or prevent them from splitting up; but if times get hard, a written agreement can do wonders to reduce paranoia and confusion and help each partner deal with one another fairly. There are no national statistics on how many unmarried, cohabiting couples enter into living together contracts, but many lawyers report such contracts are on the rise as a result of more couples living together and new legal rulings that support the validity of living together agreements.

The Law and Living Together Contracts

Before the 1970s, couples who lived together without getting married existed in a legal vacuum. Across the United States, the law generally held that money and property belonged to the person who earned it or originally owned it. Contracts to share earnings or property usually weren't enforced by courts on the ground that the agreements were based on "meretricious consideration." Consideration is the price paid in a contract; meretricious means "having the nature of prostitution."

What the courts were saying was that living together contracts were illegal contracts, trading nonmarital sex for compensation (remember, cohabitation was illegal in all states until 1970), and illegal contracts cannot be enforced. This meant that unmarried couples were unable to enforce their agreements to share or divide property upon separation or death.

All this began to change in the mid-1970s, when the California Supreme Court decision in the case of *Marvin v. Marvin*, 557 P.2d 106 (1976), gave unmarried couples in California the right to make contracts to jointly own property or to support each other. (See "The *Marvin* Case," below.)

Because the *Marvin* case has often been referred to in the press as a defining event regarding the right of unmarried couples, many people assume that the decision is the law everywhere. This is an exaggeration. The California Supreme Court has no legal authority outside of California, except by way of example. However, the case's general proposition—that unmarried couples are subject to the principles of contract law—has been universally accepted (with some variations) by courts of every state.

This change in the law was significant. Now, contracts between people living together are no longer illegal.

The *Marvin* Case

The California Supreme Court decision in *Marvin v. Marvin*, 557 P.2d 106 (1976), thrust the issue of contract rights for unmarried couples into the media spotlight. This case rose to prominence partly because of the late actor Lee Marvin's fame, and partly because of the sweeping nature of the decision. The case arose from a dispute between Lee Marvin and Michelle Triola Marvin, the woman he lived with and supported for a number of years. Even though they never married, she took his last name, resulting in endless confusion as to how an unmarried couple had the same last name!

After they broke up, Lee supported Michelle for a while, but then stopped. She sued him, claiming that they had an oral agreement—in exchange for her giving up her career as a dancer to be a full-time homemaker and companion, he said he would support her for the rest of her life.

The trial court initially ruled against Michelle, stating that living together contracts between unmarried couples were illegal and unenforceable. Michelle appealed to the California Supreme Court, which handed down the well-known *Marvin* decision, adopting several significant new legal rules for unmarried couples in California. Most importantly, it stated that unmarried couples did indeed have the right to make contracts that could be enforced in court.

The *Marvin* decision did not rule that an unmarried partner is automatically entitled to marital assets or financial support (which the media termed "palimony") just as a divorcing spouse would be entitled to alimony. Instead, the unmarried partner must prove a legal basis for such a claim—such as a contract.

Palimony isn't a legal term; it was coined by journalists to describe the division of property or alimony-like support given to an unmarried partner after the couple breaks up.

Some General Legal Rules Regarding Living Together Contracts

Here are some of the basic principles governing living together contracts, established in the *Marvin* case and other court decisions.

Unmarried Couples Don't Have the Same Rights as Married Couples

The court in *Marvin* held that California divorce laws—alimony and the division of property—don't apply to unmarried couples. This means that a court can't turn to state divorce laws when your relationship ends; a court instead will divide up your property based on contract law principles. Without a contract of some kind, neither party will have any rights to the other's assets or to postseparation support—unless the couple lived in a state that recognizes common law marriage (see above) and held themselves out to be married. In this case, the relationship must be ended by divorce and marital rules will apply.

The general rule that marital property rules do not apply to unmarried couples has been widely adopted in other states. However, a few states that do not recognize common law marriage have nevertheless found ways to provide some relief to a long-term unmarried partner when a relationship ends. For example, several courts in the State of Washington have applied marital community property law to unmarried couples, even though the state doesn't recognize common law marriage, as an equitable guide to resolving nonmarital disputes. (*Connell v. Francisco*, 898 P.2d 831 (1995).) While the Washington courts have sometimes looked to marital law as a guide to how nonmarital breakups should be resolved, they only do so if the particular facts of the couple's history support this outcome—it's not a universal rule for all unmarried couples in Washington.

Unmarried Couples May Enter Into Contracts

The court in *Marvin* stated that unmarried couples may make express contracts concerning their property, money, or other assets. An express contract is one made in words—oral or written.

This was a significant change in the law: Contracts between people living together in a sexual relationship were no longer illegal. The court added a caveat that is recognized in many other states: If the contract is explicitly based on sexual services performed by one partner, the contract is invalid. (See "Don't Mention Sex," below.)

The courts of nearly every state and the District of Columbia now enforce written contracts between unmarried partners. Most states also recognize oral (spoken) contracts but only if they can be proven, which is not a simple task. (Texas and Minnesota are the only states that have passed laws requiring contracts to be in writing, but courts in other states—including New York and New Mexico—have been unwilling to recognize implied agreements.) However, if one partner says there was an oral contract while the other emphatically denies it, a judge is unlikely to find that a contract was made, unless other evidence (such as a witness to the discussion about the contract) supports the contract claim.

In some rare instances, courts have even recognized contracts that can be implied from the circumstances of the couple's relationship and their actions (such as, jointly contributing to purchase expensive items, for example) or upon their actions (regularly supporting a partner while you're living together) but only if they can be proven. In these cases, the court acknowledges that the couple did not explicitly agree to a contract, but that the couple acted as if a contract existed—that there was an unspoken agreement. Courts have found such implied contracts even when the cohabitation was part time. For example, in a case involving the famous lawyer Johnnie Cochran, the court ruled that even though Cochran spent as little as one night per week with a woman to whom he was not married, there could still be a valid and enforceable agreement for lifetime support. (*Cochran v. Cochran*, 89 Cal.App.4th 283 (2001).) In that case, Johnnie Cochran lived with Patricia, to whom he was not married, and their son, on a part-time basis for many years. During some of those years, Cochran was married to other women. Cochran provided Patricia and their son with monetary support. When Cochran stopped paying support, Patricia sued. Cochran argued that even if there was an implied agreement for lifetime support, it couldn't be enforced because the *Marvin* case only applied to cohabiting couples, and he and Patricia never cohabited. The court disagreed, ruling that even part-time living together was enough to meet the *Marvin* standards of cohabitation—and sent the case back to the trial court to hear evidence as to whether there was, in fact, an implied agreement for lifetime support.

> **CAUTION**
>
> **Illinois, Georgia, and Louisiana couples beware.** These states are all exceptions to the general rule of acceptance of contract rights for unmarried couples. There the courts still hold that the "immoral" nature of living together prevents a couple from forming a contract. (*Hewitt v. Hewitt*, 394 N.E.2d 1204 (1979).) However, some progress has been made: At least one Illinois court has held that contracts not based entirely on living together, and not resembling marriage claims, may be enforced. (*Spafford v. Coats*, 118 Ill.App.3d 566 (1983).) Changes in social attitudes also suggest that courts in the future will be less hostile to these claims.

Concepts of Fairness (Equity) Sometimes Protect the Rights of Members of Unmarried Couples

The courts of some states, including the California Supreme Court in the *Marvin* case, have recognized that the legal concept of "unjust enrichment" also may apply to disputes between unmarried couples. In this context, unjust enrichment means that if one person contributes something (usually labor, such as housework) to make the other's property more valuable, with the reasonable expectation of receiving a benefit in return, that expectation will be honored. This concept often overlaps with the legal notion of implied contract, but is somewhat different. If the circumstances of a couple's property dealings look like a contract to share ownership—like an unspoken agreement—the court will find an implied contract, whereas no such arrangement is necessary when it comes to the doctrine of unjust enrichment.

> **EXAMPLE:** Janet works to repair and refinish Todd's boat for nine months, expecting a share of the resulting increased value. After they split up, Todd refuses to give her a cent. If Janet sued Todd to recover her share of the boat she would probably argue that Todd had been unjustly enriched by her work and that she should be paid for her labor.

Although the legal theory of unjust enrichment has been recognized by many states besides California, including Arizona and Florida, other states, such as New York, reject it. (*Morone v. Morone*, 50 N.Y.2d 481 (1980).) And, even in states that do recognize it, the practical problems inherent in trying to win a lawsuit based on unjust enrichment mean that it's rarely worth the trouble to file suit, unless large amounts of money are at stake.

The lesson to be learned: Unmarried partners should record all of their important understandings (their contracts) in writing and should never rely on courts to bail them out later.

Why You Need to Put Your Living Together Agreement in Writing

By now, one thing should be clear: You can avoid a host of legal problems by putting your living together agreement in writing. A written contract covering who owns what is the only way to protect yourself and honor your collective intentions—whether you want to keep all your property separate or share some or all of it. Without some type of written agreement, you may face serious and potentially expensive battles if you separate and can't agree on how to divide what you have acquired.

> EXAMPLE: After they break up, Miriam sues Eric. She demands $100,000, an amount she claims Eric agreed to pay her if they should break up within one year of Miriam's moving 500 miles to live with Eric. When Eric emphatically denies that he had made any such agreement and Miriam can produce no evidence to back up her claim, the court rules for Eric.

Putting your contract in writing needn't be time-consuming or dreary (and it's certainly better than having a judge write one for you as part of an expensive court fight). There is no requirement that your living together agreement be prepared by an attorney, or even that it be notarized. Approach the task in the spirit of clarifying your understanding and preserving the shared memory of two fair-minded people. The details of how to accomplish this are in Chapter 3.

Sometimes one or both partners can be reluctant to sign a contract, believing it demonstrates a lack of trust in the other partner's word. To the contrary, we believe it's a healthy dose of realism, recognizing that over time memories fade and feelings change, and a written contract can make you feel secure that your intentions at the time you made it won't be forgotten.

And even if the agreement never has to be discussed in a court, it can provide an opportunity to discuss the tough financial issues, which itself can be healthy for your ongoing relationship. Without a written living together agreement, it is almost impossible to enforce a claim of an oral contract in court. If your partner isn't willing to sign an agreement, don't rely on the oral promise—it's best to consider yourself to be without a contract at all.

Cases Based on Implied Contracts and Unjust Enrichment

Oregon. *In re Raimer and Wheeler*, 119 Or. App. 118, 849 P.2d 1122 (Or. Ct. App. 1993). The couple in this case lived together for six years and jointly operated several businesses, including a ranch. Shirley Wheeler owned the ranch and did the bookkeeping for the ranch. Rondal Ray Raimer worked the ranch, installed an updated irrigation system (which Wheeler reimbursed him for), brought additional acres under irrigation, and spent a substantial amount of his money on ranching supplies and equipment. When they split up, the Oregon courts awarded Raimer one-half of the appreciation of the ranch and reimbursement for the items he had purchased for the ranch because both parties had jointly operated it and treated it as a joint asset while living together.

Wisconsin. *Watts v. Watts*, 137 Wis.2d 506, 405 N.W.2d 303 (1987). Here, one partner gave up a career to move in with the other and become a full-time homemaker and mother. The court said she could sue under any theory available to noncohabitants, including implied contract (they had an unspoken agreement that she'd be paid for her services), unjust enrichment (he benefited from her efforts and should compensate her), or partition of the jointly held property.

Cases Based on Implied Contracts and Unjust Enrichment (continued)

North Carolina. *Suggs v. Norris*, 364 S.E.2d 159 (1988). As in the *Watts* case above, the court allowed one partner to sue the other's estate under any legal theory available to noncohabitants. She chose unjust enrichment, claiming that they had a joint business, all the proceeds went to him, and she should be paid for her work. She was.

California. *Byrne v. Laura*, 52 Cal.App.4th 1054 (1997). After Byrne died, his cohabiting partner sued his estate for a portion of his property. The trial court rejected Laura's claims as an effort to get marital support. The Court of Appeal reversed, finding that if Laura could prove, as she alleged, that Byrne promised to take care of her for the rest of her life, she might be entitled to half of his assets based on an oral or implied contract.

Connecticut. *Boland v. Catalano*, 202 Conn. 333, 521 A.2d 142 (1987). This couple lived together for nine years, pooling assets and earnings. The court found an implied contract to share income and the "fruits of joint labor."

Indiana. *Turner v. Freed*, 792 N.E.2d 947 (2003). A couple lived together on and off for more than five years, during which time the woman did all of the housework and raised the couple's son as well as taking care of her partner's son from a previous relationship. In addition, she helped her partner with his work for less-than-market rate pay. All of this allowed the partner to build his water-softening business, and when the couple broke up, the court found that the woman was entitled to a payment on the basis that, otherwise, the man would be unjustly enriched by her help.

New Jersey. *In re Estate of Roccamonte*, 174 N.J. 381, 808 A.2d 838 (2002). The Court of Appeal held that evidence showing the two parties had a marital-type relationship supported an argument that the male partner had promised to support his female cohabitant for life, and the promise was enforceable against the man's estate. The court also held that it wasn't necessary for the woman to be completely economically dependent on the man in order for a valid palimony agreement to exist—the promise itself was enough.

Don't Mention Sex

A living together contract that is explicitly based on sexual services per-formed by one partner may be ruled invalid if you end up in court. Explicit does not mean you used sexually explicit language in your agreement. It means that you made reference somewhere in your agreement to the fact that the two of you are having sex. The courts are very sensitive to any implication that they are legitimizing any act of prostitution (what is some-times called "meretricious consideration"). If a court can imply from the wording of your contract that either party agreed to perform any sexual acts in order to receive a benefit from the contract, it may not be enforced. Even referring to one's partner as a "lover" has been held sufficient grounds to throw out a living together contract.

> EXAMPLE: Dianne and Val lived together for many years in a state that didn't recognize common law marriages. Dianne died without leaving a will, and Val sued the estate for a share of the accumulated property, alleging that he gave up his career as a mountain-climbing guide to live with Dianne and be her lover, companion, and homemaker in exchange for a share in the property. Because the word "lover" implies that sexual services are an inseparable part of their agreement, some courts would rule that Val can't recover a share of the property.

However, other courts have ruled that, in some situations, a word such as "lover" can be deleted from the contract retroactively, while the rest of the agreement is enforced.

What Happens to Your Written Living Together Agreement If You Get Married?

Let's suppose you take our advice and write your own living together contract (using one of the forms in Chapter 3). Several years later you decide to tie the knot—either by getting married or registering. Is your living together contract enforceable after marriage? Generally, it still applies to whatever assets you acquired prior to getting married, but not to any assets or debts that came into your lives after your marriage. As for those postmarital assets, it would only be valid, if it was created shortly before your marriage or at a time when you planned to be married, and only if it meets your state's standards for a premarital agreement—which probably wasn't the case for your agreement. To be enforceable, premarital (prenuptial or premarriage) contracts must be made in contemplation of marriage and must be completed in accordance with the strict marital laws of your state. That means that most couples who prepared living together agreements will have to sign a new premarital agreement if they decide to marry and want to keep the same arrangements they've had for their postmarital assets and property.

What's the Relationship Between a Living Together Contract and a Premarital Agreement?

Premarital agreements allow people who plan to marry to modify the contract imposed by state marital law. You can establish your own property ownership rules, different from the state's marital property laws, in a premarital agreement. But you have to explicitly state that you aren't going to follow marital law rules—something that unmarried couples don't say in their agreements. So if you do want the property ownership terms of your living together agreement to apply during your marriage—for example, if you're an older couple and want to keep property separate—you can normally do this by rewriting your agreement as a premarital agreement, describing which marital laws you don't want to follow. You can also agree in advance as to how much support (if any) one person will pay the other in case of divorce by using a prenuptial agreement.

Twenty-seven states have adopted the Uniform Premarital Agreement Act, which lets couples make premarital written contracts concerning ownership, management, and control of property; disposition of property at separation, divorce, and death; alimony; wills; and life insurance beneficiaries. (See "States That Have Adopted the Uniform Premarital Agreement Act," below, for the list.) The states that haven't adopted the Act have other premarital agreement laws, which often differ in only minor ways from the Act. In every state, couples are prohibited from including provisions about child custody or support—the court, not the couple, must make these decisions.

Premarital agreements are different from cohabitation contracts, as they are a modification of marital rights and duties, rather than the voluntary acceptance of contracted duties. They are usually upheld by courts unless either spouse shows that the agreement is likely to promote divorce (for example, by including a large alimony amount in the event of divorce), was written and signed with the intention of divorcing, or was unfairly entered into (for example, a spouse giving up all rights to the other's future earnings without the advice of an attorney).

Here are the main provisions of the Uniform Act.

(a) *Parties to a premarital agreement may contract with respect to:*
    (1) *the rights and obligations of each of the parties in any of the property of either or both of them whenever and wherever acquired or located;*
    (2) *the right to buy, sell, use, transfer, exchange, abandon, lease, consume, expend, assign, create a security interest in, mortgage, encumber, dispose of, or otherwise manage and control property;*
    (3) *the disposition of property upon separation, marital dissolution, death, or the occurrence or nonoccurrence of any other event;*
    (4) *the modification or elimination of spousal support;*
    (5) *the making of a will, trust, or other arrangement to carry out the provisions of the agreement;*
    (6) *the ownership rights in, and disposition of, the death benefit from a life insurance policy;*
    (7) *the choice of law governing the construction of the agreement; and*
    (8) *any other matter, including their personal rights and obligations, not in violation of public policy or a statute imposing a criminal penalty.*
(b) *The right of a child to support may not be adversely affected by a premarital agreement.*

States That Have Adopted the Uniform Premarital Agreement Act		
Arizona	Illinois	New Mexico
Arkansas	Indiana	North Carolina
California	Iowa	Oregon
Connecticut	Kansas	Rhode Island
Delaware	Maine	South Dakota
District of Columbia	Montana	Texas
Florida	Nebraska	Utah
Hawaii	Nevada	Virginia
Idaho	New Jersey	Wisconsin

How to Convert a Living Together Contract Into a Premarital Agreement

If you wish to marry and convert your living together contract into a premarital agreement, you will need to follow these steps:

1. Use your upcoming marriage as an opportunity to take another look at your agreement; make any agreed-upon updates and changes.
2. Rewrite your agreement with references to which marital laws you are opting out of. Call it a prenuptial or premarital agreement, and state that it is made in contemplation of marriage and does not take effect until you marry.
3. Because even a small mistake can result in a court later refusing to enforce your agreement, have your new agreement reviewed by an attorney experienced in this area. In most instances, it makes sense that each partner should have his or her own attorney review the agreement. In some states, the agreement is presumed invalid if not prepared and reviewed by independent lawyers, one for each spouse.
4. Sign your agreement in front of a notary public.

📄 **FORMS**

More information about premarital agreements. See *Prenuptial Agreements: How to Write a Fair & Lasting Contract*, by Katherine E. Stoner and Shae Irving (Nolo).

Special Issues for Seniors

The fastest-growing demographic group among unmarried couples is seniors (one source says that over the past decade, the number of unmarried partners over the age of 65 has increased by 70%). All of the same reasons that younger couples give for not marrying may apply to seniors as well—not wanting to repeat experiences from a bad marriage or not wanting the government involved in the relationship, for example—but for many seniors, finances are the biggest issue preventing legal matrimony. There are a number of common concerns that seniors have about tying the knot.

Social Security and pensions. If you are divorced and you remarry before age 60, you'll lose Social Security income from a previous marriage to which you would have otherwise been entitled. (However, you may get more from your new spouse's Social Security payment, so use the calculator available from the Social Security Administration at www.ssa.gov to figure out whether this is a real problem for you.) The same is often true of pension benefits awarded to you as part of a divorce settlement, or pension benefits paid to you as the survivor of a deceased employee.

Marriage can also affect the amount of taxes you're required to pay on your Social Security benefits when you begin receiving them. A single person can earn $25,000 per year before being taxed on those benefits, while a married couple can have total income of only $32,000 before taxes are levied.

Estate planning. If you have college-age children, your marriage may result in your new spouse's income being counted for financial aid purposes, which in turn may reduce the aid your child is eligible for. And if you have adult children and want them to inherit the bulk of your estate, you must use careful estate planning to ensure that your wishes are carried out. Spouses have certain inheritance rights in many states, and if you want to limit those rights you must make sure your documents are in good order. Signing a cohabitation agreement also may reassure your children that your new partner isn't going to grab too much of your assets.

Alimony. If you were in a long-term marriage that ended in divorce and you're receiving alimony, you'll most likely have to give that up when you remarry—check your divorce order.

Medical and nursing home expenses. When you marry, you take on responsibility for your partner's support and care. If your new spouse has serious health concerns, or ends up living in a nursing home, you may not want to take on that financial responsibility. Unmarried couples, no matter how intimately connected in personal and financial ways, don't take on this same responsibility. Marrying also can disqualify you from certain public benefits.

With all of these potential concerns, it's no wonder seniors are cohabiting in droves. If you are considering getting hitched, and especially if either of you have significant assets or adult children, we'd recommend seeing an attorney or tax professional who can advise you about the pros and cons of marriage in your particular circumstances.

Living Together Agreements: Why and How They Work

Ten Tips for Writing a Living Together Agreement...39

Property Agreements 43

    Agreement to Keep Property Separate 44

    Prepare a Separate List of Items You Own... 48

    Address Domestic Partnership Issues (If Relevant) 49

    Agreement to Share Property...50

    Signing a Property Agreement or Other Living Together Contract.............51

Agreement to Share Ownership of a Joint Purchase...57

    How to Prepare an Agreement for a Joint Purchase...................................57

    Buying a Car Together..63

    How to Transfer Ownership in Property.. 64

Agreement Covering Joint Projects...65

Agreement Covering Homemaker Services 67

Agreement for Artists, Writers, and Inventors...71

Agreement for People in School 75

**Agreement to Protect Person Who Moves a Long Distance
or Gives Up a Job**...79

FORMS IN THIS CHAPTER

Chapter 3 includes instructions for and samples of the following forms:

- Agreement to Keep Property Separate
- Attachment A (Separately Owned Property)
- Agreement to Share Property
- Attachment B (Jointly Owned Property)
- Agreement for a Joint Purchase

The Nolo website includes downloadable copies of these forms. See the appendix for the link to the forms in this book.

Chapter 3 also includes several sample agreements: Sample Joint Purchase Agreement When Only One Partner Is the Legal Borrower; Sample Agreement Covering a Joint Project; Sample Agreement Covering Homemaker Services; Sample Agreement for Artists, Writers, and Inventors; and Sample Agreement for People in School.

n case you didn't get the message from Chapter 2, it's extremely important to spell out your financial and property arrangements in a written agreement—what we call a living together contract or living together agreement. Among other things, an agreement can help avoid problems when you commingle money and property; make clear what your intentions and expectations are regarding property ownership, caring for children, covering household expenses, and the like; it helps you sort things out while you're living together, and will ease the division of your assets during a breakup.

Examples of problems unmarried couples face if they don't have a living together agreement are discussed throughout the remainder of this book. For example, in Chapter 4, you'll learn why it's important to put in writing your agreement to commingle or keep your property separate. Chapter 6 discusses why you should have a contract if you plan to jointly own a home, and Chapter 10 explains how not having a written agreement can cause major problems if you break up. We recommend that you read all of these chapters before you prepare any of the agreements included in this chapter.

Of all the reasons to write out your agreement, avoiding a court fight is probably the most important. From a practical perspective, little gets resolved in court without costs and legal fees eating up the lion's share of the money and property in dispute. Those of you who have been through a contested breakup or divorce already know this. Once you add up the time, emotional pain, and bitterness that are always a part of our adversary process, you should be reaching for your pen (or keyboard).

Obviously, you don't need a living together contract if you have no assets or are in a short-term relationship. But in a long-term and serious relationship, whether you're basking in the glow of just having "joined forces" or you've been together 20 years, you should consider the legal consequences of how you live. This is especially true if you are buying a house together or relying on each other for your basic financial needs.

This chapter on living together contracts is designed to help you clarify your understanding about your life as a couple. We strongly believe that talking out (and writing down) your intentions should bring you closer, and help you overcome any fears or concerns you may have about money, property, and your future. And if you do split up, having an agreement helps you avoid litigation. For one thing, all of the agreements here include a clause providing for mediation for disputes arising out of the contract. Then, if a lawsuit is filed, the judge will focus on interpreting your written agreement, not on trying to infer an implied contract from your behavior or determining who's right if one of you claims you had an oral contract and the other disagrees.

Your living together contract need not be like the fine-print treatises forced on you by car salesmen or insurance agents. A simple, comprehensive, and functional document using common English is much better than one loaded with "heretofores," "pursuants," and other legalese. You can, and should, design your agreement to say exactly what you both want, in words you both understand. And, while many people can draft their own living together contracts (rather than have a lawyer write one), it's often a good idea to have a lawyer review your agreement—for example, if a lot of money or property is involved. The following section, "Ten Tips for Writing a Living Together Agreement," covers situations when legal advice is especially useful.

This chapter shows how to do just that, and includes a variety of contracts for different situations, including:

- basic property agreements (one for pooling property and assets and one for keeping them separate), covering issues such as how you're sharing costs and property ownership and what happens to your property if you break up or one of you dies
- more narrow agreements for sharing ownership of specific items, such as a computer, and
- contracts designed to cover specific situations, such as when one partner puts the other through school.

All of our contracts are written in plain English and are easy to follow. Please read (or at least skim) all the contracts in this chapter before deciding which one to use. You may choose to use one of our contracts verbatim, customize one to meet your specific needs, or use a particular contract as a starting point for your own agreement.

 RELATED TOPICS
Chapters in this book provide agreements covering other aspects of your relationship, including:

- Renting a home together (Chapter 5): How to prepare an agreement spelling out your responsibilities to each other as tenants, covering who pays what portion of the rent and expenses, who gets the place if you split up, and the like
- Buying or owning a house together (Chapter 6): How to write a contract for owning a house together, including sharing costs and ownership, what happens to the house if you break up or one of you dies, and how to deal with disputes over the house
- Having children together: How to prepare paternity statements (Chapter 7) or custody agreements (Chapter 8)
- Preparing a will and other estate planning documents (Chapter 9)
- Drafting a settlement agreement should you separate (Chapter 10).

Ten Tips for Writing a Living Together Agreement

The rest of this chapter provides specific instructions and forms you will need to prepare a living together agreement. Here are some basic tips to keep in mind as you go:

1. Talk it out and reach an understanding. Before you can prepare a written agreement covering ownership of your property and other assets, the two of you must agree on how you will conduct your financial affairs. This is especially true if either of you makes sacrifices for the relationship, such as moving a long distance or giving up a job to care for small children or if one of you is earning a lot more than the other one. How you reach an understanding about money and property issues is up to you. We suggest that before trying to reach an agreement, you carefully read the rest of this chapter (and if real property is involved, Chapter 6) so you understand your options.

Many people find that creating a contract forces them to deal with the very guts of their relationship. This is a healthy thing to do now and then—but it can also be challenging. Take your time; don't expect to finish it in an evening, and be prepared for some emotional challenges. Remember, a good contract often involves compromise and accommodation. Preparing your contract should be an affirmative act, but it's up to you to make it so. If you get bogged down in trading this for that and wonder why you're dealing with all of this legal mumbo-jumbo, take a break and get back to it when you're both feeling more cheerful.

2. Cover the basics—property and assets, such as money. A living together contract can be comprehensive, covering every aspect of your relationship, or it can be specific, covering only your new car or a home purchase. Living together contracts can include a wide variety of economic arrangements. You can keep all of your assets and property separate, or agree that what belongs to either of you belongs to both. Or perhaps your agreement will be somewhere in between—with you keeping the property and assets brought into the relationship separate, but agreeing to share expenses equally and make joint purchases after you start living together. But regardless of how detailed your contract is or how much you decide to include, you must deal with two basic issues: money and property.

Property and Assets Defined

Virtually anything one can own is considered property. Generally, we think of items that have monetary value as **property**—including both tangible things you can see and touch (furniture, houses, cars, and jewelry) and intangible items (such as business goodwill, the right to receive future pensions, or the copyright in a book). The term **real property** refers to houses and other real estate. In the legal realm the term **personal property** is used to refer to any kind of asset other than real property, and includes furniture, money, or even artwork. **Assets** is another term for property of all kinds.

3. Don't try to cover everything in one contract. Relationships and people are complicated. If you try to cover too much ground in one contract, you'll get bogged down and never figure it all out. It's often better to have several smaller agreements covering specific issues. For example, your property agreement should be separate from whatever agreement you have to support a partner who's in school. Your agreement on sharing housing costs and ownership should also be separate, as explained in Chapters 5 and 6.

4. Don't get too personal. As we've explained in Chapter 2, agreements between unmarried partners are generally enforceable to the extent they cover property, payment for services (excluding sex), or payment in exchange for a person giving something up, such as a job or a house. A court is unlikely to enforce an agreement that covers nonmonetary issues. The contracts included in this chapter pertain only to property and finances. They do not cover the day-to-day details of your relationship, such as who will do the dishes, who will walk the dog, how many overnight guests you'll allow, and whose favorite painting goes in the living room. A court won't—and shouldn't be asked to—enforce these kinds of personal agreements. If your agreement includes personal as well as financial clauses, a court might declare the entire contract illegal or frivolous and refuse to enforce any of it—including the more important financial clauses. Obviously, you need to be clear with your partner on things such as housecleaning and cooking. Just don't mix up these day-to-day issues with the bigger legal issues of living together.

5. Don't mention sex. A living together agreement that is explicitly based on sexual services performed by one partner—even a reference somewhere in the agreement to the fact that the two of you are having sex—may be ruled invalid if you end up in court. And you shouldn't condition any payment or obligation on a duty to be monogamous— issues of fidelity are best dealt with as personal concerns, not legal promises in a contract.

6. Consult an attorney before preparing a living together agreement about sharing property if one or both of you are married to someone else. In many states, if either partner who is still married is permanently separated from his or her spouse, it may be possible to create a legally valid living together contract to share property. Unfortunately, however, little is certain in this legal gray area where there are few court rulings. Therefore, if one of you is still married to someone else, it's best to agree in writing to keep all your property separate until the divorce is final. At a minimum, get good legal advice before signing anything, if you find yourself in this situation. Then you can write a new agreement, pooling your property if you both wish to do so. For more on legal issues that arise when you live with someone while you're still married, see Chapter 8.

7. Get legal advice before signing an agreement if a lot of money or property or complicated estate planning is involved. This is just common sense—particularly if one partner has substantially more assets than the other.

8. Get legal help if bargaining power isn't equal. A living together contract might not be enforced if a judge concludes that one partner has taken unfair advantage of the other. For example, a court is unlikely to uphold a one-sided living together contract between an experienced lawyer and an unsophisticated, but wealthy, 19-year-old who just moved to America and speaks little English, under which the immigrant agrees to support the lawyer.

9. Get legal help if you live in Illinois. In Illinois, it's doubtful that any living together contract is enforceable. As explained in Chapter 2, courts in Illinois remain an exception to the general acceptance of contract rights for unmarried couples. You may be able to create a legal living together contract in Illinois by stating, in writing, that your agreement is simply a contract to share the ownership of certain property and has nothing to do with your personal relationship. See a lawyer for advice.

10. Agree in advance to mediate disputes that may arise over your agreement. We recommend mediation because it is cheaper, faster, more effective, and usually less painful than litigation. All of the contracts in this chapter include a general clause stating that you agree to bring in a third party to mediate any dispute that may arise out of the contract. (For an example, see Clause 6 in the Agreement to Share Property, below.) The same clause provides that one partner may request formal arbitration should mediation prove unsuccessful. To learn what's involved with mediation or arbitration be sure to read Chapter 10, which provides detailed information on dispute resolution.

RESOURCE

Find a lawyer at www.nolo.com/lawyers. You can check out Nolo's Lawyer Directory, which offers comprehensive profiles of the lawyers who advertise there, including each one's education, background, areas of expertise (such as family law), fees, and practice philosophy. Lawyers also indicate whether or not they're willing to review documents or coach clients who are doing their own legal work. You can also submit information about your legal issue to several local attorneys who handle legal issues for unmarried couples who live together, and then pick the lawyer you'd like to work with. See Chapter 11 for advice on finding and working with a lawyer. You should not assume that family law attorneys—who regularly handle marital law disputes—know the rules for unmarried couples.

What Happens to Your Living Together Agreement If You Get Married?

Your living together contract probably will not be enforceable after marriage unless it was created shortly before your marriage at a time when you both planned to marry and meets the local standards for a premarital contract. To be enforceable, prenuptial (or premarital) contracts must be made in contemplation of marriage and they must meet the applicable state standards for premarital agreements wherever you live. For more details, including how to turn your living together contract into a prenuptial agreement, see Chapter 2.

Property Agreements

This section includes two living together agreements designed to cover major areas of concern to most unmarried couples—ownership of personal property, such as furniture, cars, and the like, and assets. Chapter 6 includes legal agreements relevant to buying or sharing ownership of real property (a house or condominium) together. In some states you can have a written contract that extends some of the rights of ownership to someone who is not on the title, but in most instances "owning" property means being listed on the title, either at the outset when the property is purchased, or by being added to the title later on.

You have several options when it comes to ownership of personal property with an unmarried partner:

- You can keep the property or items that each of you owned before your agreement to separate or you can share them; and you can transfer ownership of none, some, or all of your property to your partner.
- You can agree to split income and expenses in many different ways, some equal, some not.
- You can keep separate bank and checking accounts, credit cards, and insurance, or create joint accounts.
- Most crucially, you can decide in advance who gets what should you separate, or alternatively, you can agree to a process for resolving any disputes that come up should you separate.

We suggest you start with one of our basic contracts:

- Agreement to Keep Property Separate, or
- Agreement to Share Property.

Read both contracts and see which one works better for you, editing as appropriate as discussed in "Signing a Property Agreement or Other Living Together Contract," below.

FORMS
Sample copies of the Agreement to Keep Property Separate and the Agreement to Share Property, as well as Attachment A (Separately Owned Property) and Attachment B (Jointly Owned Property), are shown below, and the Nolo website includes downloadable copies of these forms. See the appendix for the link to these forms.

Agreement to Keep Property Separate

Especially in the first year or two after they get together, most unmarried couples keep all or most of their money and property separate—with the occasional exception of a joint account to pay household bills or an agreement to purchase one or more items jointly. This is especially true for younger couples, but applies to older pairs as well.

Agreement to Keep Property Separate

_____Rose Jackson_____ and ___Alan Lewis_____ agree as follows:

1. This contract sets forth our rights and obligations toward each other. We intend to abide by the provisions in a spirit of cooperation and good faith.

2. All assets and property (including real estate and personal property and financial assets) owned by either of us as of the date of this agreement will remain the separate property of its owner and shall not be transferred to the other partner unless this is done in writing. Except as so approved in writing, neither of us will assert any claim to any property or assets titled in the other party's name. We have each attached a list of our major items of separate property to this contract. (See Attachment A, Separately Owned Property.)

3. The income each of us earns—as well as any assets, items, property, or investments either of us purchases with our income—belongs absolutely to the partner who earns the money unless there is a written joint ownership agreement as provided in Clause 6.

4. We will each maintain our own separate bank, credit card, investment, and retirement accounts, and neither of us will in any way be responsible for the debts of the other. If we register as domestic partners in a jurisdiction that makes this option available and, by so doing, the law requires us to be responsible for each other's basic living expenses, we agree to assume the minimum level of reciprocal responsibility required by the law. We will not, however, be entitled to any of the other's savings or assets if we later end our relationship.

5. Expenses for routine household items and services, which include groceries, utilities, rent, and cleaning supplies, will be shared equally, or as we so agree from time to time. Neither of us shall be obligated to reimburse the other for any excess contributions to these expenses, except as agreed to in writing.

6. From time to time, we may decide to keep a joint checking or savings account for a specific purpose (for example, to pay household expenses), or to own some item jointly (for example, to purchase a television). If so, the details of our joint ownership agreement will be put in writing (either in a written contract or a deed, title slip, or other joint ownership document); if not, the funds in the account will be owned 50/50.

7. Should either of us receive any real or personal property by gift or inheritance, the property belongs absolutely to the partner receiving the gift or inheritance and shall not be transferred to or shared with the other partner or deemed to be shared with the other partner unless we agree to do so in writing.

8. In the event we separate, each of us will be entitled to immediate possession all of our separate property, including any real property or financial assets.

9. In the event of a separation, neither of us will owe any postseparation financial support to the other, regardless of our financial circumstances, including any real property or financial assets or any difference in our incomes.

10. Any dispute arising out of this contract will be mediated by a third person mutually acceptable to both of us. The mediator's role will be to help us arrive at a solution, not to impose one on us. If good faith efforts to arrive at our own solution to all issues in dispute with the help of a mediator prove to be fruitless after two mediation sessions, either of us may make a written request to the other that the dispute be arbitrated. In that case, our dispute will be submitted to arbitration under the rules of the American Arbitration Association, and one arbitrator will hear our dispute. The decision of the arbitrator will be binding on us and will be enforceable in any court that has jurisdiction over the controversy. By agreeing to arbitration, we each agree to give up the right to a jury trial.

11. This agreement represents our complete understanding regarding our living together and replaces any and all prior agreements, written or oral. It can be amended, but only in writing, and any amendments must be signed by both of us.

12. If a court finds any portion of this contract to be illegal or otherwise unenforceable, the remainder of the contract is still in full force and effect.

Rose Jackson _____ 3/2/xx _____
Rose Jackson Date

Alan Lewis _____ 3/2/xx _____
Alan Lewis Date

Attachment A
Separately Owned Property

The following is the separate personal property of ___Rose Jackson___ :

Living room furniture: blue sofabed, red armchair, oak rocking chair, and glass coffee table

Apple personal computer and incidental equipment

King-size bed

Cuisinart food processor

Condominium unit located at 235 Bank Street in Chicago, Illinois

Prius automobile

Retirement and savings accounts in America Bank and Silver Investment institution

The following is the separate personal property of ___Alan Lewis___ :

Oriental rugs in living room and dining room

Pine dining room table and six chairs

Stereo system, TV, and all media equipment

Kitchen table and matching chairs

Harley Davidson motorcycle

Investment accounts in America Bank and Silver brokerage office

You may think that keeping your property ownership separate is so simple that you don't need a written agreement. Think again. Because most states recognize oral contracts between unmarried couples (as discussed in Chapter 2), the lack of a written agreement can be an invitation for one partner to later claim the existence of an oral property-sharing agreement. This is what commonly occurs in the so-called palimony cases that regularly hit the headlines.

To avoid the possibility of future misunderstandings concerning property ownership, use the Agreement to Keep Property Separate form shown above to confirm that each of you plans to keep your property and income separate unless you make a specific written agreement otherwise. This agreement keeps all of your property separate, including property you brought into the relationship as well as property you purchased with your own money or received by gift or inheritance while living together.

> **TIP**
>
> **Want to keep your property separate?** Be sure to read "Buying and Investing Together" in Chapter 4 for other ways to maintain your financial independence.

Prepare a Separate List of Items You Own

Here are a few things to keep in mind if you're using the Agreement to Keep Property Separate.

Clause 2 states that you will attach a separate list of major items you own to the Agreement. Prepare an attachment, such as the sample Separately Owned Property form shown here, listing the personal property each of you owns. If this is the first attachment to your contract, label it Attachment A as shown here. (See "How to Edit or Modify a Living Together Agreement," below, for advice on preparing attachments.) This sample is just a partial list of what most couples own.

You should be very specific as to any items of significant value—at least list all items worth $500 or more. Be sure to update your list of separately owned items from time to time—once a year is a good period.

Making an agreement about the property you bring into the relationship may seem unnecessary, but it's not. Think about trying to separate it all ten years from now, when you've both been referring to everything around the house as "ours."

> **TIP**
>
> **Value of property inventory.** Detailed lists of property you own will also come in very handy for insurance purposes should your property be stolen or damaged in a fire, flood, or other natural disaster.

Address Domestic Partnership Issues (If Relevant)

Clause 4 of the Agreement to Keep Property Separate specifies that if you register as a domestic partner in a program that is not "marriage-equivalent," but nonetheless makes you responsible for each other's basic living expenses, you agree to only the minimal level of reciprocal financial responsibility. We include this language because, as discussed in Chapter 2, registering as domestic partners may imply that you intend to share ownership of property unless you include this type of disclaimer. Of course, if no domestic partnership programs are available to you or you do not intend to register as domestic partners, you can delete this sentence of Clause 4.

Clause 5 provides that you will share expenses for household items and services equally. If you have a different arrangement, or want to spell out how you will split expenses of nonhousehold items, such as insurance or car repairs, you can edit Clause 5 accordingly.

Clause 6 refers to a joint ownership agreement that you may prepare from time to time—for example, if you purchase a television or computer together. There's a sample agreement below that you can use for this purpose. It covers issues such as what happens to the jointly owned property if you separate.

Clause 10 provides mediation should a dispute arise over your agreement, with arbitration as a backup should mediation fail. See Chapter 10 for a detailed discussion of mediation, arbitration, and other ways to resolve disputes.

If you are buying a house together but keeping everything else separate, it probably makes the most sense to draft a separate house ownership contract and refer to it in this agreement. Alternatively, you can combine the separate-assets provisions with the house co-ownership terms in the same agreement. In either event, you should be sure that the titling of the house is consistent with your written agreement. See Chapter 6 for advice and forms on buying a house together.

Which Agreements Do I Need?

Many couples feel it's unnecessary for them to spell out the details of their household arrangements, and they are willing to keep their furniture and income structure unwritten as well. If that's your approach, you will only need to complete one of the house co-ownership agreements described in Chapter 6. On the other hand, if you have entered into specific agreements about other assets, or you want to be sure to clarify that you are keeping those other assets separate, then you should either draft a separate agreement for the non-real-estate issues, or combine the provisions of the non-real-estate terms in to your house co-ownership agreement. Again, be sure that the names on the title are in sync with the terms of your agreement.

Agreement to Share Property

Especially if you have been together several years or more and have begun to purchase property jointly (a new car or bed, for example), you may want to do what a fair number of unmarried couples do—abandon (in whole or in part) your agreement to keep property separate, and instead treat property that either of you purchases as jointly owned. If this is your understanding, write it down.

Use the Agreement to Share Property form to establish that all newly acquired property—except that given to or inherited by one partner, or that which is clearly specified in writing as separate property—is to be jointly owned by both, and equally divided should you separate. If you are buying a house together, you should include the provisions of the home ownership contract (see Chapter 6). If you're sharing a significant amount of earned income or making large gifts of assets to each other, you should be sure to consult with a tax advisor, since you aren't entitled to tax-free asset transfers that married couples enjoy.

To complete the Agreement to Share Property, simply fill in your names, fill in (or modify) the blank in Clause 2, and sign the agreement.

Note that Clause 3 assumes that you will attach a list of the property each of you owned prior to the date of your agreement. (See sample Attachment A, Separately Owned Property, above.) Clause 3 also assumes you will attach a list of jointly owned property. (See sample Attachment B, Jointly Owned Property.) You may be as detailed as you want in preparing these separate property lists, but at least include major items (valued at $500 or more). Be sure to update your lists from time to time—either when you make a major purchase or at least once a year.

Signing a Property Agreement or Other Living Together Contract

Whether you use one of our living together contracts or design your own, photocopy (or print an extra copy of) the final draft (including all attachments) so you and your partner each have a copy. If you alter one of our forms by writing or typing in changes after you've printed it out, be sure that you and your partner initial each change before signing the agreement.

Sign and date both copies of your agreement. It makes no difference who keeps which—both are "originals."

Make sure you print your agreement out—don't just save it on your computer or store in your hard drive or "in the cloud." Courts still like to see real-life signatures on real pieces of paper.

Keep your agreement in a safe place, along with copies of other important documents, such as insurance papers, title slips to jointly held property, lease, copies of wills, important financial papers, and the like.

Agreement to Share Property

Beth Spencer and _Rich Portman_ · agree as follows:

1. This contract sets forth our rights and obligations toward each other. We intend to abide by this agreement in a spirit of cooperation and good faith.

2. All earned income received by either of us after the date of this contract and all assets acquired or property purchased with this income shall belong in equal shares to both of us (regardless of how it is titled or held) with the following exceptions: _____

   _____

   Earned income includes contributions for retirement accounts, stock options, or other forms of compensation for our labor. Income from prior investments shall not be considered earned income.

3. All real or personal property earned or accumulated by either of us prior to the date of this agreement (except jointly owned property listed in Attachment B of this agreement), including all future income this property produces, is the separate property of the person who earned or accumulated it and shall not be transferred to the other except in writing. Attached to this agreement in the form of Attachments A, Separately Owned Property, and B, Jointly Owned Property, are lists of the major items of property each of us owns separately and both of us own jointly as of the date of this agreement.

4. Should either of us receive real or personal property by gift or inheritance, that property, including all future income it produces, belongs absolutely to the person receiving the gift or inheritance and cannot be transferred to the other except in writing.

5. In the event we separate, all jointly owned property will be divided equally. Each of us shall retain our separate property, and neither shall owe any postseparation support to the other, regardless of financial conditions or differences in our incomes.

6. Any dispute arising out of this contract will be mediated by a third person mutually acceptable to both of us. The mediator's role will be to help us arrive at a solution, not to impose one on us. If good faith efforts to arrive at our own solution to all issues in dispute with the help of a mediator prove to be fruitless after two mediation sessions, either of us may make a written

request to the other that the dispute be arbitrated. In that case, our dispute will be submitted to arbitration under the rules of the American Arbitration Association, and one arbitrator will hear our dispute. The decision of the arbitrator will be binding on us and shall be enforceable in any court that has jurisdiction over the controversy. By agreeing to arbitration, we each agree to give up the right to a jury trial.

7. This agreement represents our complete understanding regarding our living together and replaces any and all prior agreements, written or oral. It can be amended, but only in writing, and any amendments must be signed by both of us.

8. If a court finds any portion of this contract to be illegal or otherwise unenforceable, the remainder of the contract is still in full force and effect.

Beth Spencer _____ 9/15/xx _____

Beth Spencer   Date

Rich Portman _____ 9/15/xx _____

Rich Portman   Date

Attachment B
Jointly Owned Property

The following property is jointly owned by ___Beth Spencer and Rich Portman___
in equal proportions except as otherwise noted:

Sony video camera

All garden tools and equipment

Deck furniture including table, umbrella, and six chairs

All kitchen equipment and dishware

All linens and towels

Household checking account

2 bicycles

How to Edit or Modify a Living Together Agreement

One of the property agreements or other living together contracts in this book may meet your needs perfectly. However, it's more likely you'll want to make some changes to fit your circumstances—either the first time you prepare an agreement or sometime down the road.

Editing a form in this book. Many unmarried couples will be able to use one of our living together agreements as is, simply printing out a copy, filling in a few blanks, and signing it. You may decide to edit or delete part or all of a particular clause. Or you may want to add a clause. Be sure you renumber clauses as needed.

Changing a form after you've signed it. Modifications of a contract should always be in writing. This is because historic, but still applicable, legal doctrines make most oral modifications of a written contract invalid. In addition, our contracts expressly state that any changes must be in writing. A modification can simply state that you agree to change your contract, and then set out the change. Date and sign all modifications. But if you're making really major changes, tear up the old agreement and start over.

You should evaluate your living together agreement from time to time (maybe once a year on your anniversary) as your relationship or your situation changes.

 SEE AN EXPERT

See a lawyer if you're making major changes to a living together agreement—or if lots of money or a major real estate purchase is at stake. By the time you finish modifying one of our agreements, your changes may pretty much replace the original. If that's the case, and especially if it refers to significant amounts of money or if property is involved, have a lawyer look at your living together agreement.

Optional Clauses to Add to Living Together Agreements

Here are some clauses you may want to add to your property agreement or other living together contract.

Property Division at Death. It's legal (but not required) to include a clause stating that if one partner dies, the survivor keeps the jointly owned property. We include this type of provision in some, but not all, of our contracts, depending on whether we think it's likely to be desired. (For example, see Clause 6 of the Sample Joint Purchase Agreement, below.) If a contract does contain a clause stating that the survivor becomes the sole owner of a particular piece of property when the first partner dies, it takes precedence over any provision in a will that says otherwise. In some states, however, you must make this provision on the title (as joint tenants with right of survivorship) or in a valid will or trust.

If there is no mention of what happens to property at death in a living together agreement that covers jointly owned property, each person can leave his or her portion by will or other estate plan to anyone (including, of course, one's partner). We discuss how to do this in Chapter 9. It's always best to have the terms stated in the agreement *and* in a valid will or trust document so there's no doubt as to your intentions. The one major exception to this rule is for property (such as a house) held in joint tenancy with right of survivorship, which automatically goes to the surviving joint tenant(s) when one joint tenant dies. (Chapter 6 discusses this issue in detail, and Chapter 9 covers wills and estate planning.)

If a clause covering property division at death is not in an agreement and you want it to be, or if you want to delete this language from a form, modify your agreement accordingly.

Agreement to Attend Counseling Before Separating. None of the agreements in this book contain a provision requiring that a couple attend counseling together if one of them wishes to separate. Unless both partners are willing to participate at the time the problems arise, making this commitment in advance serves little purpose, and, in our opinion, doesn't belong in a legal contract. If you want to include such a provision, here is sample language:

If either of us wants to end our relationship and the other doesn't, before splitting up we agree to participate in good faith in at least three conciliation sessions with a mutually acceptable third party. If, after a minimum of three sessions, either of us still wants to end our living together relationship, it will end.

TIP

Notarization is optional. Usually, having your agreement notarized isn't necessary. However, in some states you must notarize the agreement if it covers issues affecting real estate. If that is the case, sign the agreement before a notary. Then if you wish, you can record the agreement at your county records office. (Chapter 6 explains how to notarize and record a house ownership contract.) Notarization doesn't make a contract legal or enforceable. It simply proves that your signatures aren't forged, which can never hurt.

Agreement to Share Ownership of a Joint Purchase

Many people make purchases item by item, understanding that whoever makes the purchase owns the property. George buys the kitchen table and chairs, and Edna buys the lamp and stereo. If they split up, each keeps the property he or she bought. In this situation, George and Edna would use the Agreement to Keep Property Separate, above.

Purchases also can be shared, and this makes sense if you are pooling your incomes (or some portion of your incomes). Edna and George can jointly own everything bought during the relationship, and divide it all 50-50 if they separate. In this case, the Agreement to Share Property, above, would be appropriate.

While consistent approaches to property ownership may simplify things, they aren't legally required. Some items may be separately owned, some pooled 50-50, and some shared in proportion to how much money each contributed toward the purchase price or how much labor each put into upkeep.

How to Prepare an Agreement for a Joint Purchase

Many unmarried couples opt for a basic keeping-things-separate approach, at least when they first get together. However, an unmarried couple will often want to own one—or sometimes several—major items together, as would be the case if they pool their incomes to buy a car and an expensive audio system. Clause 6 in the Agreement to Keep Property Separate allows you to easily do this.

Agreement for a Joint Purchase

___Amy Randolph___ and ___Brett Bow___ agree as follows:

1. We will jointly acquire and own a _Sony flat-screen television and Blu-ray_ _disc player_ (the Property) at a cost of $ _2,500_ .
2. We will own the Property in the following shares [*fill in*]:
   ___Amy___ will own _50_ % of the Property and ___Brett___ will own _50_ % of the Property.
3. Should we separate and cease living together, one of the following will occur:
   a. If one of us wants the Property and the other doesn't, the person who wants the Property will pay the other the fair market value (see Clause 4) of his or her share of the Property.
   b. If both of us want the Property, the decision will be made in the following way [*choose one*]:
      ☒ (1) Right of First Offer. ___Amy___ shall have the right of first offer and may purchase ___Brett's___ share of the Property for its fair market value (see Clause 4). ___Amy___ will then become sole owner of the Property.
      ☐ (2) Coin Toss Method. We will flip a coin to determine who is entitled to the Property. The winner, upon paying the loser for his or her share of ownership, will become the sole owner of the Property.
      ☐ (3) Other. _____ .
4. Should either of us decide to end the relationship, we will do our best to agree on the fair current value of the Property. If we can't agree on a price, we will jointly choose a neutral appraiser and abide by that person's decision, or use the average price listed on eBay for an equivalent item.
5. Should we separate and neither of us wants the Property—or if we can't agree on a fair price—we will advertise it to the public, sell it to the highest bidder, and divide the money according to our respective ownership shares as set forth in Clause 2.
6. Should either of us die while we are living together, the Property will belong absolutely to the survivor. (If either of us makes a will or other estate plan, this agreement shall be reflected in that document.)
7. This agreement can be changed, but only in writing, and any changes must be signed by both of us.

8. Any dispute arising out of this contract will be mediated by a third person mutually acceptable to both of us. The mediator's role will be to help us arrive at a solution, not to impose one on us. If good faith efforts to arrive at our own solution to all issues in dispute with the help of a mediator prove to be fruitless, either of us may pursue other legal remedies.

9. If a court finds any portion of this contract to be illegal or otherwise unenforceable, the remainder of the contract is still in full force and effect.

Amy Randolph   _2/17/xx_
Amy Randolph   Date

Brett Bow   _2/17/xx_
Brett Bow   Date

Sample Joint Purchase Agreement When Only One Partner Is the Legal Borrower

Marcus Lyons and Karen Moore agree as follows:

1. Marcus has entered into an agreement with Macy's to purchase a bedroom set consisting of one king-size bed, one double dresser, two night stands, and two lamps at a total cost of $5,000.

2. Marcus has agreed to pay to Macy's that sum in monthly installments of $500, including interest, for 12 months, due on the first of every month beginning January 1, 20xx.

3. We intend that this bedroom set will be owned equally by both of us and that we each will pay one-half the monthly payment cost.

4. Karen will pay Marcus $250 per month at least one week before each monthly payment is due. Marcus will pay the entire installment due to Macy's in a timely manner.

5. Should either of us fail to make his or her share of the payment, the other will have the right to do so, and the ownership percentage of this person will be proportionately increased. If, for example, Karen makes sixteen payments (all of hers and four of Marcus's), she'd own $^{16}/_{24}$, or $^2/_3$, of the furniture.

6. Each of us shall keep a record of payments made. All payments shall be made by check.

7. If we stop living together, Marcus may buy the bedroom set from Karen by agreeing to be solely responsible for the rest of the monthly payments to Macy's and by paying Karen one-half of the difference, if any, between the bedroom set's current resale value, and the amount of money still owed to Macy's.

8. If Marcus does not want the furniture under the terms set out in Paragraph 7, Karen may buy the bedroom set by paying the full amount still owed to Macy's, so that Marcus no longer is obligated to make payments to Macy's, and by paying Marcus one-half of the difference, if any, between the bedroom set's current resale value and the amount of money still owed to Macy's. Alternatively, Karen may enter into an arrangement with Macy's to take over the payments herself, and pay Marcus one-half of the difference between the bedroom set's current resale value and the amount of money still owed.

9. If neither person wants the bedroom set, the furniture will be sold. The balance owed Macy's shall be paid from the proceeds of sale, and any remaining debt will be divided between us equally or, if either of us has made extra payments under Paragraph 5 of this agreement, according to our ownership share.

10. Should either of us die while we are living together, the furniture will belong absolutely to the survivor. If either of us makes a will or estate plan, this agreement will be reflected in that document.

11. This agreement can be changed, but only in writing, and any changes must be signed by both of us.

12. Any dispute arising out of this contract will be mediated by a third person mutually acceptable to both of us. The mediator's role will be to help us arrive at a solution, not to impose one on us. If good faith efforts to arrive at our own solution to all issues in dispute with the help of a mediator prove to be fruitless, either of us may make a written request to the other that the dispute be arbitrated. If such a request is made, our dispute will be submitted to arbitration under the rules of the American Arbitration Association, and one arbitrator will hear our dispute. The decision of the arbitrator will be binding on us and will be enforceable in any court that has jurisdiction over the controversy. By agreeing to arbitration, we each agree to give up the right to a jury trial.

13. If a court finds any portion of this contract to be illegal or otherwise unenforceable, the remainder of the contract is still in full force and effect.

Marcus Lyons   *February 3, 20xx*
Marcus   Date

Karen Moore   *February 3, 20xx*
Karen Moore   Date

You can prepare an Agreement for a Joint Purchase using the form shown above. Simply fill in the details of your joint purchase, including the item or property bought, the percentage of ownership (such as 50-50 or 60-40) each of you has, and how you will deal with the property should you split up. For example, you may specify that one person automatically has the right (of first refusal) to buy out the other's share. You may agree to do a simple coin toss or come up with your own approach depending upon the particular property.

FORMS

The Nolo website includes a downloadable copy of the Agreement for a Joint Purchase shown above. See the appendix for the link to this form.

You can edit this Agreement for a Joint Purchase as you see fit, or use it as a starting point to prepare your own agreement. For example, if one of you purchased the jointly owned item by credit card, you may want to add details to Clause 2, clarifying that one person made the purchase, but that the item is jointly owned. See the Sample Joint Purchase Agreement When Only One Partner Is the Legal Borrower, above, for ideas.

CAUTION

Only the partner whose name is on the credit card is legally obligated to pay the bill, even if you have a private agreement splitting the cost. If only one of you signs a credit agreement to purchase an item, only that person is legally obligated to pay the creditor. This is true even if you and your partner sign a private agreement to share ownership and payments. The creditor will accept money from anyone and properly credit the account, but if a payment isn't made, the creditor will pursue only the person whose name is on the account. Thus, Karen doesn't have to pay Macy's if Marcus stops paying the bill for the furniture he purchased with Karen but charged to his account. Karen has a legal contract with Marcus, but not with Macy's. Of course, the store doesn't care who pays the bill. Karen can send the money and the store will credit Marcus's account.

Buying a Car Together

It's not uncommon for unmarried couples to purchase a car together. If you do so, be aware that buying a car means entering into a series of agreements with third parties (for example, a car dealer, a bank, and an insurance company) that are binding regardless of the status of your relationship.

It pays to understand all of your options and choose an arrangement that is financially viable.

Sole ownership. If you intend that the vehicle will belong to only one partner, but the other partner will advance part or all of the down payment in the form of a loan, the borrower should sign a written contract to repay. This contract is a called a "promissory note." A sample promissory note and directions for use are included in Chapter 6. If you choose this option, you should register the vehicle in the borrower's name only.

If you decide that only one of you will own the car, you can include the other partner as an "additional driver" on the car insurance. One advantage to sole car ownership: If the car is involved in an accident, only the partner who owns the car can be sued. (But if the other partner was driving, that person could be sued for negligent actions.)

Joint ownership. If you intend to own the vehicle jointly, you'll need a written agreement outlining the details. This is especially important if only one of you signed for the loan but both of you will be contributing toward its repayment. When you register the vehicle with the state, put it in both names. Depending on state law, you often have three options with car registration:

Option 1. "Thomas Finnegan or Keija Adams." This creates a joint tenancy in many states; if one person dies, the other automatically inherits the car without going through probate. However, depending on state law (see Option 3, below), the "or" form of ownership lets either party sell the vehicle without the knowledge or consent of the other.

Option 2. "Thomas Finnegan and Keija Adams." This establishes a tenancy in common; both signatures are required to transfer title of the vehicle. At death, however, each person can leave his or her share to anyone he or she wishes. If no estate plan is made, the nearest blood relative inherits the deceased person's share by intestate succession. If you want your partner to inherit your interest in the car, include it in your will (discussed in Chapter 9), or consider Option 3, below.

Option 3. "Thomas Finnegan and Keija Adams, as Joint Tenants With Right of Survivorship." Not only does this let the survivor automatically inherit the car without going through probate if one of you dies, but it also requires both signatures to transfer title while you're both alive.

Car leases. The same rules (as joint ownership) apply to leased cars: The one who signs the contract is responsible for the payments, even if his or her partner is using the car. Be careful here, as lease payments can exceed a car's value if you default early in the contract.

> **CAUTION**
>
> **State vehicle ownership rules can vary.** Before relying on the general vehicle ownership rules described above, check with your state's motor vehicle department. Most have information online. Your state's rules regarding the words that should be used to establish the different types of joint ownership of motor vehicles may be slightly different from those outlined above.

How to Transfer Ownership in Property

If one of you already owns property, such as a car, you may want to give the other a full or partial interest in your property. If the property comes with a title slip (for example, a car or boat), you can change the names on it to reflect the new joint or transferred ownership. If you don't have a title slip, simply make one up. A sample is shown below. Be sure to include the names, dates, and any amount paid, and sign and date it.

It's particularly important to create a title slip (or change a state-provided slip) when you transfer or change ownership of valuable property. If you split up, having clear records of who owns what will make your financial disentanglement much easier.

> **TIP**
>
> **Transferring ownership of real property has its own special rules and is usually, but not always, handled in a separate, written agreement.** Several samples are included in Chapter 6. Be particularly careful in this area, as there may be significant tax consequences to a transfer.

Sample Title Slip

I, Shirley Letterman (owner), give one-half of my right, title, and interest in MegaBoom VII Sound Experience Home Theater System, model number 123456789, to Fred Leno, for the sum of $500.

Shirley Letterman
_____
Shirley Letterman

September 2, 20xx
_____
Date

Fred Leno
_____
Fred Leno

September 2, 20xx
_____
Date

Agreement Covering Joint Projects

John and Martha live together. They have no property to speak of, but they have a dream—to build a boat and sail around the world. They know it will take a lot of time, energy, and cooperation, and they want to protect their vision should any of life's disappointments affect their relationship.

A sample Agreement Covering a Joint Project is shown below. You can use this as a guide in crafting your own agreement. (If you're building a house, many of the ownership and financing issues are the same as if you were buying a house together. See Chapter 6 for advice.)

In making your own agreement for a joint project, be sure you spell out completely:

- what the project is—for example, construction of a sailboat (Clause 1)
- how much each partner will contribute in terms of income, labor, or something else (Clauses 2 and 3)
- how the joint project will be divided should you separate (Clauses 4, 5, and 6); for example, in Clause 4 of the Sample Agreement Covering a Joint Project, you could reverse the provision giving Martha the first option to keep the boat, or include a provision on how you will make this decision, such as by flipping a coin for that right, and
- the effect on the agreement if one partner fails to contribute his or her promised share to the project (Clause 7).

You can add other relevant terms to your agreement—for example, you may want to cover contingencies such as what happens if the project costs more than originally estimated.

Sample Agreement Covering a Joint Project

John Ito and Martha Silver agree as follows:

1. We intend to jointly construct a 30-foot sailboat to be jointly owned upon completion.

2. We each will contribute $12,000 for the purchase of necessary supplies. This money will be kept in a joint bank account and both signatures will be required to withdraw any money from this account.

3. We each will work diligently on the boat (this means at least 20 hours per month). We will each keep records of all hours worked.

4. Should we separate, Martha will have the first opportunity to buy out John's share for an amount of money equal to John's actual cash investment plus $50 per hour for each hour he has worked on the boat.

5. If we separate and Martha decides not to buy out John's share under the terms of Paragraph 4, John will have the opportunity to buy out Martha's share on the same terms.

6. Should neither of us elect to purchase the other's share of the boat at separation, we will sell the boat and divide the proceeds equally.

7. If either of us fails to work on the boat at least 20 hours per month for three consecutive months, the other may buy out the nonworker's share at that time under the terms of Paragraph 4.

8. Should either of us die while we are living together, the survivor becomes sole owner of the boat. (If either of us makes an estate plan, this agreement will be incorporated in that document.)

9. This agreement can be changed, but only in writing, and any changes must be signed by both of us.

10. Any dispute arising out of this contract will be mediated by a third person mutually acceptable to both of us. The mediator's role will be to help us arrive at a solution, not to impose one on us. If good faith efforts to arrive at our own solution to all issues in dispute with the help of a mediator prove to be fruitless, either of us may make a written request to the other that the dispute be arbitrated. If such a request is made, our dispute will be submitted to arbitration under the rules of the American Arbitration Association, and one arbitrator will hear our dispute. The decision of the arbitrator will be binding on us and will be

enforceable in any court that has jurisdiction over the controversy. By agreeing to arbitration, we each agree to waive the right to a jury trial.

11. If a court finds any portion of this contract to be illegal or otherwise unenforceable, the remainder of the contract is still in full force and effect.

John Ito
Signature

July 2, 20xx
Date

Martha Silver
Signature

July 2, 20xx
Date

SEE AN EXPERT

If your project is a business, get legal advice. If you and your partner are opening a business together, you will be investing a great deal of your time—and probably your money. You will also need to decide on the form of business entity (such as a partnership or corporation). The Business Formation section on www.nolo.com is a good place to start reviewing your options. In most cases, you'll need a formal partnership agreement. We recommend *Form a Partnership: The Complete Legal Guide*, by Denis Clifford and Ralph Warner (Nolo), to do this. You should also have your agreement checked by a lawyer with experience in small business issues.

Agreement Covering Homemaker Services

In some relationships, one person works outside the home while the other partner cooks, cleans, shops, and otherwise takes care of the home. This sort of division of labor can raise questions such as whether the homemaker should be compensated. One option is to treat it as income; the other option is to pay the expenses of the stay-at-home partner in lieu of a weekly salary. Be careful here, as the IRS might consider these payments as taxable income, rather than a tax-free gift.

Let's take the example of Ted and Joanne. Ted is 45, divorced, and has custody of his two children. He's a physician with an annual after-tax income in excess of $350,000. Joanne is 38, also divorced, with custody of her child. Her ex-husband only occasionally pays child support. Ted and Joanne decide to live together and agree that Ted will earn the money and Joanne will take care of the children and of the household full time. They want to write a contract that will provide Joanne with fair compensation for housework and child care, but not give her any rights to Ted's property should they separate.

One preliminary problem Ted and Joanne face is valuing Joanne's services. Should her pay be based on what the cheapest local domestic workers charge or what a high-quality teacher gets paid, or should it be based on Ted's income? Also, should Joanne have some responsibility to provide some of the household and child care services without compensation? After all, she and her child live there too.

Although there is no one answer to these questions, it often helps to list all factors that either one feels ought to go into deciding how much the stay-at-home worker should be paid, and then to work out a compromise agreement that feels good to both. In our view, the two most important factors are that:

- the household worker have enough income (money of his or her own) to achieve a substantial measure of financial independence, and
- both members of the couple feel the amount is more or less reasonable.

The sample Agreement Covering Homemaker Services shown below provides one model you can follow for this type of situation. In this example, Ted and Joanne would not need to prepare the Agreement to Keep Property Separate, and Attachment A (Separately Owned Property), described earlier in this chapter, since those issues are already covered in this Agreement Covering Homemaker Services.

Note: It may seem old-fashioned to have a "stay-at-home" partner (male or female), but as high-end work obligations seem to increase exponentially, this isn't a totally outmoded family arrangement.

Sample Agreement Covering Homemaker Services

Ted Corbett and Joanne Lewis agree that they plan to live together. They intend to remain in a committed, long-term relationship that will provide love and nurturing for both themselves and their children, but for personal reasons, have decided not to get married. In a spirit of fairness, and to help them further their joint goals, they agree that:

1. Ted will continue to work as a physician. He and Joanne expect that he'll work 50–60 hours a week and he will have little time or energy to care for the home or their children.

2. Joanne will devote her time in the home raising the children and doing most of the domestic chores including the cleaning, laundry, cooking, and gardening. Ted will contribute an extra $800 a week to a joint account, which Joanne can draw on to cover her expenses, over and above all of the costs of running the home as set out in Paragraph 7. These payments will be adjusted from time to time to reflect changes in the cost of living. If Ted elects to make a gift to Joanne in any year, the value of this gift will be deducted from this obligation. In such event, no taxes or Social Security payment will be due.

3. If the partners decide that Ted will make payments directly to Joanne instead of depositing them in their joint account, Ted will make Social Security and other legally required employer payments for Joanne as his employee and he will pay for medical insurance coverage for her and her son, Tim. Joanne will be responsible for any income tax owing on these payments.

4. All real and personal property owned by either Ted or Joanne prior to the date of this agreement will remain the separate property of its owner and cannot be transferred to the other person unless this is done in writing. We have each attached to this contract a list of our major items of separate property.

5. As of the date of this agreement, all property owned, earned, or accumulated by Ted or Joanne will belong solely to the person earning or accumulating it. The home and furnishings will be provided by Ted and wiill be owned solely by him. All property purchased by Joanne with her earnings will belong to her.

6. The separate assets and property of either Ted or Joanne, owned now or acquired in the future, shall not become the separate property of the other, or the joint property of both, except under the terms of a written agreement signed by the person whose separate property is to be reclassified.

7. Ted will deposit reasonable amounts of money into the joint account each month to provide food, clothing, shelter, and recreation for the entire family as long as he and Joanne live together. By doing this, Ted assumes no obligation to support Joanne or her son upon termination of this agreement.

8. Either Ted or Joanne can end this agreement by giving the other two months' written notice. No reason is necessary. During the two-month notice period, Ted will continue to provide Joanne with a home and if he has been paying her a salary, he will continue to pay her salary. No further postseparation support will be owed by either party.

9. Any dispute arising out of this contract will be mediated by a third person mutually acceptable to both of us. The mediator's role will be to help us arrive at a solution, not to impose one on us. If good faith efforts to arrive at our own solution to all issues in dispute with the help of a mediator prove to be fruitless after two mediation sessions, either of us may make a written request to the other that the dispute be arbitrated. If such a request is made, our dispute will be submitted to arbitration under the rules of the American Arbitration Association, and one arbitrator will hear our dispute. The decision of the arbitrator will be binding on us and will be enforceable in any court that has jurisdiction over the controversy. By agreeing to arbitration, we each agree to give up the right to a jury trial.

10. This agreement represents Ted and Joanne's complete understanding regarding their living together and replaces any and all prior agreements, written or oral. It can be changed, but only in writing, and any changes must be signed by both parties.

11. If a court finds any portion of this contract to be illegal or otherwise unenforceable, the remainder of the contract is still in force and effect.

Ted Corbett	_April 24, 20xx_
Ted Corbett	Date
Joanne Lewis	_April 24, 20xx_
Joanne Lewis	Date

> (!) CAUTION
> **IRS warning. Don't ignore the tax implications of your arrangements!**
> Giving your partner more than $14,000 per year can trigger a gift tax obligation
> (though in most instances, no tax is owed until as much as $5,490,000 is given over
> a lifetime). Paying "wages" to a partner for domestic services can trigger Social
> Security and income tax withholding obligations (for more on this, see the "Social
> Security" section in Chapter 4). In some instances, therefore, it may be more
> prudent simply to have the higher-earning partner pay more (or all) of the joint
> expenses rather than giving money to the lower-earning or unemployed partner.

Agreement for Artists, Writers, and Inventors

Creative people often work on inventions, software programs, artwork, or books for a long time. While the work is in progress—and even when it's done—it is usually unclear how much monetary value, if any, the finished product will have. If you keep all your property and income separate, and you include creative work in your definition of property, valuing creative works won't be a problem. Each person owns what he or she has created.

If you agree to pool the property you accumulate while living together, however, valuing creative work—if you split up—can be a real problem. Suppose, for example, you're a successful writer who's been working on a novel for two years. Who knows whether this yet-to-be-published book will sell 5,000 copies, a million copies, or some number in between? If you and your partner break up, even if you easily agree to divide your property, you may have real difficulty doing it fairly.

If you're determined to share some or all of your property, you will face some important issues when it comes to creative works protected by copyright, trade secret, or patent laws (also known as intellectual property laws). For example, co-owning a painting is quite different from co-owning the copyright in that painting. The owner of the painting makes money when the painting is sold; the owner of the copyright makes money when the image is licensed for use on postcards, books, posters, or other merchandise. If you are an inventor, the rules can be even more complex. Under patent law, for example, each co-owner has the right to license the invention without paying the other co-owner.

If you and your partner wish to share in the income from artistic or inventive property, we recommend that you create an agreement that establishes: (1) that ownership in any intellectual property rights will be retained by the partner who created the work; and (2) that income from the sale or licensing of the works will be shared equally between the partners for a fixed time period, after which the owner no longer has to share the income with the other partner.

This arrangement provides for sharing of income but allows the creator of the creative work to control the sales and licensing deals—an important factor for every writer, artist, or inventor. The use of a fixed time period guarantees that the split will not go on forever; keep in mind that copyright protection, for example, lasts over 100 years.

The Sample Agreement for Artists, Writers, and Inventors, shown below, includes the options discussed above. This is just one of many ways that intellectual property can be divided.

SEE AN EXPERT

See an IP lawyer. If you and your partner are concerned about the rights and income associated with a creative work, have a lawyer familiar with intellectual property law review any agreement you prepare before you sign on the dotted line.

> **EXAMPLE:** Terri and Chris have been together for three years. Terri is a toy inventor and Chris is a photographer, but both have other part-time jobs to make ends meet. They recently moved in together and have decided to alternate earning an income and taking time off to focus on their artistic ventures. This way, they can both be creative and they can also pay their rent and groceries.
>
> Terri and Chris have prepared their own agreement for this purpose. (See the Sample Agreement for Artists and Inventors shown below.)

TIP

A loan and promissory note is another option. If only one person wants to take time off, the working partner may simply lend the other money, using a promissory note such as the one shown in Chapter 6. No matter what you arrange, you must specify how much time equals how much money and, if appropriate, set a method of repayment.

Sample Agreement for Artists, Writers, and Inventors

Terri McGraw and Chris Macklin agree as follows:

1. Each of us will keep as our separate property, all assets and property (and any income generated by that property) each of us owns as of the date of this agreement. We have each attached a list of our major items of separate property to this contract. (See Attachment A, Separately Owned Property.)

2. Starting as of the date this agreement is signed and continuing for as long as we live together, any property or income, including salaries or financial returns from artistic pursuits, earned by either of us while we are living together (except for inheritances and gifts—see Paragraph 3—and except as set forth in paragraph 8) belongs equally to both of us. All joint funds will be kept in joint bank or securities accounts.

3. Money or property inherited by either of us or gifts given to either of us during the time we live together will be and remain the separate property of the person inheriting it. Separate property belonging to one of us cannot become the separate property of the other or the joint property of both without a written agreement signed by the person whose separate property is to be reclassified.

4. We agree to take turns working at regular full-time jobs in order to earn enough money for the two of us to live on. While one person works, the other will be free to pursue his or her creative endeavors. Terri will work for the first six months, Chris the next six months, and so on, alternating six-month periods of work and creative time for the duration of this agreement. If we modify our schedule, our actual working schedule shall be deemed to be our agreed-upon schedule, unless either party objects in writing within one month of the schedule change.

5. All of our household expenses and personal and medical expenses will be paid by the partner who's employed at the time the expense is incurred.

6. Should our living together relationship end at a point when one partner has been employed for a longer period of time than the other, then if a written objection has been sent, the partner employed for less time will reimburse the other partner for one-half of the living expenses incurred during the extra months that the other partner has worked.

7. Should our living together relationship end, each of us will keep our separate property (property we owned prior to living together, income from that

property, and any property inherited or received as a gift while we are together). All property, other than intellectual property, that was acquired or created while we lived together will be considered to be jointly owned and will be evenly divided.

8. During our living together relationship each of us may create works that can be protected by copyright, patent, trade secret, or trademark laws (intellectual property). The rights to the intellectual property, and the works themselves, shall be owned by the creating partner. However, all income from the sale, license, or exploitation of the intellectual property, individually or collectively, will be shared equally between us as long as we continue in a living together relationship. Should our living together relationship end, all income from the intellectual property will be shared by us for a period of three years from the date of separation, and the creating partner will be entitled to any income or royalties after that period. In the event that we jointly create a work, we will enter into a separate co-ownership agreement that establishes each partner's ownership interest based upon their contribution, but absent such an agreement, it will be deemed owned 50/50 by the two of us.

9. This agreement represents our complete understanding regarding our living together and replaces any and all prior agreements, written or oral. It can be changed, but only in writing, and any change must be signed by both of us.

10. If a court finds any portion of this contract to be illegal or otherwise unenforceable, the remainder of the contract is still in full force and effect.

11. Any dispute arising out of this contract will be mediated by a third person mutually acceptable to both of us. The mediator's role will be to help us arrive at a solution, not to impose one on us. If good faith efforts to arrive at our own solution to all issues in dispute with the help of a mediator prove to be fruitless after two mediation sessions, either of us may make a written request to the other that the dispute be arbitrated. In that case, our dispute will be submitted to arbitration under the rules of the American Arbitration Association, and one arbitrator will hear our dispute. The decision of the arbitrator will be binding on us and will be enforceable in any court that has jurisdiction over the controversy. By agreeing to arbitration, we each agree to give up the right to a jury trial.

Terri McGraw	*October 15, 20xx*
Terri McGraw	Date
Chris Macklin	*October 15, 20xx*
Chris Macklin	Date

A variation of this Sample Agreement for Artists, Writers, and Inventors can be used for any situation where one partner wants to take time off—for example, to work on an invention, make a film, or write the Great American Novel. If one partner is taking time off to raise a child, you may not need an "equal time off" agreement or a loan, as both partners are contributing to the relationship in different ways, and if you are both legal parents, the ordinary obligations of child support will apply to you if your relationship comes to an end.

Agreement for People in School

It's common for one partner to help the other with educational expenses or support while he or she is in school, even for older couples who are going back to school for retraining, especially after a divorce. It is important to have a written agreement in this situation.

Agreements providing that one member of an unmarried couple will help support the other while he or she goes to school can take many different forms. Usually, the aim of such an agreement is to make clear that the person going to school will owe the other partner (who pays all or some of the school bills and supports the student while in school) a certain amount of money. That way, if the couple breaks up shortly after the student finishes school, the nonstudent partner won't have paid school bills and supported the student for nothing.

One way to plan for a fair monetary result is to provide that the person going to school owes the other partner any money expended for tuition and living expenses. This can take the form of a simple promissory note for all money paid out, plus reasonable interest. (See Chapter 6 for a sample promissory note.) Assuming the student goes to school for several years, the amount owed will have to be updated periodically. Be sure to discuss—and include in the agreement—how you intend to handle student loan debt. Only the student borrower is legally liable for a student loan, but sometime the couple uses some of the loan funds to pay for their joint living expenses. If this is the case, it's only fair that the nonborrower reimburse the borrower for some percentage of the debt if the couple breaks up before the loan is paid in full.

Sample Agreement for People in School

Carol Thayer and Bill Fujimoto agree as follows:

1. We are living together and plan to continue to do so indefinitely.

2. All property and assets owned by either of us prior to the date of this agreement (including all future income earned from this property) shall be the separate property of its owner. We have attached a list of our major items of separate property to this contract. (Attachment A, Separately Owned Property.) In addition, all money or property inherited by or given to either of us shall be his or her separate property.

3. We will take turns going to school so that the one not in school can support the other until he/she gets a degree. We will flip a coin to decide who goes first. The "loser" will be responsible for a portion of the "winner's" educational expenses, up to a total of $18,000 per year, for three years. At the end of three years, the person who has already attended school will assume these responsibilities for the other, for three years, up to a total of $20,000 per year.

   If we split up during the first three-year period, all agreements by either of us to provide the other with future education expenses will terminate. The student shall sign a promissory note agreeing to repay the full amount the other partner has expended for the student's education at the rate of $800 per month. However, if we live together for more than three years, our continuing financial obligations to support each other while in school shall not be affected by subsequent separation. Thus, if a separation occurs during the fourth, fifth, or sixth year, the nonstudent still must pay the other's tuition and other school-related expenses up to a total of $20,000 for that year. All tuition is to be paid in the month due.

4. During the first six years we live together, beginning with the date we sign this agreement, all income and property acquired by either of us (excluding inheritances, gifts to one of us, and income produced by previously owned separate property) shall be jointly owned. The person who is the primary income producer at the time will manage the funds and pay all necessary household bills. After six years, we will inventory our accumulated property and divide it equally. Thereafter, each person's earnings shall be his or her separate property and neither of us will have any interest in the present or future property of the other.

If we separate before the end of six years, all jointly owned property shall be divided according to the fraction of time each of us has provided the primary support (if Carol supports Bill for three years and Bill supports her for two, Carol is entitled to three-fifths of the property).

5. Should we separate, neither will owe any continuing financial obligation to the other except as set out in Paragraph 3, with one exception. If any of the student loan money either of us receives is used to pay joint living expenses, that portion of the loan will be a joint obligation, and the nonborrower will reimburse the borrower for that portion of the loan repayments on an annual basis.

6. Any change in the ownership status of any property (from the separate property of one person to joint property, or from the separate property of one person to the separate property of the other) shall be made in writing and signed by the person making the transfer.

7. This agreement is our complete understanding regarding our living together and replaces any and all prior agreements, written or oral. It can be amended, but only in writing, and any writing must be signed by both.

8. If a court finds any portion of this contract to be illegal or otherwise unenforceable, the remainder of the contract is still in full force and effect.

9. Any dispute arising out of this contract will be mediated by a third person mutually acceptable to both of us. The mediator's role will be to help us arrive at a solution, not to impose one on us. If good faith efforts to arrive at our own solution to all issues in dispute with the help of a mediator prove to be fruitless, either of us may make a written request to the other that the dispute be arbitrated. In that case, our dispute will be submitted to arbitration under the rules of the American Arbitration Association, and one arbitrator will hear our dispute. The decision of the arbitrator will be binding on us and will be enforceable in any court that has jurisdiction over the controversy. By agreeing to arbitration, we each agree to give up the right to a jury trial.

Bill Fujimoto
Bill Fujimoto

January 2, 20xx
Date

Carol Thayer
Carol Thayer

January 2, 20xx
Date

EXAMPLE: Soon after Alvin and Siena move in together, they agree that Siena will attend pharmacy school while Alvin works, supports them both, and pays a portion of Siena's tuition. (Siena will take out a student loan for the rest.) Alvin and Siena agree in writing that if they break up while Siena is in school or within three years after she graduates, she will owe Alvin $10,000 for each year he has supported her, with no interest to be charged until she graduates, at which point interest will be figured at a rate of 5%. They also agree that Siena will have five years to repay Alvin in equal monthly installments.

Of course, more complicated agreements are possible. In the Sample Agreement for People in School, above, Carol plans to become a veterinarian, and Bill is an aspiring dentist. To maximize both career opportunities and their personal relationship, they provide that each shall help the other finish his or her education.

What Is the Best Living Together Contract for Senior Cohabitants?

The legal issues for seniors are not fundamentally different from those of younger couples, but the realities of the lives of older partners calls for a somewhat different approach when it comes to drafting a living together agreement. Most likely a "Keeping Things Separate" approach, will be most appropriate for an older couple, possibly with an additional clause providing for a joint household bank account to cover day-to-day expenses. (See the Agreement to Keep Property Separate section earlier in the chapter.) And, if you are sharing a house that is owned solely by one partner, you should add a paragraph that confirms the shared living situation—specifying who is the owner, allocating the expenses of home ownership, maintenance, and occupancy, and providing that if there's a breakup the nonowner will move out promptly. Older couples also need to pay special attention to the drafting of wills or trusts, and they should talk openly with each other about their respective estate plans.

Agreement to Protect Person Who Moves a Long Distance or Gives Up a Job

Occasionally, one partner moves a considerable distance to be with the other. Sometimes, doing this is a welcome adventure. Other times, however, it's more traumatic, especially if the person who is moving decides to give up a good job and a supportive network of family and friends, or a low-cost apartment rental. Despite the hopes and wishes of both partners, there's always a fear that the relationship won't work out and the person who moved will either have to return to his or her original location or cope with being alone in a new town. Obviously, these concerns increase if the moving partner has small children.

To deal with this potential problem, some couples agree that the person who moved or gave up a job will be compensated if the relationship dissolves within a relatively short time. Here are two slightly different clauses that can be included in any living together contract in this book:

As a condition of Sarah giving up her job and moving with John to Chicago, John agrees that if, for any reason, they cease living together before September 1, 20xx, John shall immediately pay Sarah $5,000 to help her establish a separate household.

or

John and Sarah agree that as a condition of John giving up his present employment and moving to New York to live with Sarah, she will immediately pay him the sum of $2,500.

CAUTION

Consider tax implications. If these payments are significant, the IRS could treat them as reportable gifts or taxable income.

Debt, Credit, Taxes, and More:
Practical Aspects of Living Together

Debt and Credit..83

   Debts 84

   Joint Bank Accounts.. 84

How (and Why) to Check Your Credit Report 86

   Joint Credit Card Accounts 87

   Authorized Users of Credit Cards..89

Buying and Investing Together.. 90

   Property Acquired Before Getting Together 90

   Property Acquired After Getting Together.......................... 90

Discrimination 92

   Credit Discrimination..92

   Discrimination in Employment.. 94

   Discrimination When Traveling Together 96

Sharing Your Last Name..97

   Change of Name by Usage..98

   Change of Name by Court Order...98

Income Taxes... 99

   Tax Rates and the Standard Deduction 100

   Income Tax and Social Security 101

   Dependents and Taxes... 101

   Income Tax on the Sale of Your Home: Capital Gain Exclusion 102

Social Security 103

Retirement Plans.. 105

   Naming a Beneficiary... 105

   Your Will Doesn't Govern Your Retirement Plan 106

   Rollovers 107

Public Benefits..108

Insurance 109

    Life Insurance 109

    Homeowners' Insurance 110

    Renters' Insurance 110

    Automobile Insurance...111

    Health Insurance 111

    Workers' Compensation Insurance...112

    Unemployment Insurance...113

Liability for Medical Care of a Partner 114

Making Medical and Financial Decisions for Your Partner 114

    Health Care Directives..115

    Durable Power of Attorney for Finances...117

Wrongful Death and Loss of Consortium Lawsuits..119

hen you and your partner decide to live together, you are probably acting on romantic impulses. Unfortunately, practical
problems inevitably tag along in the wake of romance.
Although most of these problems aren't legal and certainly don't
demand the input of lawyers, some day-to-day issues are connected with
the law. This chapter focuses on the everyday legal situations unmarried
couples face—from the pros and cons of joint accounts to legal rules about
discrimination against unmarried couples to paying your income taxes.

RELATED TOPICS
Related topics covered elsewhere in this book include:
- How to write living together agreements covering property, cars, and
  other joint purchases: Chapter 3
- Renting or buying a home together: Chapters 5 and 6
- Having or adopting a child together: Chapter 7
- Writing wills and planning your estates: Chapter 9
- Handling disputes regarding property when separating: Chapter 10.

Debt and Credit

While most of us aspire to rise above crass material concerns, the reality
is that all couples benefit from clearly agreeing in advance who will pay
for the rent, car installments, or groceries. When you live together, you
must also decide whether to pool your money and the property you buy
with that money, or keep it all separate. Keep in mind that sharing a
home doesn't mean your financial lives must become one. If you want to
combine finances, be sure you really know and trust your partner. Don't
feel pressured to combine everything when you're just starting out simply
because the unmarried couple upstairs—who have been together 15
years—have only one bank account. Remember, remaining financially
independent is one of the "privileges" of being unmarried.

This section provides an overview of an unmarried couple's rights and
responsibilities when it comes to debt and credit. Once you understand
these issues, you'll be better prepared to write out your agreement about
sharing money and property—equally, partially, or not at all. Chapter 3
shows you how to do this.

Debts

A debt is a sum of money owed to someone else, whether it is owed to an individual or a bank, including credit card debts.

Unlike marriage, living together does not make you legally responsible for your partner's debts. Should your partner declare bankruptcy or face other debt problems, you won't lose your property as long as you've kept it separate and haven't voluntarily agreed to be liable. Your wages cannot be attached and your property cannot be taken to pay for your partner's overdue bills or debts, and your credit rating will not be negatively affected by your partner's financial problems.

But this financial independence may suddenly disappear if:
- you sign a joint purchase agreement
- you cosign a loan with your partner obligating yourself to pay the debt if the person taking out the loan fails to do so
- your partner's debt is charged to a shared or joint account or to your own personal account, or
- you register as domestic partners, in some jurisdictions, especially if you register in a marriage-equivalent form of domestic partnership.

Joint Bank Accounts

There are many different ways to pool money—not at all, completely, or on a limited basis. It's up to you. You might decide to combine all of your finances, to keep them entirely separate, or to shoot for something in between.

You should not face any problem opening a joint checking or banking account under both your names. In general, joint accounts make sense if you limit their purpose (for example, for specific household expenses, paying for a jointly owned asset, or for travel) and keep adequate records. Many unmarried couples have peacefully maintained joint bank accounts for years.

But having a joint account is also a risk. In most states, each person has the right to withdraw or spend all the money, even if they didn't contribute any funds to the account, and both partners are responsible for all activity involving the account. You're equally liable for bounced checks, overdrafts, and all the rest. This can cause big problems if one of you is a habitual overspender.

Joint Accounts May Imply a Contract to Share Income

As we discuss in Chapter 2, in some states, including California, enforceable contracts between unmarried couples to share earnings and other property can be made orally or sometimes even implied from the circumstances of a relationship. Sharing credit and bank accounts might be a factor a court would consider in deciding whether a couple had an implied contract to share income and other property. So if you want to do everything possible to keep property ownership separate, it's best not to open joint accounts. If you do, sign an agreement, such as the Agreement to Keep Property Separate in Chapter 3.

In theory, you can prevent your partner from bouncing checks and the like by requiring both signatures on checks and withdrawals. But this is usually cumbersome and inconvenient, and many banks won't be willing to go along with this requirement.

Record keeping can pose another problem with joint accounts. It's often difficult to keep track of how much money is in the account when two people are writing checks and making withdrawals. You'll have to set up a reliable method of tracking these things and then resolve to stick to it, including honoring whatever agreement you've made about how much each of you is going to contribute to the account.

CAUTION

Transfers of assets between unmarried partners may be taxed. Be careful if you are shifting valuable property or a lot of money to your living together partner. If the asset is worth more than $14,000, you will likely need to file a federal gift tax return, though you won't owe any taxes on the transfer until the amounts become significant. So, get some good tax advice in advance. See Chapter 9 for more on this issue.

How (and Why) to Check Your Credit Report

If you've lived together for a long time or have had joint credit card or bank accounts, it's possible that your credit report has become intertwined with that of your partner or has information on it that belongs only to him or her, and not to you. This is usually not to your advantage, especially if your partner has bad credit.

Your credit report contains your credit history. Credit reports are maintained by credit bureaus—companies that collect information related to your creditworthiness, including your bank and credit card accounts, loans (such as mortgages, car loans, and student loans), payment history on those loans and accounts, delinquencies on accounts, bankruptcy filings, criminal arrests and convictions, current and previous employers, lawsuits and judgments against you, and tax or other liens. Creditors, landlords, employers, banks, and collection agencies can request and review your credit report.

Unfortunately, many credit reports contain inaccurate or outdated information. If you have some joint accounts with your partner or have been living together for a long time, the credit bureaus may have included information on your credit record about your partner's separate accounts. Information about separate accounts should only appear on the report of the partner responsible for that account. Information about joint accounts should appear on both reports. One of the added benefits is that you will clear up who is really the borrower on the account and who is considered the primary borrower on a joint card account.

Each partner should request a copy of his or her credit report and review it for errors or outdated information. It's a good idea to do this every year. Contact one of the three major national credit bureaus to get your report.

The federal Fair Credit Reporting Act (FCRA) now requires each major national credit bureau—Equifax, Experian, and TransUnion— to provide you one free copy of your credit report each year. You can request your free report by one of these means:
- Telephone—877-322-8228
- Internet—www.annualcreditreport.com, or
- Mail—Annual Credit Report Service, P.O. Box 105281, Atlanta, GA 30348-5281.

You must provide your name, address, Social Security number, and date of birth when you order. You also may be required to provide information that only you would know, such as the amount of your monthly mortgage payment.

You may be entitled to additional free copies of your credit report in any of the following circumstances:

- You have been denied credit or insurance because of information in your credit file. (In that case, you are entitled to a free copy of your report from the credit bureau that reported the information. A creditor that denies you credit or insurance will tell you the name and address of the credit bureau reporting the information that led to the denial.)
- You are unemployed and planning to apply for a job within 60 days following your request for your credit report.
- You receive public assistance.
- You believe that your credit file contains errors due to fraud, such as identity theft.

If you find errors on your report (for example, a car loan for which your partner is the only signatory) or outdated information, notify the credit bureau in writing. The bureau is required by law to correct your report. If the bureau investigates the item and disagrees with you, at the very least you can include a brief explanation on your report about the disputed item.

For more information on what information can appear on your credit report and for how long, how to correct errors, and how to rebuild credit after a financial setback, see the Debt Management section of www. nolo.com. The Nolo book *Credit Repair*, by Margaret Reiter and Robin Leonard, includes more detailed information on the subject.

Joint Credit Card Accounts

As with bank accounts, you may want to keep your credit accounts separate and each deal with creditors on your own terms. In that way you don't have to worry about the other person's purchases and any potential damage to your credit rating. Nevertheless, many unmarried couples open joint credit card accounts in which both partners are authorized by the credit lender to charge up to a credit limit.

You can open a joint account for broad purposes, such as paying household expenses or to fund a distinct project—for example, remodeling a kitchen, saving for a vacation, or making a joint investment. Or you may use a joint card solely for household purchases, and use your individual cards for all other expenditures. You can get a joint charge account where you pay the entire monthly balance at once, like some American Express accounts, or a credit account where you are only obligated to pay a monthly minimum, such as a Visa or department store account. We strongly discourage putting one person's solo expenses solely on the credit card of the other person—it simply creates too great a risk of default.

It's fairly easy to put two names on a credit card. You simply fill out a joint credit card application. Many companies have changed the blanks from "spouse" to "co-applicant" or "co-applicant/spouse." If the application form only says "spouse," cross off the word "spouse" and write in "co-applicant." Don't claim to be a spouse—that term has a specific legal meaning (having to do with liability and responsibility), and lying on a credit application is fraud.

As long as one of you has sufficient income or savings to be considered a good credit risk—that is, you appear to be able to pay the bills—you'll probably get the credit card. Creditors are generally willing to open joint credit accounts—and why shouldn't they be? A joint account means more people are responsible for a debt. For example, if Roger and Jane have a joint credit card, and Roger lets his sister Fiona charge $2,500 on it, Roger and Jane are both legally obligated to pay the bill—even if Jane didn't know about Fiona using the card or knew about it but opposed it. Similarly, if Jane retaliates by leaving Roger and going on a buying binge using the joint credit card, Roger is legally responsible for all the charges Jane makes.

If one of you has a poor credit history, you may be denied a joint card, even if the other's credit is perfect. The partner with better credit may have to reapply in his or her name only. If this is what you end up doing, remember that only the official borrower is legally responsible for the debt.

CAUTION

If you break up, immediately close all joint bank and credit accounts.
All too often, one person feels depressed about a breakup and tries to pamper
himself or herself with "retail therapy." Don't just divide up the cards, each keeping a few. You're both still liable for all accounts—and you could get stuck paying
for your partner's "therapy" bill. And if a joint account becomes delinquent,
your credit record will suffer—even if you didn't incur the charges. Chapter 10
discusses important breakup tasks such as closing a joint account.

Authorized Users of Credit Cards

Most credit cards will allow you to add another person as an "authorized
user" of your account. For example, if Jane adds Roger as an authorized
user of her Visa credit card, Roger will get his own card with his name
on it and he may use it to charge purchases, but Roger is not legally
responsible for paying the bill (Jane is). If this is your plan, we encourage
you to have a side agreement that obligates Roger to repay Jane for any
bills she has to pay—though if Roger is broke this agreement won't be
of any benefit to Jane. It's crucial that you monitor the expenditures
regularly to be sure that you aren't taking on more of your partner's debt
than you agreed to—and if so, you need to be prepared to cancel your
partner's rights as an authorized user option.

Another option is for Jane to add Roger as a joint account holder, or
for the couple to take out a joint card. Keep in mind that each account
holder is fully liable for the entire bill—and if Roger is unwilling or
unable to pay his share of the bill, Jane will still be stuck for the entire
amount. Adding someone to the account or opening a joint account
requires credit approval for both partners, so the credit card company
may or may not approve this, based on Roger's credit history.

As with joint accounts, if Jane and Roger break up, Jane should
immediately remove Roger's name as an authorized user of her Visa
card. Generally, it's not possible to close an account altogether until all
charges on that card have been paid in full.

Buying and Investing Together

Many couples make purchases and investments together, such as houses and cars (issues covered in Chapters 3 and 6). Here we cover joint ownership of and investment in other assets.

Property Acquired Before Getting Together

Except as you otherwise agree in writing, each person retains sole ownership of all property (TV, furniture, dishes, CDs, books, cars, and the like) owned before getting together. In several of the property agreements set out in Chapter 3, we provide a section for each person to list his or her separate property. It isn't legally necessary to do this (the property is already separately owned), but it's a good way to avoid later confusion. You can, of course, give your partner an equal or partial interest in some or all of your property. We also explain how to do this in Chapter 3.

Property Acquired After Getting Together

As an unmarried couple, you have the choice of either keeping your property separate or merging it (what lawyers call commingling). Whatever you decide, be sure to put it in writing, using the property agreements in Chapter 3. This will help avoid confusion if you separate.

How to Keep Your Property Separate

It is imperative to keep property separate if one of you is having debt problems or is not covered by comprehensive medical insurance. But even if you and your partner both have excellent credit ratings and good medical coverage, you can avoid potential complications by keeping property separate.

Here's how to maintain your financial independence and keep most of your assets and debts separate:

- Write a simple property agreement, such as the one in Chapter 3, outlining your intention to keep your income and property separate.
- Don't open joint accounts or make joint purchases unless absolutely necessary or for limited purposes. Keep the bulk of your money in your own name and don't add extra signatures to your account.

- Don't cosign a loan or credit agreement for your mate unless you're willing to pay the entire debt in full if your partner can't, or won't. You can always make a gift, but you should be sure you know the value of what you are giving, and be certain that the gift is limited, rather than being unlimited by the amount of the credit card authorization.
- Don't pass yourselves off as husband and wife or use the same name—especially if you live in a state that recognizes common law marriage.
- It's not a good idea to register as domestic partners (if this is an option), even with the registrations that are not "marriage equivalents," as some registration forms declare that you will be financially responsible for each other's basic needs and living expenses. If you want to take advantage of the benefits and protections of a domestic partner ordinance, check your state law or consult with an attorney to see what effect registration will have on keeping your property separate.

How to Mix or Commingle Your Property

It's fairly common for unmarried partners to pool their incomes to purchase a car, furniture, or other expensive item. Even if only one of you takes out a loan to finance the purchase or uses separate money to buy it, you can both be legal owners, if that's what you want.

If you intend to own an item jointly, you'll need a written agreement outlining the details, especially if only one of you signs for a loan but both of you will be contributing funds toward the repayment. Again, Chapter 3 includes sample agreements for owning property jointly. The contracts cover important issues, such as how property is to be paid for, your joint ownership or investment percentages, what happens to the property if you break up, and whether the survivor becomes the sole owner if one of you dies.

How to Share Costs, But Not Ownership, of Property

In some situations, one partner may lend the other money for a major purchase, such as a car, without intending to share ownership of the property. In this case, the partner borrowing the money should sign a promissory note agreeing to repay the loan. Chapter 6 includes a sample promissory note you can use for this purpose. To keep the property separate, register the car in the borrower's name only.

Discrimination

This section covers various forms of discrimination you may face as an unmarried couple. Legal discrimination still exists in some locales, despite the increased numbers of unmarried couples. And even in places that provide legal protection, the law is not always followed entirely.

 RELATED TOPICS

More information on discrimination. Chapter 5 covers legal rules regarding discrimination in rental housing. Chapter 6 covers discrimination in house purchases.

Credit Discrimination

A credit grantor generally will provide credit to anyone who is a good financial risk. A person with no apparent source of income, with a history of long periods of unemployment, who regularly pays bills late or misses payments, or who has recently declared bankruptcy, isn't a good risk. A person with a low income and many dependents and expenses also may not be a good risk. These are legitimate considerations for a lender. However, creditors are not permitted to consider factors that are unrelated to income or ability to pay, such as marital status.

The Equal Credit Opportunity Act (ECOA) prohibits creditors from discriminating on the basis of marital status (and on the basis of race, national origin, religion, sex, age, or because all or part of a person's income comes from public assistance). (15 U.S.C. § 1691.) Ability to pay should be the criterion used.

Specific federal regulations say that a creditor:

- cannot inquire about marital status for individual unsecured credit unless the applicant lives in a community property state or is using as collateral property located in a community property state
- cannot require the use of a married name, but must allow credit to be issued in either your given name or a combined surname

- can require you to reveal alimony and child support payments for which you are responsible, but not payments you receive, unless you rely on them to establish your income for credit purposes
- may not ignore your income from child support or alimony payments in determining your creditworthiness, but may consider how likely it is that you will actually receive that income
- may not ignore income from a part-time job
- may not ask questions about your birth control practices, or whether you intend to have children
- may not terminate your account or require a reapplication if you change your name or marital status unless there is evidence that you're unwilling or unable to pay your bill, and
- must inform you of any reason you are denied credit.

A creditor that illegally discriminates in extending credit may be liable for up to $10,000 plus any money that's actually lost as a result of the discrimination.

But the law is not completely cut and dried. Under the ECOA, asking a person's marital status is not discrimination if the inquiry is made in order to determine "the creditor's rights and remedies applicable to a particular extension of credit"—for example, whether the creditor will require a cosigner or guarantor, or whether property you are claiming as an asset for purposes of your credit application is jointly owned. However, the inquiry is illegal if it is made solely for the purpose of discriminating on the basis of your status. In addition, because the ECOA allows a creditor to consider state property laws in its decision to extend credit, in some states a creditor may be able to ask about marital status in certain situations. For example, if a loan will be secured by real property, and state law gives the applicant's spouse an interest in the property, the creditor can ask if the applicant is married.

Few cases have tested the Equal Credit Opportunity Act. Since its passage, however, unmarried couples have had fewer obstacles in opening joint accounts.

For more information on the ECOA, visit the Federal Trade Commission's website (www.ftc.gov) and look in the Consumer Protection area.

RESOURCE

Questions about credit-related discrimination? If you feel you have been the victim of discrimination, contact the consumer affairs division of one of these federal agencies for advice:

- **Non-bank-related problems.** Federal Trade Commission Website: www.ftc.gov; Phone: 877-FTC-HELP (382-4357)
- **Bank-related problems.** Federal Reserve Board Website: www.federalreserve.gov; Phone: 888-851-1920.

Discrimination in Employment

It's unlikely that a private employer will care about your marital status. The exception might be if you're in an extremely important or politically or culturally sensitive position—for example, you're an unmarried, pregnant private school teacher or if you work for a religious institution. In situations like these, some courts have allowed employers to fire employees based on their unmarried status. (For example, the court supported the employer when an unmarried pregnant North Carolina woman who lived with her lover was fired from her job at the YWCA because she was "setting a bad example." *Harvey v. YWCA*, 533 F.Supp. 949 (N.C. 1982).) In other cases, they haven't. (In Virginia, a school forced an unmarried pregnant teacher to take a leave of absence. A court found that the school violated the teacher's constitutional rights. *Ponton v. Newport News School Bd.*, 632 F.Supp. 1056 (E.D. Va. 1986).)

If you work for one of the rare employers that does object to your cohabitation and threatens to fire or demote you because of it, whether you have protection depends on several things: (1) whether your employer is a federal agency, private company, or local or state government agency; and (2) the law in your state. In any case, don't ever lie about your marital status—as firing someone for lying is allowed under the laws of every state.

Private Companies and Local or State Government Agencies

There is no federal law that prohibits firing or job discrimination against people because they are unmarried and living with a partner. However, many states have passed laws that prohibit this type of discrimination. If you work for a private company or a local or state government agency and you live in a state or locality that prohibits employment discrimination based on marital status, you probably cannot be fired for cohabiting.

Keep in mind that many of these state and local laws only apply to employers with a minimum number of employees, such as five or more. Also, some state courts have ruled that the "marital status" provisions do not protect cohabitors, only employees who are married or single. Finally, state laws change all the time, so before you assume your state does or doesn't protect you, check with the state agency that governs employment discrimination—this is often the state fair employment practices agency. Or, do some legal research on your own. (See Chapter 11 for information on legal research.)

If your state doesn't have a statute that prohibits marital status discrimination in employment, you may still get protection from the courts. For example, federal district courts in Michigan and Arkansas have upheld the right of police officers to cohabit. (*Biggs v. North Muskegon Police Dept.*, 563 F.Supp. 585 (Mich. 1983); *Swope v. Bratton*, 541 F.Supp. 99 (Ark. 1982).) However, other courts have allowed employers to fire employees because they cohabited. For example, a court in Texas allowed a police department to take disciplinary action against officers for off-duty dating and cohabitation. (*Shawgo v. Spradlin,* 701 F.2d 470 (5th Cir. 1983).) And in 1977, a Pennsylvania court held that a public library employee's living in "open adultery" was reason enough to warrant firing. (*Hollenbaugh v. Carnegie Free Library*, 436 F.Supp. 1328 (W.D. Pa. 1977).)

Finally, don't forget to check your employer's personnel manual. Many employers have internal policies prohibiting discrimination on the basis of marital status. If your employer has such a policy, it must follow it, even if state law doesn't prohibit marital status discrimination.

States That Prohibit Employment Discrimination Based on Marital Status

States that have nondiscrimination laws include Alaska, California, Connecticut, Delaware, District of Columbia, Florida, Hawaii, Illinois, Maryland, Massachusetts, Michigan, Minnesota, Montana, Nebraska, New Hampshire, New Jersey, New Mexico (with 50 or more employees), New York, North Dakota, Oregon, Virginia, Washington, and Wisconsin.

Federal Government Agencies

Federal law states that most federal agencies aren't allowed to discriminate on the basis of marital status in hiring, firing, assignments, or discipline. And court decisions involving federal employees usually give cohabitants protection on the job.

Discrimination When Traveling Together

In most parts of the country, an unmarried couple will encounter no problems when traveling together. Many hotels and motels require only one name and signature on the register, though you'll have to state the number of people that will be occupying the room. Even if you both must sign the register, you are still very unlikely to have problems. Clerks, after all, are used to the fact that many married women do not adopt their husband's last name.

A very few places may hassle you if you register under two different surnames, and refuse to provide lodging if you say you're unmarried. But this is very unlikely, especially if you stay in a name-brand hotel or motel.

CAUTION

Don't register under a false name or false pretext of marriage. In some jurisdictions (like Maine and the District of Columbia) it is illegal to register in a hotel under a false name. (Me. Rev. Stat. Ann. tit. 30-A, § 3822; D.C. Code Ann. § 22-3224.) And, if you are in North Carolina or Arkansas and a hotel does inquire as to your marital status, you might want to think twice before claiming that you are married. Under those states' laws, it's illegal to falsely register or represent yourself as a married couple when you are not in fact married. (N.C. Gen. Stat. § 14-186; Ark. Code Ann. § 20-26-203.) The only reported case of prosecution under the Arkansas statute dates back to 1947. But the North Carolina statute was revisited and amended as recently as 1994.

Sometimes travel discount rates are available only to married couples. Most are extended to any two adults traveling together, but occasionally you may be able to save a few dollars by saying you're married. Do you run any legal risk by doing this? Probably not, but that doesn't make it morally or legally correct. And claiming an untrue status in order to get the cheapest rate could create problems if anyone gets injured and makes an insurance claim. At the same time, because many married couples use different last names these days, no one is likely to ask for proof that you're married.

> **CAUTION**
> **Legal remedies for discrimination.** What happens if a hotel or motel discriminates against you because of your marital status? Do you have any legal recourse? Unless there is a local ordinance prohibiting discrimination in public accommodations on the basis of marital status (these exist in many major cities and university towns), the answer is usually no. For more information on researching local ordinances, see Chapter 11.

Sharing Your Last Name

Normally, each partner in an unmarried couple keeps his or her own last name. It's easy, legal, and creates few, if any, practical problems. Occasionally, however, members of an unmarried couple want to use the same last name—his name, her name, a hyphenated version of the two names, or a completely new name for both.

This can be done with little difficulty, as it's fairly simple to change your last name by getting a court order. In most states, by contrast, someone who is getting married can change their last name as part of the marriage license process, without having to obtain a court order.

Bear in mind that you cannot change your name to defraud creditors, for any illegal purpose, to benefit economically by the use of another person's name, or to invade someone's privacy (don't name yourself Madonna or Bill Clinton). Also, you can't take on a name that is likely to incite violence (such as a racial epithet) or is inherently confusing (such as a string of numbers). Otherwise, you can change your name for any reason and assume any name you wish.

! CAUTION

Using the same last name may have undesired legal repercussions.
In some states, it can show intent to establish a common law marriage. If your
state recognizes common law marriage (see Chapter 2) and you use the same
last name, you may create an implication that you intend to be married—
especially if you tell others that you are married. If you live in a common law
marriage state and want to use the same name, but don't want to be married,
it's a good idea to sign a brief Agreement of Joint Intent Not to Have a Common
Law Marriage, like the one included in Chapter 2. Also, don't hold yourselves out
to family and friends as a married couple.

Using the same last name combined with other factors, such as a claim by one
of you that you orally agreed to pool income, may imply that you intend to share
your earnings and property. If you wish to keep all property separate but share your
last name, it's an extremely good idea to sign an agreement to keep your property
separate by using one of the living together agreements included in Chapter 3.

Change of Name by Usage

In some states, it is legal to change your name by simply using a new
name and gradually changing your official documents to match the
name you are using. However, given the rising incidence of identity
theft and the focus on security after the terrorist attacks of September
11, 2001, we no longer recommend the usage method of changing your
name, even if you live in a state that allows it. Most government agencies
will no longer just take your word for the fact that you've changed your
name, but will require a court order with a judge's signature, especially
when it comes to getting a driver's license or a passport. And you don't
want to run afoul of the Patriot Act or any other new "homeland
security" rules by having documentation in two different names. It's far
better to just spend the few hundred dollars and take the time to change
your name legally through the court petition method.

Change of Name by Court Order

The second way to change your name is by court order. Getting a court
order is usually pretty simple: You fill out, and file at the courthouse,

a short petition, publish legal notice of your intention to change your name in a local legal newspaper, and attend a routine court hearing.

Once you obtain the court order changing your name, you must still change your records, identity cards, and documents. All you need to do is show the various bureaucrats the judge's order. Keep in mind that if you break up and want to reclaim your prior name, you will need to go back to court—unlike with marital divorces, which allow a name change as part of the dissolution process.

CAUTION
Each state has its own laws governing the court order method. While the procedures are similar, if you're serious about changing your name by court order, check your state laws (Chapter 11 shows how). *How to Change Your Name in California*, by Lisa Sedano and Emily Doskow (Nolo), will help you do the job quickly and efficiently in that state.

TIP
Rather not say why you're changing your name? If you live in a state where you must give a reason for the change and you'd rather not tell the judge that you're changing your name to your partner's, you don't have to. You can state that your new name will make it more convenient for business or simply say that you like the new name better.

Income Taxes

In most cases, being unmarried does not negatively affect the amount of taxes you pay. In fact, some unmarried couples pay less in federal and state income taxes than married couples, because married couples are generally taxed at a higher rate as a richer "family" than they would be taxed as single people. In addition, some unmarried partners can claim the other partner as a dependent, which qualifies them for an additional exemption. And when it comes to selling your home, if you and your partner are unmarried and you each own half the home, you can often reap the same tax benefits as married couples, although the eligibility requirements are a little tougher to satisfy.

Common law marriage may count as a real marriage as far as taxes are concerned. If you live in a state that recognizes common law marriage and you hold yourself out to be married, you are also married for federal tax purposes and should file accordingly. (See Chapter 2 for a list of states recognizing common law marriage.) However, if you and your partner live together with no intent to be married, you may (and should) file as single individuals even if you live in a state recognizing common law marriage.

Tax Rates and the Standard Deduction

For many years, unmarried couples that lived together paid less in federal income tax—often substantially less—than did their married counterparts. This was especially true for higher-income couples. If both people worked, getting married often was expensive income tax-wise. For example, two single wage-earners, each with net taxable income of $50,000 per year, would have been in a 28% tax bracket in 2000. But if these people were married, their combined $100,000 net taxable income would have put them in a 31% bracket.

Compounding this so-called "marriage penalty" was the standard deduction, which disproportionately favored single people. An individual who filed as a single person in 2002 could claim a standard deduction of $4,400 (and two single people living together would get $8,800). The same couple, if married and filing jointly, was entitled to a combined standard deduction of only $7,350.

This discrepancy (why wasn't the married couple entitled to a standard deduction of $8,800?) didn't lead to an actual revolt by married taxpayers, but their vocal displeasure eventually brought about some changes, and the marriage penalty was largely eliminated beginning in 2003. This was accomplished by making the standard deduction for married taxpayers exactly twice that of single taxpayers. However, for some couples with significant disparities in income, the total taxes they would pay as a married couple remain higher than the total taxes paid by the two of them as single taxpayers.

Income Tax and Social Security

When it comes to taxing Social Security, the marriage penalty is very much alive and well. Older married couples in which the partners have modest incomes and receive Social Security benefits must pay tax on a portion of their benefits if their "base amount" is more than $32,000. (The "base amount" is the married couple's combined adjusted gross income, as reported on their tax return, plus interest from tax-exempt investments, plus 50% of their combined Social Security benefits.) In contrast, each partner in an unmarried couple pays taxes on Social Security benefits only if his or her "base amount" is more than $25,000. That would mean that, as a couple, their base amount could be as high as $50,000 before they had to pay taxes on Social Security benefits.

 RESOURCE
Tax rules relating to older people. See IRS Publication 554, *Older Americans Tax Guide,* available from the IRS at 800-829-1040 or www.irs.gov.

Dependents and Taxes

In some circumstances, one partner in an unmarried couple can claim a cohabitating partner as a dependent and qualify for an additional exemption ($3,700 in 2011). The IRS defines dependents as either close relatives or unrelated persons who live in the taxpayer's household as the principal place of abode and are supported by the taxpayer.

Claiming Your Partner as a Dependent

Your partner may qualify as a dependent if you provide over one-half of his or her total support (for food, shelter, clothing, medical and dental care, education, and the like) during the year, he or she has earned less than $4,050 in 2017 (not including tax-exempt income, such as welfare or Social Security benefits), and he or she is a U.S. resident or citizen who has lived with you the entire year. In addition, your partner cannot file a joint return with someone else (for example, a spouse if he or she is still married).

> **TIP**
>
> **More details on dependents and taxes.** See IRS Publication 501, *Exemptions, Standard Deductions and Filing Information*. To get this publication, contact the IRS at 800-829-1040 or visit its website at www.irs.gov.

Claiming Child Household Members as Dependents

Unmarried partners may also claim "head of household" filing status when they support a dependent other than an adult with whom they are living. So, for example, if your child lives with you and your partner, you could file as head of household and get many of the same credits available to married filers, such as the earned income credit for the working poor, and child and dependent care credits. By filing as head of household, an unmarried taxpayer could claim both the child and the other adult as dependents, for a total of three exemptions.

When parents are divorced or just live apart, the question of who gets to take the dependency exemption for federal income tax purposes often arises. Section 152 of the Internal Revenue Code provides that if the parents were once married, the parent who has physical custody for the greater part of the year gets to claim the exemption. You can change this by waiving your right to claim the exemption in a written agreement (for example, in a divorce, separation, or child custody agreement) or by filing a declaration with the IRS. For more information on how to handle this situation, see IRS Publication 504, *Divorced or Separated Individuals*, which you can download for free at www.irs.gov.

If you were never married, the child qualifies by living with you for more than half the year as long as the child didn't provide more than half of his or her own support.

Income Tax on the Sale of Your Home: Capital Gain Exclusion

Current tax law allows married couples to avoid taxes on the first $500,000 of capital gain (usually the difference between the original purchase price and the selling price) when they sell their home, as long as at least one spouse has owned the home, and both spouses have resided in the home, for two out of the five years preceding the sale.

Unmarried individuals are each entitled to a $250,000 gain exclusion on their portion of the home owned with someone else which, at first glance, looks the same as for two married spouses. However, in the case of an unmarried couple, both individuals must have owned and lived in the home for two of the five years preceding the sale. Some unmarried partners have tried to avoid this tax by claiming they had been equitable co-owners even though not on title, but this is risky, as the IRS does not always accept this argument. The loss of this exemption is one of the most frequent tax penalties incurred by unmarried couples.

> **TIP**
> **More information on the capital gain tax break.** See "Check Out Legal and Tax Issues Before Transferring a Share of Your House" in Chapter 6. For advice on tax rules and to get the IRS publications mentioned above, contact the IRS at 800-829-1040 or visit the IRS website at www.irs.gov. If you claim your partner as a dependent, the IRS objects, and you want to fight it, we recommend that you get a copy of *Stand Up to the IRS*, by Frederick W. Daily (Nolo).

Social Security

Unmarried couples that live together are often at a disadvantage when it comes to Social Security benefits—especially if one partner stays at home caring for children or running the household, or has lower income.

Typically, you each will qualify for Social Security benefits based on your own earnings record. However, if you don't work at a job that requires payment of Social Security tax, you don't earn credit toward Social Security benefits. But married couples get a benefit—spouses are eligible for certain Social Security benefits based on the other spouse's earnings record. These are called dependents' benefits (which you get if your spouse qualifies for retirement or disability benefits) and survivors' benefits (which you get if your deceased spouse or ex-spouse qualified for retirement or disability benefits). So, for example, if a husband stays at home and takes care of the kids for a number of years or has lower income, he may still be able to collect Social Security benefits based on his wife's earnings record.

TIP

A common law marriage is valid for purposes of receiving Social Security. Common law marriage is just as valid as a formal marriage for Social Security purposes. This means if you lived with someone covered by Social Security in a state that recognizes common law marriage (see Chapter 2) and your partner has recently died or become disabled, you may be able to claim you were married and, as a result, qualify for benefits.

Adults who live together, but are not married, are not eligible for their partner's dependents' or survivors' even though their children are dependents of both. This presents an obvious disadvantage when one partner in a living together arrangement works outside the home and the other works in the home caring for kids or taking care of the household, or has lower income.

A stay-at-home partner could earn Social Security credits, however, if the other partner employed him or her to take care of the home and children. The "employer partner" would pay wages to the stay-at-home partner and pay Social Security tax on the stay-at-home partner's behalf. Both partners would have to comply with other requirements. For example, the stay-at-home partner would have to pay state and federal income tax on the wages. And in many states, the "employer partner" would also have to pay disability insurance and other types of insurance or taxes. (See the "Agreement Covering Homemaker Services" in Chapter 3 for a contract that provides for this type of arrangement.)

TIP

Living with someone doesn't end Social Security benefits derived from a former marriage. If your spouse has died and you are receiving survivor's benefits or if you are divorced, you can get benefits on your ex-spouse's Social Security account if your marriage lasted at least ten years and, in some cases, if you have been divorced for at least two years (it makes no difference whether a former spouse has remarried or you are living with someone). Similarly, if you qualify for benefits as a divorced spouse and your ex has died, you can receive survivor's benefits as early as age 60 (50 if you're disabled). This same protection applies if you state-register as domestic partners, to the extent the federal agencies don't recognize the registration as a marriage.

RESOURCE

Advice on Social Security rules and benefits. Contact a local office of the Social Security Administration or check their website at www.ssa.gov. For a clear explanation of Social Security benefits—what's available and how to claim them—see *Social Security, Medicare & Government Pensions: Get the Most Out of Your Retirement & Medical Benefits,* by Joseph Matthews with Dorothy Matthews Berman (Nolo).

Retirement Plans

For those lucky enough to have them, retirement plans are valuable assets that provide security to the retiring worker, of course, and can also provide for a surviving spouse if the worker dies prematurely.

In most instances, unmarried couples can use retirement plans in much the same way—to provide for a surviving partner. But unmarried couples need to jump through a few more hoops to accomplish the same thing.

Naming a Beneficiary

Whether you have an IRA, a 401(k), or another type of retirement plan, you may name any beneficiary you want. But you must do exactly that—name the beneficiary by filling out a beneficiary designation form that states your wishes. Generally, your financial institution will require you to complete a beneficiary designation form when you first open an IRA. But in the case of an employer's plan, you might have to request a form from your plan administrator. Signing a cohabitation agreement or executing a will are not substitutes for the legal requirement of a formal beneficiary designation.

Many employer plans name a surviving spouse as a default beneficiary in the event a worker fails to designate a beneficiary in writing. However, unmarried partners will not be default beneficiaries, so it is important that you complete a form, then keep a copy of the form in your files and give one to the plan administrator. Under some plans, designating an unmarried partner can have financial impacts in comparison to naming a spouse as a beneficiary.

Naming a beneficiary of your retirement plan accomplishes several things. First, it ensures that the assets are distributed to the people you intend. Second, designating a beneficiary might protect the retirement plan from probate. (In many states, retirement plan assets are not subject to probate, provided there is a clear designation of beneficiary. Without such a designation, assets might be forced through probate to identify the appropriate heir.) Third, when you name a beneficiary of your retirement plan, the individual or individuals who inherit the plan will have more control over how quickly the assets are distributed, potentially saving your beneficiary a bundle in taxes.

Bear in mind that naming a beneficiary is not an irrevocable action. You may change your beneficiary at any time by completing a new beneficiary designation form.

The rules for pensions work differently. Some plans don't allow you to provide survivor benefits to a nonspouse, whereas others do—but at a lower benefit rate than if the survivor is a spouse. Some employers (like the federal government) often require that you be married for a minimum of five years before the employee retires for the spouse to get full pension benefits, so be sure to learn about these rules if either of you are entitled to receive a good-sized pension.

Your Will Doesn't Govern Your Retirement Plan

Some people make the mistake of failing to name a beneficiary or simply naming "my estate," believing their will should take care of everything. But in the case of a retirement plan or IRA, it is the beneficiary designation form, not the will, that governs what happens to the assets. So, for example, if your beneficiary designation names your brother as beneficiary of your IRA, but in your will you indicate that you want your IRA assets to go to your partner, the IRA assets will go to your brother, because his name is on the beneficiary designation form. Similarly, if you fail to name a beneficiary on the beneficiary designation form, you are deemed not to have named a beneficiary of the plan, even if you try to leave the retirement funds to someone in your will. In that case the funds will go to your legal next of kin—who is not your unmarried partner.

Rollovers

As we mentioned above, married couples enjoy some advantages over unmarried couples when it comes to inherited retirement plans. For example, and perhaps most important, a spouse who inherits a retirement plan is permitted to roll it over into a retirement plan of his or her own. Having done so, the spouse can then treat those assets as if they had always been part of his or her own retirement account.

In comparison, the surviving partner in an unmarried couple cannot roll over his or her deceased partner's retirement assets into the survivor's retirement plan. If the survivor attempts to make such a transaction, the assets would immediately be subject to tax and penalties.

The picture is not completely bleak, however. If you inherit an IRA from your partner, you are not required to take all the money out immediately and pay taxes on it (although you may if you wish). Instead, you are permitted to spread distributions over your life expectancy, thereby reducing the tax burden.

You can achieve much the same result if you inherit your partner's interest in an employer's retirement plan. You may roll over your partner's retirement plan assets into an IRA and then take distributions over your life expectancy. For this to work, you must satisfy the following conditions:

- You must have the retirement plan assets transferred to a new IRA, not an existing one.
- The new IRA must be in your partner's name, not your name. (This allows the IRS to distinguish between IRAs inherited by a nonspouse and those belonging to the original owner or a spouse; different distribution rules apply so the IRS needs to know which is which.)
- The transfer must take place as a trustee-to-trustee transfer, meaning you can't take the money out and then put it into a new IRA—it has to be rolled over directly from one savings vehicle into the other.
- The employer plan must allow the rollover.

There's more good news. Even if the plan provides that your partner's interest must be paid out within five years (the five-year rule), you can void that requirement by taking your first required distribution from the employer plan on or before December 31 of the year after your partner's death and rolling over the balance into a new IRA in your partner's name—usually it will be titled to include your name as well; for example, it might say: "John Doe (deceased) IRA, for benefit of Jane Doe." If you roll over the assets into the new IRA in the year of death, you may roll over the entire amount and take the first required distribution the following year. But again, for all of this to work, the employer's retirement plan has to permit the rollover to an IRA.

Another benefit of being unmarried is that, in most instances, cohabitation won't cut off your entitlement to the survivor pension benefits awarded to a deceased spouse.

RESOURCE

More information about inheritance and taking money out of retirement plans and IRAs. See *IRAs, 401(k)s & Other Retirement Plans: Taking Your Money Out,* by Twila Slesnick (Nolo).

Public Benefits

People who receive public benefits often worry that they will be cut off if their partner moves in. If you receive benefits based on your financial condition and a physical or mental condition—aid to the aged, blind, or disabled, for example—you don't risk any loss. Broadly speaking, these programs function like Social Security—once you qualify, you're largely left alone. When it comes to benefits based on financial condition alone (and not on a physical condition), however, living with someone may affect your food stamp eligibility or the amount of aid you receive. This issue usually arises when a woman with children who is receiving welfare wants to live with her boyfriend. In large part because the federal government now delegates welfare rules to the states, which in turn are experimenting with all sorts of policies, the best advice we can give you is to call your local social service department and make sure you understand the rules that affect you.

Depending on where you live, here is what you may find:

- Cash contributions made by a living together partner may reduce the amount of a welfare grant—but it can depend on how much is contributed and the purpose of the contribution.
- Contributions toward household expenses—such as paying the rent or buying the food—made by someone you are living with will not affect the amount of your grant.
- In a few states, a legal responsibility for all living together partners to contribute to the so-called "Welfare Unit" is presumed. This means if you live with someone in these states, your welfare grant will be reduced even if the person doesn't, in fact, chip in on expenses.
- If you have registered as domestic partners, you may have signed a statement saying you will provide for one another. This could, in theory, be used to deny one of you public benefits, especially if the other person earns substantial income.

Insurance

Generally speaking, unmarried couples can purchase most types of insurance at competitive rates. This is usually easy to do, especially if you co-own property. Be sure to shop around, because prices can vary dramatically, and in some instances, unmarried couples can end up paying more than married couples for the same level of insurance coverage.

This section won't help you decide whether or not you need a particular type of insurance, but will help you sort out some of the issues involved when buying insurance with a partner.

Life Insurance

Many people get life insurance as a benefit of employment or buy their own insurance policy. Either way, you can name your partner as beneficiary. If either of you is vulnerable to estate tax liability, you should consider buying a policy on each other's life, which you can do if you co-own property.

> ⓘ **CAUTION**
> **Don't claim to be married if you aren't.** If you have a life insurance policy in which you've incorrectly stated that you are married, change it.

See Chapter 9 for more details on life insurance as it relates to estate planning.

Homeowners' Insurance

Homeowners' (or hazard) insurance is sold to homeowners when they buy a house. It insures the house against fire, flood, and other acts of destruction. It used to be difficult for unmarried couples to buy homeowners' insurance together, but this is no longer true. Many companies now write policies for unmarried couples at the same rates offered to married couples.

However, if you're the sole owner of the house, your partner's belongings won't be automatically covered by your policy. If your partner has valuable personal property, check with your homeowners' insurance company to see whether he or she can be added as an occupant and covered under the same terms as you are. Otherwise, your partner should purchase a separate renters' insurance policy.

Renters' Insurance

Renters' insurance protects tenants against the loss of their property due to theft or some act of destruction. Like homeowners' insurance, renters' insurance is easy for an unmarried couple to obtain together. Insurance companies insure the property, not the owners of the property. And the rates are related to the age and security of your building, the neighborhood you live in, and how well your landlord maintains the building. Shop around. You should be able to find one policy that covers both of you, although a few companies may try to charge you more or require that you each buy your own policy.

Automobile Insurance

Purchasing automobile insurance jointly can be a problem for unmarried couples, but not to the extent it once was. If you each own a car, you should have no trouble getting separate insurance. For unmarried couples who jointly own one vehicle, obtaining one policy will be cheaper than getting two (one for each partner). But you may have to shop around to find an agent and company that will allow you to do this.

If you jointly own two or more cars, it's often cheaper to get one policy covering all of your cars. Married couples are always allowed to do this—and thereby get discounts and other special benefits. But again, not all insurance agents or companies will offer these benefits to unmarried couples. Shop around. If you have significant assets, you might want to buy an umbrella policy that provides coverage for high-liability accidents. In most instances you will each have to obtain your own policy.

If all else fails, consider transferring ownership of both cars to one person (call your department of motor vehicles and ask how you can change the title slip) and listing the other person as a secondary driver. Also, see Chapter 3, which covers joint ownership of cars.

Health Insurance

Unmarried couples often cannot get employer-paid health insurance coverage for their partner. This is changing, however. Some cities and states are offering domestic partner benefits to their employees, even for unregistered cohabitants, and more and more private employers are doing the same. A majority of the country's largest corporations offer domestic partner benefits. You can find a list of Fortune 500 companies that provide domestic partner benefits, as well as other information on benefits, at the Human Rights Campaign website, www.hrc.org. Some companies only cover same-sex couples, and some only cover state-registered couples, so be sure to learn the specific requirements of your employer.

If your employer doesn't provide domestic partner health benefits, and your partner doesn't get benefits through a job (or doesn't work), see whether your employer will agree to cover your partner on its health plan if you pay for the premiums. Group plans available through employment are usually less expensive, and often provide better coverage, than individual plans.

Even if your employer does provide domestic partner health benefits, the premium paid to cover the domestic partner will be considered taxable income, not a pretax deduction from income as it is when the employee is covering a spouse. Also, be aware that the federal COBRA (Consolidated Omnibus Budget Reconciliation Act) health insurance rules don't apply to your partner if you lose or leave your job, or if you break up. Under COBRA, your employer must allow you to continue health insurance coverage for a certain period of time, as long as you pay the premiums, but your partner is not entitled to continue domestic partner benefits as would be the case if you were married.

The new health care reform law should take some of the pressure off unemployed or self-employed partners, as they should be able to retain their former insurance plan or obtain their own coverage, without having to be added to their better-employed partner's plan. And, it's usually better for each partner to have his or her own insurance coverage, so that a change in the relationship status doesn't jeopardize anyone's health care.

But the laws in this area are subject to political trends and could change dramatically in the future, so be careful. Also, as noted in earlier chapters, some employers are shutting down their domestic partnership benefit programs now that same-sex couples can legally marry. For that reason, unmarried partners should never assume that such coverage will continue indefinitely into the future.

Workers' Compensation Insurance

In some states, the dependent of a worker who is killed on the job can obtain death benefits from the state workers' compensation insurance program. Because "dependent" is often broadly defined, in several instances courts have allowed unmarried partners to recover these benefits. For example, a Maryland court awarded workers' compensation benefits to a woman who lived with the deceased worker for a number of years—giving up her job to take care of the house and raise the children while the deceased provided financial support. (*Kendall v. Housing Auth.*, 76 A.2d 767 (Md. Ct. Spec. App. 1950).) In California, a court awarded benefits to a woman who lived with the deceased worker because she was a "good faith" member of his household, even though she was married to someone else. (*State v. Workers' Compensation Appeals Bd.*, 94 Cal.App.3d 72 (Ct. App. 1979).) And in Oregon, the Workers' Compensation statute itself states that unmarried cohabitants are entitled to compensation as long as the couple had children together and lived together for more than one year before the worker was injured. (Or. Rev. Stat. § 656.226 (1991).)

However, not all courts have been so generous. In South Carolina, a woman living with and dependent on a deceased worker was denied workers' compensation benefits because she was married to another man. (*Palm v. General Painting Co.*, 370 S.E.2d 463 (S.C. Ct. App. 1988).) And in Nevada, a court denied death benefits to the unmarried cohabitant of a deceased worker, even where the cohabitant had previously been married to the deceased worker, because she no longer had a "legally recognizable relationship" with him. (*Banegas v. State Indus. Ins. System*, 19 P.3d 245 (2001).)

Unemployment Insurance

In many states, an employee may obtain unemployment insurance benefits for quitting a job for "good cause." Often, the unemployment board will consider a spouse's decision to leave employment in order to accompany the other spouse to a new home to be "good cause." In several cases, this benefit has been extended to unmarried partners as well. For example, the Massachusetts Supreme Court ruled that a woman who left her job in order to remain with her living together partner of 13 years who was relocating his business had compelling reasons to quit and was entitled to unemployment insurance benefits. (*Reep v. Commissioner of Dep't of Employment & Training*, 593 N.E.2d 1297 (Mass. 1992).) The California Supreme Court also awarded unemployment benefits to an unmarried woman who quit her job in order to follow her partner to another state. (*MacGregor v. Unemployment Ins. Appeals Bd.*, 37 Cal.3d 205 (1984).) However, in that case, the court's decision was based in large part on the fact that the unmarried couple had a child together. It's unclear whether the California Supreme Court would rule the same way if an unmarried couple did not have children together.

Liability for Medical Care of a Partner

Generally, one member of a married couple is liable to pay for all, or at least a substantial portion of, health and nursing home care for the other, over and above what is reimbursed by public or private insurance, as a function of the duty of married spouses to provide basic support for one another. Some state laws allow a healthy spouse of modest means to keep (exempt) a portion of the combined property, but on the whole there is joint liability for these obligations.

Fortunately, the legal situation is far better for unmarried couples. If one partner has large medical bills or moves to a nursing home, the other's property is not at risk of being grabbed to pay the bills—unless the couple has voluntarily mixed their property together, as with a joint bank account. If the institutionalized person exhausts his or her property, including that person's half of jointly owned property, Medicaid pays the rest, and the other member of the couple need not exhaust any savings or sell property to raise money. For more information, see *Long-Term Care: How to Plan & Pay for It*, by Joseph Matthews (Nolo).

Making Medical and Financial Decisions for Your Partner

If you ever become unable to make your own health care decisions or manage your own finances—because of injury, serious illness, or advanced age—you probably want your partner to step in and take care of you. Unfortunately, unmarried couples, unlike their married counterparts, often aren't permitted to handle medical or financial decisions for each other without signed authorization.

There are a few simple legal documents you should prepare if you want to ensure that critical decisions stay in the hands of your partner.

These are called health care directives and durable powers of attorney for finances. Without these documents, your partner may face substantial obstacles to acting for you in the event of a medical emergency or handling a simple financial transaction on your behalf. At worst, your health care and finances may be placed in the hands of a biological relative who won't consider your partner's input, and may well make decisions contrary to what you want.

Fortunately, the documents you need are straightforward and usually easy to complete.

Health Care Directives

Every state has laws authorizing individuals to create simple documents setting out their wishes about the type of medical treatment they do (or do not) want to receive if they are unable to communicate their preferences. These documents may also name someone to make medical decisions on the signer's behalf.

These documents are particularly important for unmarried partners. If you don't take the time to prepare them and you become incapacitated, doctors will turn to a family member designated by state law to make medical decisions for you. Most states list spouses, adult children, and parents as top-priority decision makers, making no mention of unmarried partners. The strict rules limiting access to medical records by nonpatients make it especially crucial that your directive include medical record access.

Registered domestic or civil union partners are always given priority as surrogate decision makers. And a few states that don't offer registration make room for unmarried partners on their list of potential decision makers, though they are not always given priority. But no matter what state you live in, you can save your partner a great deal of time and trouble by planning ahead.

There are two documents that permit you to set out your health care wishes, both grouped under the broad label "health care directives." First, you need a written statement you make directly to medical personnel that spells out your wishes for medical care if you become incapacitated. Your statement functions as a contract with your treating doctor, who must either honor your wishes for health care or transfer you to another doctor or facility that will honor them.

The second document is usually called a "durable power of attorney for health care." In this document you appoint the person you choose—most likely your partner—to see that your doctors and other health care providers give you the kind of medical care you want to receive. You can also use your durable power of attorney for health care to give your partner (who may be called your "attorney-in-fact," "agent," or "proxy" depending on where you live) other rights to participate in your medical care, including:

- directing your health care under any circumstances that you don't specifically address in your declaration
- hiring and firing medical personnel
- visiting you in the hospital or other facility even when other visiting is restricted
- having access to medical records and other personal information, and
- getting court authorization to enforce your health care wishes if a hospital or doctor refuses to honor them for any reason.

In some states, your statement of wishes and appointment of a proxy will be combined into a single document, often called an "Advance Health Care Directive."

A Health Care Directive by Any Other Name …

Depending on the state, your health care documents may be called by one of several different names: Advance Health Care Directive, Medical Directive, Directive to Physicians, Declaration Regarding Health Care, Designation of Health Care Surrogate, or Patient Advocate Designation. The document that describes your health care wishes may also be called a "living will," but it bears no relation to the conventional will used to leave property at death.

You can make valid health care directives if you are at least 18 years old and of sound mind. Being of sound mind essentially means that you are able to understand what the document means, what it contains, and how it works. Physically disabled people may make valid health care documents; they can direct another to sign for them if they are physically unable to do so.

As long as you are of sound mind, you can change or revoke your health care directives at any time.

Durable Power of Attorney for Finances

A durable power of attorney for finances allows you to name someone you trust (called your "attorney-in-fact" or "agent") to handle your finances if you become unable to take care of yourself. Every state recognizes this type of document.

As with documents directing medical care, you should seriously consider making a durable power of attorney for finances if you want your partner to manage your money if you can't. If you don't prepare the document and you later become incapacitated, your partner or other family members will have to ask a court for authority over your financial affairs. These proceedings, called "conservatorship proceedings," can be time-consuming and expensive—and they can be disastrous for unmarried couples if the court names another family member to take over, especially if your finances have been intertwined with those of your partner for a long time.

You can make your financial power of attorney effective immediately or you can specify that it should go into effect only if you become incapacitated; the latter is called a "springing" power of attorney. While some people are more comfortable making a springing document, an immediately effective document holds a potential advantage for unmarried couples in a long-term trusting relationship. If you make your document effective immediately, your partner can handle financial transactions for you at any time, even when you are not incapacitated. This can be useful if you are out of town, under the weather, or temporarily unavailable for any other reason.

When you make a durable power of attorney for finances, you can give your partner (or other attorney-in-fact) as much or as little control over your finances as you wish. The powers you grant may include:

- using your assets to pay your bills and everyday expenses
- buying, selling, maintaining, paying taxes on, and mortgaging real estate and other property

- collecting benefits from Social Security, Medicare, or other government programs or civil or military service
- investing your money in stocks, bonds, and mutual funds
- handling transactions with banks and other financial institutions
- buying and selling insurance policies and annuities
- filing and paying your taxes
- operating your small business
- claiming property you inherit or are otherwise entitled to
- hiring someone to represent you in court, and
- managing your retirement accounts.

Whatever powers you give your attorney-in-fact, he or she is legally required to act in your best interests.

Like health care directives, you can make a durable power of attorney for finances if you are at least 18 years old and of sound mind. And as long as you continue to be of sound mind, you can change or cancel your document at any time.

Two cautionary warnings: Be careful here, as a power-of-attorney could be abused by a greedy partner, and check with your bank or stock broker, as some plans insist on your using their customized forms.

RESOURCE

Where to get the forms you need. There are a number of ways to find the proper health care and power of attorney forms for your state. You don't usually need to consult a lawyer to obtain or prepare them. Here are some likely sources for forms and instructions:

Quicken WillMaker Plus (Nolo) is software for Windows that allows you to prepare a health care directive and a durable power of attorney for finances. It also lets you make a will, living trust, and many other useful legal documents.

Caring Connections offers health care forms for every state. You can download forms for free at www.caringinfo.org. For more information call the organization at 800-658-8898.

You may also be able to obtain health care forms from local senior centers, hospitals, your regular physician, or your state's medical association.

Wrongful Death and Loss of Consortium Lawsuits

When a person is killed as a result of a negligent or intentional act, the law of every state recognizes the right of a spouse and relatives to file suit and recover money and other economic benefits they would have received from the deceased person if the person had lived. Called "wrongful death statutes," these laws have traditionally not allowed unmarried partners to sue, even where the relationship has lasted many years. The unfair result can be that a blood relative whom you don't even live with may be compensated, while a person you have lived with for 20 years—and who may have suffered both emotional and economic losses as a result of your death—can't be.

More recently, however, many legal commentators have agreed that it's time for the wrongful death law to catch up with social reality. And in a closely related area of the law, a few courts have granted so-called "bystander" rights—traditionally limited to spouses and blood relatives—to unmarried couples. (*Dumphy v. Gregor,* 642 A.2d 372 (N.J. 1994) and *Binns v. Fredendall,* 513 N.E.2d 278 (Ohio 1987).) Bystander rights come into play to compensate a person who suffered emotional distress as a result of witnessing a loved one being killed or seriously injured.

In 2003, New Mexico became the only state in which an unmarried cohabitant can make a claim for "loss of consortium"—usually defined as the loss of the companionship of a spouse as a result of injury. (*Lozoya v. Sanchez,* 133 N.M. 579, 66 P.3d 948 (2003).) The court ruled that factors to be considered in determining whether an unmarried partner's claim should be granted include the length of the relationship and the degree to which the partners' lives are intertwined.

Renting and Sharing a Home

Discrimination on the Basis of Marital Status.. 122

Housing Rights of Unmarried Couples 123

Practical Tips for Dealing With Potential Landlords.. 124

Leases and Rental Agreements 125

Moving In Together... 126

Cotenants' Legal Obligations to the Landlord.. 126

Cotenants' Obligations to Each Other.. 128

The Tenant and Subtenant Arrangement 129

Dealing With Objections When Moving Into the Rental Home

of One Partner 132

Getting the Landlord's Permission 135

More Roommates, More Rent.. 136

Security Deposit Increases.. 136

Getting Your Security Deposit Back 138

FORMS IN THIS CHAPTER

Chapter 5 includes instructions for and samples of the Agreement Covering Rented Living Space and the Letter Requesting Permission to Add a Roommate.

The Nolo website includes downloadable copies of these forms. See the appendix for the link to the forms in this book.

Chapter 5 also includes two sample notices (one for tenants with a month-to-month rental agreement and the other for use with a lease): Sample Tenant's Notice of Intent to Move Out and Substitute New Tenant.

I f you're going to live with someone and you're both renters, you have to get a place. That means renting an apartment or house together, or having one partner move into the other partner's rental. Here we focus on the special legal issues encountered by unmarried couples renting together.

RESOURCE

Other landlord-tenant questions? For complete details on your rights as a tenant and landlord-tenant law, including security deposit rules, privacy rights, habitability requirements, occupancy limits, rent control, roommates, and how tenancies end, see *Every Tenant's Legal Guide,* by Janet Portman and Marcia Stewart. Californians should see *California Tenants' Rights,* by Janet Portman and J. Scott Weaver. Both are published by Nolo. The Tenants' section on www.nolo.com provides many useful articles and state-specific resources for tenants.

RELATED TOPICS

Related topics in this book include:

- States with laws prohibiting cohabitation by unmarried couples: Chapter 2
- Buying a house together, or moving into your partner's house: Chapter 6
- Dealing with problems regarding rental property—and each other—if you separate: Chapter 10.

Discrimination on the Basis of Marital Status

Most landlords are interested in your money, not your morals. As long as you pay rent on time, keep the rental clean, and don't fight with the neighbors, they don't care in which beds you sleep. There are, of course, exceptions—people who still refuse to rent to unmarried couples. Some landlords (despite the divorce statistics) believe that unmarried couples are inherently less stable than married ones. Others may refuse to rent to you on religious grounds. Unfortunately, in most states, landlords can get away with these kinds of choices.

This section summarizes the law on housing discrimination against unmarried couples and provides practical tips on avoiding problems with landlords.

Housing Rights of Unmarried Couples

Do you have a legal right, as an unmarried couple, to rent a place? Not under federal law. The federal Fair Housing Acts (42 U.S. Code §§ 3601–3619) prohibit discrimination on the basis of race or color, religion, national origin, gender, familial status (having children and pregnancy), and physical or mental disability. Marital status is not one of the protected categories under federal law. (Public housing is an exception. Several courts have interpreted federal law to protect unmarried couples from discrimination there.)

State law is not much better. The majority of states don't have any legal provisions protecting people from discrimination based on marital status, meaning landlords may legally ask questions about your relationship and may refuse to rent to you if you are an unmarried couple.

While some 20 states plus the District of Columbia ban discrimination on the basis of marital status, most of these states' laws extend protection to married couples only (meaning that landlords cannot treat married tenants differently from single tenants). Only a few states—Alaska, California, Massachusetts, and New Jersey—have clearly ruled that the term "marital status" includes unmarried couples. Oddly, courts in Maryland, Minnesota, New York, and Wisconsin have ruled that the term "marital status" only protects married people from being treated differently from single people, not vice versa.

Some landlords resist renting to unmarried couples on the grounds that cohabitation violates their religious beliefs. Courts in California, Massachusetts, Michigan and New Jersey have refused to allow landlords to reject unmarried couples as tenants for this reason.

Your best protection against discrimination may be a city or county ordinance prohibiting discrimination on the basis of sexual orientation. Although usually passed to protect the housing rights of gay and lesbian tenants, most local laws forbidding discrimination based on sexual orientation also protect unmarried heterosexual couples as well.

If you suspect (or know for sure) that a landlord won't rent to you because you're not married, first find out whether your city or state has a law that has been interpreted to prohibit discrimination against unmarried couples in rental housing. If the answer is yes, you have a decent chance of winning if you fight back.

TIP
Remember that landlords are allowed to discriminate for legitimate business reasons. Even if you live in a state that prohibits discrimination on the basis of marital status, it's no guarantee you'll get the place you want. Landlords may reject you for legitimate business reasons, such as a bad credit history or negative references from other landlords.

RESOURCE
For up-to-date information on housing discrimination rules in your area, call your local city attorney's office or check your state laws and local ordinances. (Check under the heading "Housing Discrimination.") For information on federal fair housing laws and links to state and local fair housing agencies, visit the website of the Department of Housing and Urban Development (HUD) at www.hud.gov (click the "State Info" tab), or call the agency's Housing Discrimination Hotline at 800-669-9777. Your state consumer protection agency may also provide useful information on housing discrimination laws; find yours at www.usa.gov/directory/state-consumer.

Practical Tips for Dealing With Potential Landlords

If your state or city has no law prohibiting discrimination on the basis of marital status, you'll have to decide how open you want to be with your landlord. Here are some suggestions:

- Act in a highly responsible and respectable manner. Be ready to present financial and credit information and personal references, especially from former landlords. If you convince a landlord that you'll be excellent tenants, other factors, such as your marital status, will be less important.
- Don't flaunt the fact that you're not married. In an age when many married women use their own last name, many landlords will assume you are married and won't ask. Most won't care.
- In conservative parts of the country particularly, it may help to go with the flow. In every city, and most large towns, there are

neighborhoods with lots of unmarried people. This often tends to be true near universities. If you are new to an area, ask around.

You may not want to rent from a landlord who obviously disapproves of unmarried couples living together. This is especially true if the landlord lives nearby. Life is too short for all the hassles you're inviting by renting from someone who's inappropriately interested in tenants' private lives. If at all possible, look elsewhere.

Leases and Rental Agreements

Before signing a lease or rental agreement, carefully examine every clause. Many lease provisions are extremely restrictive and some are downright illegal and out-of-date. For example, a rental agreement form may purport to give the landlord the right to evict you without getting a court order if you fail to pay the rent. This is illegal—only a judge can order that you be evicted.

We don't have room to list all the possible illegal lease provisions, but in particular, unmarried couples should look out for any clause prohibiting "immoral behavior." If living together is legal in your state, this clause can't be used to evict you. But if cohabitation is still illegal where you live (see Chapter 2), a landlord may attempt to use a clause prohibiting "immoral behavior" to evict you. If you are worried about this, ask the landlord to cross out "immoral behavior" language. If the landlord refuses, it's probably a signal that you'd be happier renting elsewhere.

Likewise, state laws tend to be very restrictive about the landlord's right of access to an occupied rental. If you live in one of these states, but your lease gives the landlord open-ended access to your rental, you'll know that the landlord either doesn't know the law or is deliberately breaking it. Check the laws of your state regarding tenant protections, including rights of access (details are available in the Tenants section at www.nolo.com). If your landlord offers you a lease or rental agreement that is in violation of state law, ask the landlord to revise it to comply with the law. If the landlord doesn't want to do this, once again, you've learned that your prospective landlord isn't willing to comply with the legal requirements that come with owning rental property, and you should reconsider your rental application.

Moving In Together

It's essential that you are clear as to whether you are both renting the place as cotenants or whether only one of you is the tenant and the other person is a subtenant (someone who rents from the tenant). When you are both cotenants, you have legal obligations vis-a-vis the landlord and each other that are different than the legal obligations of a tenant and a subtenant. Let's consider each of these separately.

Cotenants' Legal Obligations to the Landlord

Renting a place together and signing the same lease is the most common way that two people become cotenants. But you and your partner can become cotenants in another way, too. If you have a place and your landlord approves of an additional occupant, your partner can sign your original lease and become a cotenant. And suppose your partner (let's say his name is Sam) moves into your rental and is openly acknowledged as a resident by the landlord—the landlord knows Sam's there, accepts rent from Sam, responds to Sam's requests for repairs, and in every other respect treats Sam just like he treats you. In many states, this behavior on the part of the landlord will make your partner a cotenant, just as if Sam had formally signed a lease. This means, for example, that the landlord can expect your partner to pay the entire rent if you don't, as explained below, and it also means that you cannot evict your cotenant. If you want eviction rights, you'll have to keep your partner a subtenant, as explained below.

If you and your partner are cotenants, you're each on the hook for all rent and all damages to the rental—it doesn't matter how you split the rent or who caused the damage. You are each independently liable to the landlord for all of the rent and for complying with all terms of the lease or rental agreement.

Landlords often remind cotenants of this obligation by inserting into the lease a chunk of legalese that says that the tenants are "jointly and severally" liable for paying rent and adhering to the terms of the agreement. If one tenant (your partner) can't pay his or her share of the rent in a particular month, or simply moves out, you (the other tenant) must still pay the full rent.

EXAMPLE 1: Clem and Julie sign a month-to-month rental agreement with Oak Hill Properties for $1,500 a month. Clem and Julie agree between themselves to each pay one-half of the rent. After three months, Clem moves out with no notice to Julie or the landlord (Oak Hill). Julie is liable for all the rent until she legally ends the tenancy. Clem, of course, is equally liable, but if he's unreachable, Oak Hill will come after Julie for the entire amount. Julie can cut her losses by legally ending the tenancy (this typically requires giving the landlord 30 days' written notice). When she moves out at the end of that period, her liability ends.

EXAMPLE 2: This time, Clem just hangs about the place, refusing to pay or leave. Even if Julie gives the landlord a 30-day written notice and moves out, leaving Clem in the rental unit, she is still liable for the rent for as long as Clem remains. Oak Hill will eventually evict Clem, but is likely to try to collect all unpaid rent from Julie if she's the one with a job, including the rent for the period after she moved out. In short, Julie's best bet is to persuade Clem to get out when she does.

EXAMPLE 3: The same facts as Example 1, but the couple have both signed a one-year lease. Again, Clem and Julie are both liable for all the rent. If one won't pay, the other must, unless the landlord approves someone new to take over the lease. If Clem and Julie both leave, in most states the landlord must attempt to limit losses (called "mitigation of damages") by renting to a suitable new tenant. If the landlord doesn't make this effort, the landlord loses the right to collect lost rent from Julie and Clem. But if, despite its reasonable efforts, the landlord can't find a new tenant (or can only find one at a reduced rent), both Clem and Julie are independently liable for the difference between the amount called for in the lease and the amount the landlord actually collects.

TIP

Small claims court can be an effective way to collect from a former living together partner. If you pay the landlord more than your fair share of the rent, you have a legal right to recover from your partner only if you had an agreement, separate from your lease or rental agreement, that you would pay rent equally. If you break up and are shortchanged, try small claims court. (The Small Claims Court section of www.nolo.com provides lots of useful information. For more details, see *Everybody's Guide to Small Claims Court,* by Ralph Warner (Nolo).) However, it usually doesn't make sense to sue unless you have a rent-sharing agreement in writing, and are pretty sure you can collect the judgment (this normally means that your former partner has a job or savings). In short, if your ex is penniless, getting a small claims judgment won't put any money in your pocket.

Cotenants' joint and several liability is broader than just rent. The landlord can hold any or all cotenants responsible for the negative actions of just one, and terminate both of your tenancies with the appropriate notice. For example, you can be evicted if your partner seriously damages the property, moves in a dog (contrary to the landlord's no-pets rule), or otherwise violates the lease or rental agreement.

If your landlord approves your request to add a roommate, he or she will probably ask both you and your partner to sign a new lease or month-to-month rental agreement. Or, the landlord might ask the newcomer (identified as a cotenant) to sign the original lease. From your landlord's point of view, this is far more than a formality, as it makes the new arrival a cotenant who is 100% liable to pay rent and make good on any damage (as discussed above). It's also desirable from your perspective, because it makes it completely clear that you and your partner have the same legal rights and responsibilities.

Cotenants' Obligations to Each Other

People sharing a rental unit usually have certain expectations of each other as roommates. We recommend that you write them down. After all, you sign an agreement with a landlord almost as a matter of course—why not do the same with each other? It's a good way to make sure you're both clear as to your responsibilities to each other as tenants—who pays what portion of the rent and utilities, who gets the place if you split up, and the like.

If your relationship ends down the line, memories may have blurred and questions such as "Whose apartment is this, anyway?" may turn into serious disputes. To avoid later problems, write down your understanding when you first move in together. A sample Agreement Covering Rented Living Space is shown below.

FORMS
The Nolo website includes a downloadable copy of the Agreement Covering Rented Living Space shown below. See the appendix for the link to this form.

This agreement can stand alone or be incorporated into a more comprehensive living together contract, such as the ones discussed in Chapter 3. You can edit this agreement—for example, you can include paragraphs about living expenses, cleaning responsibilities, or anything else that is important to you. As with all the contracts in this book, the Agreement Covering Rented Living Space includes a clause requiring you and your partner to participate in mediation.

The Tenant and Subtenant Arrangement

Instead of being cotenants, you and your partner may have a tenant-subtenant arrangement. In this situation, the tenant rents directly from the landlord, and the subtenant rents from the tenant. You're likely to have this kind of arrangement if one of you moves in with the other and the landlord does not put the newcomer on the lease or otherwise acknowledge the second resident as a coequal of the original tenant, as explained above.

The main difference between the cotenant and tenant-subtenant arrangement lies in the tenant's ability to evict a subtenant. If your roommate is a cotenant, you cannot evict him or her. If your roommate is a subtenant, however, you do have eviction powers. But landlords in the know will usually object to allowing you to set up a tenant-subtenant situation. They want to retain the power to evict either or both of you, and they also want everyone living on the property to be subject to the "joint and several" liability rule described above (in a tenant-subtenant situation, the landlord cannot demand the entire rent from the subtenant, though he or she can evict both of you if the rent isn't paid).

Let's see how these rules play out. In the Clem and Julie situation, suppose Julie has not signed a rental agreement (only Clem has), and Clem wants to move out and Julie wants to remain; Julie and the landlord's legal relationship needs to be clarified. Clem should give the landlord written

Agreement Covering Rented Living Space

Julie Renoir _____ and

Clem Lawrence _____ agree that:

1. We will jointly rent ___Apartment # 4 at 1500 Peanut St., Dallas, Texas___.
   We have both signed a ___month-to-month rental agreement___ with the
   landlord, ___Oak Hill Properties___, and have each paid $ _750_ toward the
   security deposit of $ _1,500_.

2. Each of us will pay one-half of the rent and one-half of the utilities, including the
   basic monthly Internet and cable charges. Rent will be paid on the first of each
   month and utilities within ten days of when the bill is received. Utilities will be in
   the name of ___Clem Lawrence___.

3. If either of us wants to move out, the one moving will give the other and the
   landlord 30 days' written notice and will pay his/her share of the rent for the
   entire 30-day period even if he/she moves out sooner.

4. No third person will be invited to stay in the apartment without the agreement
   of both.

5. If one of us no longer wishes to live with the other, but both want to keep the
   apartment, the following will occur [check one]:

   ☒ ___Julie___ has first rights to stay in the apartment and
   ___Clem___ will move out.

   ☐ We will ask a third person to flip a coin to see who gets to stay.

   ☐ The person who needs the apartment most will retain it. Need will be
   determined by a third party whom we agree is objective, within two weeks
   of the date when one informs the other that he/she wishes to separate. In
   making this decision, the third party will consider each person's relative
   financial condition, proximity to work, the needs of any minor children, and
   [list any other important factors].

   ☐ Other. _____
   _____
   _____.

   The person who is to leave will do so within __two weeks__ of when that
   decision is made, and will have an additional __two weeks__ to pay
   his/her obligations for rent, utilities, and any damage to the apartment.

6. Any dispute arising out of this agreement will be mediated by a third person mutually acceptable to both of us. The mediator's role will be to help us arrive at a solution, not to impose one on us. If good faith efforts to arrive at our own solution with the help of a mediator prove to be fruitless after two mediation sessions, either of us may make a written request to the other that the dispute be arbitrated. If such a request is made, our dispute will be submitted to arbitration under the rules of the American Arbitration Association, and one arbitrator will hear our dispute. The decision of the arbitrator will be binding on us and will be enforceable in any court that has jurisdiction over the controversy. By agreeing to arbitration, we each agree to give up the right to a jury trial.

7. Additional agreements: _____
   _____
   _____ .

8. This agreement represents our complete understanding regarding our living together and replaces any prior agreements, written or oral. It can be amended, but only in writing, and any amendments must be signed by both of us.

9. If a court finds any portion of this contract to be illegal or otherwise unenforceable, the remainder of the contract is still in full force and effect.

Julie Renoir _____   _3/2/xx_ _____
Signature   Date

Clem Lawrence _____   _3/2/xx_ _____
Signature   Date

notice of his intent to leave (at least 30 days is usually required under state law) before he moves out. If Clem has a rental agreement, he owes no rent after the 30 days, assuming Julie is willing and able to pay. But to avoid possible problems later, should Julie be unable to pay the rent, Clem should contact the landlord and request that his name be removed from the rental agreement and Julie's officially substituted. See the Sample Tenant's Notice of Intent to Move Out and Substitute New Tenant, below.

If Clem has a lease and leaves before it expires, he still should be okay because the landlord must make reasonable efforts to limit its losses by finding a new tenant. In many states, your landlord is legally bound to accept a suitable tenant or find one without your help. Because Julie, presumably a reasonably solvent and nondestructive person, wants to stay, the landlord suffers no loss. The result is that if the landlord refuses Julie without good reason, Clem still owes no money, and any loss is the landlord's problem for refusing to limit his financial loss by letting Julie remain.

Even if you don't both sign a lease or rental agreement, you should definitely sign an agreement with each other, such as the one shown above, clarifying what happens to the rental should you separate.

Dealing With Objections When Moving Into the Rental Home of One Partner

Almost as common as two people looking for a home together is one person moving in with the other. This can be simple and smooth where the landlord is reasonable, but can raise tricky problems (and isn't recommended) if the landlord disapproves of unmarried couples or clearly doesn't want another person to move in. Don't try to argue with someone whom you know you can't convince. Use the time and energy to look for a new place for the two of you.

Sometimes, especially if the landlord lives far away or isn't likely to make waves, it seems sensible to have your partner move in and worry about the consequences later. But isn't a tenant required to get the landlord's permission before another person moves in? Usually the answer is yes, because leases and rental agreements typically limit the number of people allowed in the apartment or require landlord approval for additional roommates.

Sample Tenant's Notice of Intent to Move Out and Substitute New Tenant

(For use if you have a month-to-month rental agreement)

1500 Peanut Street, #4
Dallas, Texas

June 27, 20xx

Oak Hill Properties
10 Jones Street
Dallas, Texas

Dear Oak Hill Properties:

I live at the above address and regularly pay rent to your office under a month-to-month rental agreement. On July 31, 20xx, I will be moving out. As you know, my friend Julie Renoir also resides here. She wishes to remain and will continue to pay rent to your office on the first of each month.

We'll be contacting you soon to arrange for the return of my security deposit of $750, at which time Julie will give you a similar deposit. I would also like to have my name taken off the rental agreement and Julie's substituted. If you have any questions, or if there's anything we can do to make the transition easier, please let us know.

Very truly yours,

Clem Lawrence

Clem Lawrence

555-1234

Sample Tenant's Notice of Intent to Move Out and Substitute New Tenant

(For use if you have a lease)

1500 Peanut Street, #4
Dallas, Texas

June 27, 20xx

Oak Hill Properties
10 Jones Street
Dallas, Texas

Dear Oak Hill Properties:

I live at the above address under a lease that expires on October 30, 20xx. A change in my job makes it necessary that I leave on the last day of August. As you know, for the last six months my friend Julie Renoir has been sharing this apartment. Julie wishes to either take over my lease or enter into a new one with you for the remainder of my lease term. She's employed, has a stable income, and will, of course, be a responsible tenant.

We will soon be contacting your office to work out the details of the transfer. If you have any concerns, please give us a call.

Very truly yours,

Clem Lawrence

Clem Lawrence
555-1234

Even if your lease or rental agreement doesn't have a specific requirement that the landlord must approve additional tenants, it's normally
wise to contact your landlord before moving in another person. Your
landlord will almost surely figure it out anyway, and it's especially
important to avoid looking sneaky if you have a month-to-month
tenancy in a non-eviction-protection area where the landlord can evict
for any reason. On the other hand, if the landlord accepts rent knowing
that you have a roommate, the landlord has probably waived the legal
right to enforce the "only one occupant" clause.

Getting the Landlord's Permission

If one of you plans to move into the other's rented space, whether as a
cotenant or subtenant, here's our advice:

- Read the lease or rental agreement to see how many people
  may live on the premises and whether you need the landlord's
  permission to add a roommate.
- To help assure your landlord's approval, make sure your partner
  will meet your landlord's good-tenant criteria in terms of credit
  and financial status and rental history with other landlords. If
  you're afraid that your partner does not, in fact, meet the good-
  tenant requirements, it's still a good idea to let your landlord
  know you want to add a roommate, and try to work it out. If the
  landlord is really strict, you may end up needing to find another
  place with your partner. But even that will be better than having
  your landlord find out that you had someone new move in without
  notifying the management.
- Contact the landlord as far in advance as possible to explain your
  desire to add a roommate. Unless you are on fairly close personal
  terms with your landlord, it's a good idea to do this in writing. See
  the sample Letter Requesting Permission to Add a Roommate, below.

FORMS
**The Nolo website includes a downloadable copy of the Letter
Requesting Permission to Add a Roommate shown below.** See the appendix
for the link to this form.

If you are a good tenant and regularly pay rent on time, it's more likely that your landlord will approve your request to add a roommate, even if your landlord prefers renting to married couples.

More Roommates, More Rent

A landlord who agrees to an additional cotenant may ask for a rent increase on the theory that more people means more wear and tear. By signing a new lease or rental agreement that creates a cotenancy, you are, in effect, starting a new tenancy, so the landlord can increase rent immediately, rather than give you the usual 30 days' notice (for a month-to-month rental agreement) or wait until the lease ends.

Unless your rental unit is covered by rent control—or if the landlord is using a big rent increase as a not-so-subtle way to discriminate against you for an illegal reason—your landlord can ask for as much extra money as the market will bear.

TIP

Negotiate the rent increase. Just because your landlord asks for a big rent increase doesn't mean you have to say yes. One good approach is to counteroffer a lower amount. Let the landlord know that you may rethink adding a roommate, or even move out yourself, if you can't reach an acceptable compromise.

Security Deposit Increases

The landlord also has the legal right to change other conditions of your tenancy when you add a cotenant and sign a new agreement. One change that is particularly likely is an increase in the security deposit. However, this is one area where the sky is not the limit, because many states limit the amount of security deposits. Usually the limit is a multiple of the monthly rent. Keep in mind that if the deposit is already at the maximum, but the landlord raises the rent for the new occupant, the maximum security deposit goes up, too.

Letter Requesting Permission to Add a Roommate

1500 Peanut Street, #4

Dallas, Texas

June 2, 20xx

Oak Hill Properties

10 Jones Street

Dallas, Texas

Dear Oak Hill Properties:

I live at the above address and regularly pay rent to your office. I would like to add a second person, __Julie Renoir__ , to my __Lease__ beginning __July 1, 20xx__ . ~~He~~/She will be glad to complete a rental application and provide a recent copy of ~~his~~/her credit report and references.

I will call you soon to discuss this further. Thank you very much for considering this request.

Very truly yours,

Clem Lawrence

Getting Your Security Deposit Back

Getting your apartment security deposit back is a concern for all tenants—married couples, unmarried partners, and roommates. But special issues arise when one person moves out and the other remains. If you and your partner sign a lease or rental agreement together and only one of you moves out, your landlord does not have to return the security deposit to you. After all, one of you is still living there. It is up to the couple to work out a fair arrangement in this situation. Perhaps the remaining tenant pays the moving tenant half of the deposit. Or maybe a replacement roommate will pay the moving tenant a portion of the security deposit. It's best to decide how this will be handled before the situation arises. For example, include it in your agreement covering rented living space.

If both you and your partner are moving out of the apartment and want to ensure that you get your full (or close to full) security deposit back, follow this advice, which applies to all tenants (married or not):

Step 1: Document, in writing and with photographs, any problems that exist when you move in. Note dirty conditions, damaged rugs or appliances, faulty plumbing, and scratched, chipped, or cracked walls and floors. Get the landlord to sign your written list of problems. If the landlord refuses, have friends check the place over and sign your list.

Step 2: Thoroughly clean the apartment before you leave. Keep receipts for all cleaning supplies or services used (such as rental of a carpet cleaning machine).

Step 3: Document, in writing and with photographs or videos, the condition of the apartment after you remove your belongings and clean the place.

Step 4: Do a final inspection of the apartment with your landlord. Get the landlord to sign the document you created in Step 3. If the landlord refuses, have friends inspect the apartment and take photos.

Step 5: Understand what can and cannot be deducted from your security deposit. Your landlord cannot charge you for normal wear and tear to the apartment. However, you are responsible for any other damage. You are entitled to your full security deposit less the cost of the damage over and above normal wear and tear.

Step 6: If your landlord doesn't return your security deposit within the time period specified by your state (usually between 14 and 30 days after moving out), send a demand letter to your landlord. If you get no response, you can sue the landlord in small claims court.

RESOURCE

Information on tenants' rights. For detailed information about your rights and obligations as a tenant, including how to get your security deposit back (and the forms for doing so), see *Every Tenant's Legal Guide*, by Janet Portman and Marcia Stewart (Nolo). California tenants should see *California Tenants' Rights*, by Janet Portman and J. Scott Weaver (Nolo). You can also obtain free information on a variety of issues affecting tenants, including state laws on security deposits, at Nolo's website at www.nolo.com.

RESOURCE

Information on small claims court. If you have to go to small claims court, be sure to check out *Everybody's Guide to Small Claims Court*, by Ralph Warner (Nolo), or, for California residents, *Everybody's Guide to Small Claims Court in California*, by Ralph Warner (Nolo).

Buying a House Together

May Sellers Discriminate Against Unmarried Buyers? 144

How to Find and Work With a Real Estate Agent 145

Househunting Online 148

Home Financing and Mortgages 148

    How Much Down Payment Will You Make? 150

    What Are the Different Types of Mortgages? 152

    What Are the Best Sources of Home Loans or Mortgages? 153

    Online Mortgage Information 154

    Government Loans Available to Home Buyers 155

    How to Find the Least Costly Mortgage 156

    Loan Preapproval vs. Loan Prequalification 157

Proceeding With Your Purchase:

Offers, Inspections, Escrow, and Closing 158

    Real Estate Offers 158

    House Inspections 159

    Escrow and Closing Costs 160

Taking Title to Your New Home 161

    One Person's Name: Sole Owner 162

    Joint Tenancy 164

    Tenants in Common 167

    Changing Title 168

Contracts for Couples Owning a Home Together 170

    Editing Contracts 171

    Notarizing and Recording a House Ownership Contract 171

Contracts for Equal Ownership of a House... 172

Equal Ownership of a House—Each Partner Contributes
One-Half of the Down Payment.. 172

Equal Ownership of a House—One Person Lends the Other
Some or All of the Down Payment 180

Equal Ownership of a House—One Person Buys the House
and the Other Fixes It Up.. 185

Contract for Unequal Ownership of a House 187

**Agreement for One Person to Move Into the Other's House
and Become an Immediate Co-Owner** 192

**Agreement for One Person to Move Into the Other's House
and Become a Co-Owner Gradually**.. 199

FORMS IN THIS CHAPTER

Chapter 6 includes instructions for and samples of the following forms:

- Contract for Equal Ownership of a House
- Promissory Note
- Contract for Unequal Ownership of a House
- Agreement for One Person to Move Into the Other's House and Become an Immediate Co-Owner
- Agreement for One Person to Move Into the Other's House and Become a Co-Owner Gradually

The Nolo website includes downloadable copies of these forms. See the appendix for the link to the forms in this book.

There may come a time when you and your partner decide to purchase a house together. That means that you'll have lots to do—especially in today's dynamic real estate economy, locating an affordable house that meets your needs isn't always easy. And once you find your dream house, you must bargain with the seller for a favorable price, arrange for a good deal on a mortgage, have the house inspected for physical defects, and make decisions on dozens of other issues.

This chapter provides an overview of the most important aspects of housebuying. This generally involves four steps:

1. Finding the house.
2. Financing the purchase.
3. Working out a sensible ownership agreement between you and your partner (the buyers).
4. Transferring ownership (taking title to the house).

This chapter provides the legal information and sample agreements you'll need if you and your partner decide to purchase a house together or invest in a house already owned by or being purchased solely by one of you. We focus on how best to take title to real property and on the specific provisions you'll want to include in an agreement for owning a house together, such as how you will share costs and what will happen to the house if you break up. Our goal is to help you create a legally binding agreement that truly meets both of your needs.

RELATED TOPICS
Related topics covered in this book include:
- Writing living together contracts: Chapter 3
- Buying homeowners' insurance: Chapter 4
- Naming beneficiaries for real estate in a will: Chapter 9
- Dealing with the house if you break up: Chapter 10
- Working with a lawyer and researching real estate law: Chapter 11.

RESOURCE

For more information on buying a house and a guide to the best online real estate services—from financing to house inspections—see the Real Estate topic of Nolo's website at www.nolo.com. If it's your first house, check out *Nolo's Essential Guide to Buying Your First Home*, by Ilona Bray, Alayna Schroeder, and Marcia Stewart (Nolo). Californians should see *How to Buy a House in California*, by Ralph Warner, Ira Serkes, and George Devine (Nolo), for all aspects of home buying in the Golden State.

May Sellers Discriminate Against Unmarried Buyers?

Few, if any, sellers will care about your marital status. Occasionally, a seller might interpret the lack of a marriage license as an indication that you aren't a "serious" couple and may not be the best potential buyer, but this rarely comes up in real estate negotiations. But if a seller does refuse to sell to you simply because you aren't married, you may have little or no legal recourse in most places. In a growing number of states and in some cities, discrimination on the basis of marital status in the sale of real property is illegal. However, in many of these states, courts have ruled that "marital status" applies to married couples (or sometimes single people) but not unmarried couples. If you run into problems buying property as an unmarried couple, contact your city attorney's office, state fair housing office, or the U.S. Department of Housing and Urban Development (HUD) for advice. See Chapter 5 for contact information.

TIP

How to avoid discrimination. If you face a serious threat of discrimination, consider presenting the house purchase offer in one name alone, and then add the second name only when you are ready to close escrow. But make sure you learn the costs of doing so before you opt for this strategy.

In a few areas, you may face an unexpected obstacle: archaic zoning ordinances aimed at barring unrelated people from living together. Most of these laws prohibit groups of people from living together, but a few also prohibit two unrelated adults from living together. Several state courts, including those in Michigan, New York, and California, have interpreted their own constitutions to prohibit local communities from discriminating against unrelated adults. But unfortunately, other states' courts have been less open-minded. For example, one Missouri court evicted an unmarried couple and their children from a neighborhood zoned for single family residences, stating that "there is no state policy which commands that groups of people may live under the same roof in any section of a municipality they choose." (*City of Ladue v. Horn*, 720 S.W.2d 745 (1986).) And a Maryland court allowed a co-op to restrict residents to the immediate family of the co-op member, stating that it would provide "a more stable community." (*Maryland Commission on Human Relations v. Greenbelt*, 475 A.2d 1192 (1984).) Although it's very unlikely you'll run into this sort of problem, it still makes sense to check that the city—or neighborhood—in which you plan to buy isn't zoned only for people related by "blood, marriage, or adoption." It's our opinion that the U.S. Supreme Court's ruling in *Lawrence v. Texas*, 539 U.S. 558 (2003) renders these types of laws unconstitutional, but you may not have the time, energy, or funds for legal fees necessary to try and undo them. Also, if you're buying a co-op or a property subject to a community association, check the rules for any restrictions, and talk with your agent about how best to deal with such challenges.

How to Find and Work With a Real Estate Agent

Most homebuyers use a real estate broker (or an agent who works for a broker) to help find a home and negotiate the house purchase contract. A good agent can give you advice on prices, school districts, transportation, demographics, and economic trends in the area (for example, whether property values are going up or down). A broker or agent should also help you find the other experts you need—such as a termite inspector, a roofer, or a soil engineer—and help arrange financing and assist with the closing.

Real estate agents work usually on commission, not salary, and get paid only after you find a home, negotiate the contract, and complete the transaction. An agent's commission is a percentage of the price of the home (typically 5%–6%) for both agents combined, and is almost always paid by the seller.

Because most real estate transactions involve two brokers—one who helps the buyer and one who helps the seller—the commission is divided, usually 50-50, between the two brokerage offices. Then, within each office, the agent who handled the transaction gets a share, usually 50% of the office's total share.

In most states, brokers are allowed to represent both the buyer and the seller in the same real estate transaction, unless there is a written agreement to the contrary. (In some states, like California, the broker must inform both the buyer and seller of this dual agency in writing.) Sometimes this means that the individual broker represents both buyer and seller. Sometimes it means that different agents from the same brokerage office represent the buyer and seller. The latter situation is common, especially if a few big brokerage offices handle most of the real estate deals in the area. Either way, be aware that in this type of dual-agency relationship, your broker may be looking out for interests other than just your own.

Even if your real estate broker represents only you and not the seller, the broker's interests may conflict with your own. Your broker won't get a commission until you purchase a property. And when you do, the commission depends on the sale price. So, the broker may have an interest in (1) pushing you to buy a property very quickly, to limit the amount of work the agent must do to make the commission, (2) encouraging you to buy an expensive property to increase the commission, and (3) making sure you offer enough money on a particular property to close the deal. You, on the other hand, will be (1) looking to buy a home within your financial means and (2) trying to get the lowest price possible. Of course, a good agent knows that if you offer more than you can afford it makes very little difference (for example, if you spend an extra $10,000, the agent will probably only see about $150 more in commission) and may even jeopardize the deal if you don't qualify for the financing you need. The best agents also realize there's little to be gained from a dissatisfied customer, since customer referrals are an important part of their business.

Still, if you feel the agent is showing you homes outside of your price range or is pushing you to buy before you're ready, be sure to speak up.

To find a good agent, get recommendations from friends, family, coworkers, and others you trust. The best referrals come from those who have recently bought a home in the area where you're looking. Be sure to check an agent's reputation and references before agreeing to work with him or her. If you find your agent at an open house, in the yellow pages, or on the Internet, make sure you thoroughly check the agent's credentials and experience before you sign a contract.

Buying a House Without a Broker

For a variety of reasons, you may be tempted to proceed on your own, without a broker. But bear in mind that buying real estate takes a lot of work and patience, and involves understanding a fair amount of strange jargon and knowledge of the local customs and practices. And since it's almost always the seller who pays the entire real estate commission, it's often easier (and free) to let someone knowledgeable do at least some of the work for you. If you do decide to enter the transaction without an agent, it's only to your benefit if the seller will agree to reduce the price or give you some other concession in return, because it's the seller who normally covers this expense. So, unless the seller is willing to reduce the price a bit, we encourage you to have your own agent.

But just as you (the buyers) don't have to hire a broker, neither does the seller. A small but significant number of people sell their own homes in an effort to avoid paying the hefty real estate commission. You can find homes sold by owners—and sometimes negotiate to share some of the seller's savings —by checking newspaper and online ads or driving around and looking for "for sale by owner" or "FSBO" (so-called "fizzbo") signs. Be careful, however, if you've already started working with an agent who will represent you in the transaction. Some FSBO owners won't pay any agent commissions, which means you'll have to pay your agent's fee yourself. Of course, you can reduce the amount of your purchase offer to cover this additional cost. If neither party is using an agent, you might want to have your documents reviewed by an attorney or a consulting agent, just to be sure that everything is in order.

Househunting Online

A good real estate broker will be sensitive to your interests and show you properties that meet your needs and budget. But there's a lot that you can do on your own. Scanning listings to see which homes are available and worth a visit, how much they cost, and what they offer is now as easy as turning on your computer. You can access the Multiple Listings Service (MLS) online through sites such as Realtor.com (sponsored by the National Association of Realtors). Your state or regional realty association may also offer a website of homes for sale. These sites typically include details such as location, price, size, amenities, and other criteria, as well as pictures.

For listings of new homes and developments in major metropolitan areas, see www.move.com, operated by the National Association of Homebuilders. Online sites such as Redfin.com and Zillow.com can be very helpful, as they not only list houses for sale, but also list the closing sale prices of properties in specific neighborhoods. But be careful when it comes to online estimates of value—these sites use computerized analytics that often ignore the specific conditions of a particular house, and so they can be quite inaccurate.

To check out FSBOs (homes sold without a broker), see www.forsale byowner.com or www.salebyowner.com. Some FSBOs also appear on the MLS.

Finally, check out online editions of newspapers; many have online MLS access or similar classified sections.

Home Financing and Mortgages

It's essential to determine how much you can afford to pay before you look for a house. Many people don't understand how institutional lenders (banks, savings and loans, and credit unions) decide how much money they'll lend to you. If you don't do the calculations ahead of time, or talk to a loan broker, you may enter into a home purchase contract and then not qualify for the necessary financing. And nowadays, in many competitive markets, most sellers want to see a prequalification letter (or in some markets a preapproval letter) before they will even consider your offer.

Your Credit Score Is Important When Applying for a Home Loan

When deciding whether to approve your home loan application, most lenders will consider your credit score. Credit scores are numerical calculations between 300 and 850 that are supposed to indicate the risk that you will default on your payments. High credit scores indicate less risk and low scores indicate potential problems.

Factors that many companies use when generating credit scores include:

- your payment history
- amounts you owe on credit accounts
- length of your credit history—in general, a longer credit history increases the score
- your new credit. It helps to have an established credit history without too many new accounts. Opening several accounts in a short period of time can represent greater risk, and
- types of credit—credit scorers look for a "healthy mix" of different types of credit.

You can now get a free credit report every year, but in most cases, it won't include your score. You should be able to purchase a report including the score for less than $20. See Chapter 4 for information on how to get a copy of your credit report and correct errors, if necessary.

For more information on credit scoring, see www.myfico.com, a Fair Isaac website for consumers.

To determine how much a bank will lend you, compare your antici-pated monthly housing payments (including principal, interest, taxes, and insurance), plus your monthly payments on other long-term debts, to your gross (total) monthly income from employment and other sources. This is called the "debt-to-income ratio." Lenders normally want you to make all monthly debt payments with around 36% of your gross monthly income, though some banks will lend you up to 45% of your income. You can qualify at a lower or higher percentage depending on the amount of your down payment, the interest rate on the type of mortgage you want, your credit history, the number of other long-term debts you have, your employment stability and prospects, the lender's philosophy, and whether money is tight or fairly easily available in the U.S. economy as a whole.

Usually, lenders assume you can spend around 28% of your gross monthly income on a mortgage payment and the rest of the overall 36% on other debts. But the greater your other debts, the lower the percentage of your income lenders will assume you have available to spend each month on housing. Conversely, if you have no long-term debt and a good credit history, and are able to make a larger-than-normal down payment, a lender may approve monthly housing costs that exceed 36% of your monthly income—perhaps as high as 40%.

Remember, if both of you are going to be buyers, both of your incomes will be included in the calculations. Applications by unmarried couples are handled as two separate applications, but usually that does not affect your ability to get the loan.

The tricky part for unmarried couples is that you have separate applications and distinct credit scores, so you may be advised to list just one of you as the borrower. For a variety of reasons, we strongly discourage you from going down this path—it may seem easier at the outset, but it can create serious problems for you down the road.

RESOURCE

Mortgage calculators. Dozens of websites offer free calculators to help you quickly determine monthly payments on different size mortgages so you can learn how much house you can afford. You can find easy-to-use real estate calculators at www.nolo.com/legal-calculators, www.hsh.com, www. bankrate.com, and www.interest.com, as well as on the sites of individual mortgage lenders.

The following sections provide some background information on home financing.

How Much Down Payment Will You Make?

Unless you're eligible for a government-subsidized mortgage under a program offered by the Federal Housing Authority (FHA) or

Department of Veterans Affairs (VA), which requires either a zero or a very low down payment, or you are willing to pay a high interest rate, you'll probably need to put down 5%–20% of the cost of the house to qualify for a loan. Also, you'll have to pay the closing costs, an additional 2%–5% of the cost of the home. The days of the zero percent down payment have for the most part passed, and lenders are becoming stricter when it comes to down payments and income qualifications.

Generally speaking, the larger the percentage of the total price of a house you can put down, the easier it will be for you to qualify for a mortgage. This is because a big down payment means less money will be due each month to pay off your mortgage. And because the amount of your monthly mortgage payment (plus taxes and insurance) is the major factor in qualifying for a loan, it's easy to see that the lower this is, the more likely a lender is to say yes. It also assures a lender that if you default on your loan, there will be enough equity in the property for the lender to recover what it's owed. And of course, the lender is less worried about you defaulting, because you stand to lose more if you do. A bigger down payment often means lower interest rates, too. Finally, if your loan is for more than 80% of the home's value, your lender will require you to buy private mortgage insurance (PMI). Though you pay PMI, it protects the lender in case you default. If you put 20% down, you won't have this additional expense.

CAUTION

Feeling shaky about your relationship? If you are insecure about your romance, it makes sense to consider a house that one of you could afford on your own or one that readily accommodates a roommate. That way you won't be forced to sell the place if the relationship dissolves.

If you don't have a lot of money for a down payment, you may be tempted to ask your parents or grandparents for a gift or a loan. Whether this is wise, given your family situation, and how best to structure the transaction, are topics beyond the scope of this book. But we will note one thing: This approach will usually only help you to qualify for a mortgage loan if you do not have to pay the money back promptly (or at all). Otherwise, the amount you'll need to repay to your friends or relatives for this extra down payment money may increase your debt level so much that you won't be able to qualify for the loan. Your lender may ask your "donor" to sign a letter affirming that this is a gift, so remember, legally this won't be a loan—even if you voluntarily pay it back later on. Don't be tempted to call a loan a gift here—it will only create problems down the road. If you do receive a down payment gift, be clear about whether this is a gift to both you and your partner or just one of you.

What Are the Different Types of Mortgages?

The two basic types are fixed and adjustable rate mortgages. Here's how they differ.

Fixed Rate Mortgages

With a fixed rate mortgage, the interest rate and the amount you pay each month remain the same over the entire mortgage term, traditionally 15, 20, 30, or even 40 years.

Adjustable Rate Mortgages

With an adjustable rate mortgage (ARM), the interest rate fluctuates according to current market interest rates. Initial interest rates on ARMs are typically offered at a discounted ("teaser") rate lower than that for a fixed rate mortgage. Over time, when the initial discount ends— sometimes after only one month—the interest rate adjusts according to current market rates plus an extra amount, called a margin. ARMs can be tied to different market-sensitive financial indexes, such as one-year U.S. Treasury bills. Some indexes fluctuate up or down more quickly than others. To avoid constant and drastic changes, ARMs typically regulate (cap) how much and how often the interest rate and payments can change in a year and over the life of the loan.

Which Is Better—a Fixed or Adjustable Rate Mortgage?

It depends. Because interest rates and mortgage options change often, your choice of a fixed or adjustable rate mortgage should depend on:
- the interest rates and mortgage options available when you're buying a house

- your view of the future (generally, high inflation will mean ARM rates will go up and lower inflation means that they will fall), and
- how willing you are to take a risk.

When mortgage rates are low, a fixed rate mortgage is the best bet for long-term buyers. In the long run, ARMs are likely to go up, meaning most buyers will be better off to lock in a favorable fixed rate now and not take the risk of much higher rates later.

However, not all buyers must choose one or the other—there are other options that combine both. For example, some buyers choose hybrid adjustable rate mortgages. These mortgages start out with a fixed rate for the first few years of the loan—often five or seven years—and become adjustable after that. Usually, the interest rate offered for the fixed period is lower than what's available for other fixed rate mortgages. If you're buying a home and don't expect to stay in it longer than about seven years, or you expect to refinance the mortgage, this type of loan may work best.

What Are the Best Sources of Home Loans or Mortgages?

Many entities make home loans, including banks, credit unions, savings and loans, insurance companies, and mortgage bankers. To get the best deal, compare loans and fees with at least three or four lenders. Because many types of home loans are standardized to comply with rules established by the Federal National Mortgage Association (Fannie Mae) and other quasi-governmental corporations that purchase loans from lenders, comparison shopping is not difficult. Be sure to ask for the same size, type, and length of mortgage—such as a 30-year fixed rate mortgage for $500,000—so you're comparing apples to apples.

Current mortgage rates and fees are usually published in the real estate sections of metropolitan newspapers, and are widely available on online mortgage websites. However, keep in mind that these advertised rates usually only apply to borrowers with the best credit history, and you may not be offered the same great rates. You can also work with a mortgage broker, someone who specializes in matching house buyers to appropriate mortgage lenders. A broker will be able to compile many different options from various lenders. If your income arrangements are atypical or if either buyer has credit problems, working with a skilled mortgage broker may be the only way you can obtain a decent loan. Generally, the broker's commission is paid by the lender, so you don't have to pay for the broker's services.

Be sure to check out government-subsidized mortgages, which have no down payment and low down payment plans (see "Government Loans Available to Home Buyers," below). Also, ask banks and other private lenders about any "first-time buyer" programs that offer low down payment plans and flexible qualifying guidelines to low- and moderate-income buyers with good credit. Be careful here, as you may need to each qualify separately for such programs.

Online Mortgage Information

Dozens of websites provide a wide range of mortgage information and loans.

No-loan sites don't broker or lend mortgage money, but typically provide mortgage rate information—just what most mortgage shoppers want and need. Two of the best no-loan sites are www.hsh.com and www.bankrate.com. Offering vast libraries of mortgage information for consumers, no-loan sites are a great place to examine mortgage programs, keep daily tabs on mortgage rates, indexes, and market events that push costs up or down, learn mortgage lingo, get questions answered about the loan qualification process, and crunch numbers with online mortgage calculators.

There are also many mortgage loan sites that offer direct access to mortgage loans. You can search for a specific bank or lender or check out one of the many mortgage shopping sites that let you shop for loans among dozens of lenders. A couple of multilender shopping sites are www.eloans.com and www.quickenLoans.com.

TIP

When to stick with local lenders and brokers. If you have unconventional sources of income or if your purchase is complicated, we recommend that you use a local lender or mortgage broker, rather than an online source. In our experience, the low-cost online lenders just don't have the knowledge or patience to deal with unconventional applications.

Government Loans Available to Home Buyers

Several federal, state, and local government financing programs are available to home buyers. The two main federal loan programs are administered by the Federal Housing Administration (FHA) and the U.S. Department of Veterans Affairs (VA). State and local programs may also be available.

FHA Loans

The Federal Housing Administration (FHA), an agency of the Department of Housing and Urban Development (HUD), insures loans to all U.S. citizens and permanent residents who meet financial qualification rules. Under its most popular program, if the buyer defaults and the lender forecloses, the FHA pays 100% of the amount insured. This loan insurance lets qualified people buy affordable houses. The major attraction of an FHA-insured loan is that it requires a low down payment, usually about 3% to 5%. A drawback of FHA loans is that they usually have low loan limits, meaning you'll either have to make up the difference with a large down payment or another mortgage, or you'll have to buy an inexpensive property.

At one time, it was difficult for unmarried couples to qualify for FHA loans—the FHA would make the loan but count only the man's income in determining whether the couple qualified. The FHA no longer does this and now considers the income of both partners in both married and unmarried couples when determining financial ability.

RESOURCE
More information on FHA loan programs. Contact a regional office of HUD or check the HUD website at www.hud.gov. (Check out "Buy a Home" on the home page.)

Veterans Affairs (VA) Loans

The U.S. Department of Veterans Affairs (VA), like the FHA, guarantees loans. VA loans are available to most veterans who served a minimum time. If you default, the VA pays the lender the amount guaranteed. This guarantee makes it easier for veterans to get favorable loan terms with a low down payment. The loans are an excellent value—one of the best for moderately priced housing.

If one member of an unmarried couple is a qualifying veteran and the other isn't, the VA will guarantee only the veteran's share, which probably means the nonveteran will have to make a larger down payment. VA loans discriminate against unmarried couples—a married veteran whose spouse does not qualify can have the entire loan guaranteed.

RESOURCE

More information on VA loans. Check the VA's website at www.homeloans.va.gov, or contact a regional VA office for advice.

How to Find the Least Costly Mortgage

You can save money if you shop carefully for a mortgage. Everything else being equal, even a one-quarter percentage point difference in interest rates can mean saving thousands of dollars over the life of a mortgage.

However, don't just look at the advertised interest rate. In addition to comparing interest rates, there are a variety of fees—and fee amounts—associated with getting a mortgage. Mortgage-related costs include things like application fees, credit check fees, and points (explained below). Lenders are required to advertise the annual percentage rate (APR), which factors in the cost of these other fees. A loan that looks like it has a very low rate may in fact be quite expensive when these other costs are factored in. The downside of the APR is that it is calculated by spreading the costs of these fees over the life of loan, and many people don't keep their loans that long because they refinance or sell their homes before the mortgage is paid off.

There are sometimes benefits to taking out loans with higher fees, however. This is particularly true of a loan with points. Points make up the largest part of lender fees: One point is 1% of the loan principal. Thus, your fee for borrowing $500,000 at two points is $10,000. The benefit of paying points is that the more points you pay, the lower your rate of interest.

To decide whether to get a loan with points, factor in how long you plan to own your house. The longer you live in your house (or pay on the mortgage), the better off you'll be paying more points up front in return for a lower interest rate. On the other hand, if you think you'll sell or refinance your house within two or three years, you're probably better off obtaining a loan with no points.

A good loan officer or loan broker can walk you through all options and trade-offs such as higher fees or points for a lower interest rate. Or you can check online mortgage and financial calculators (see above) to quickly compare various combinations of interest rates and points.

You may be told you can get a better rate by having just one partner buy the house. Before you go down this path, make sure you learn the transaction costs and fees of adding the other partner later. Increasingly, we have heard of banks willing to treat just one partner as the borrower, even though both partners are on the title as co-owners. If having both partners on the loan makes it hard to qualify for a decent mortgage rate, this might be a viable option for you to consider.

Loan Preapproval vs. Loan Prequalification

Once you've done the basic calculations and completed a financial statement, you can ask a lender or loan broker for a preapproval letter. This is the lender's agreement to lend you a specific amount, based on your credit history and financial situation and subject to certain conditions like a satisfactory appraisal of the property, title report, and purchase contract. Having a lender preapprove you for a loan is crucial in a competitive market; it shows that you're in the financial position to follow through on your offer.

Don't get loan preapproval confused with loan prequalification, however. With prequalification, a lender just speculates what you're likely to be able to borrow based on the financial information you provide. The lender doesn't check your credit history or promise to lend you the money. While prequalification can help you ballpark how much you can afford, it won't give you any assurance or impress any sellers.

Proceeding With Your Purchase: Offers, Inspections, Escrow, and Closing

Finding a house you want and can afford to buy is just the first step. You must still reach a firm agreement on price and terms with the owner, arrange inspections, and go through escrow before you actually own the house.

Real Estate Offers

A legal offer to buy a house must be in writing, delivered to the seller or the seller's agent, and contain specific financial and other terms so that if the seller says "yes," the deal can go through. The seller's acceptance, too, must be in writing.

Real estate offers often contain contingencies—events that must happen within a certain period of time (such as 30 days) before the deal becomes final. For example, you may want to make your offer contingent on qualifying for financing, the house passing certain inspections, or even your ability to sell your existing house first. Be aware, however, that the more contingencies you place in an offer, the less likely the seller is to accept it. In a competitive market, the seller is more likely to take the offer that doesn't have contingencies. In most instances, you can make the offer as a solo buyer or as a couple, and then freely switch your plans about who is to be the buyer later on, during the loan approval process. But check with your agent about this issue—in highly competitive markets, the seller wants some assurance that you'll be able to complete the sale. If you're ambivalent about who is going to be the buyer, the seller might worry that you might not be able to close the deal as scheduled.

If your bid is far too low, the seller is likely to reject the offer on the spot. But even very attractive offers are rarely accepted as written. Typically, the seller will respond with a written counteroffer accepting some of the offer terms, but proposing certain changes. Most counteroffers correspond to these provisions of an offer:

- price—the seller wants more money
- occupancy—the seller needs more time to move out

- buyer's sale of current house—the seller doesn't want to wait for this to occur, and
- inspections—the seller wants you to schedule them more quickly, or in some instances waive the right to do an inspection altogether.

You may accept the seller's counteroffer, reject it, or present a counteroffer of your own. Then, the negotiations will continue until either a deal or an impasse is reached.

A contract is formed when either the seller or the buyer accepts all of the terms of the other's offer or counteroffer in writing within the time allowed. In some states, the parties will sign a more detailed contract prepared by lawyers; in other states the broker-prepared contract remains *the* contract governing the sale.

House Inspections

Inspecting the condition of a house is an important part of the home-buying process. In some states, such as California, the law requires sellers to disclose considerable information about the house, as well as potential hazards from floods, earthquakes, fires, and environmental hazards. But whether or not the seller provides disclosures, you should have the property inspected for defects or malfunctions in the building's structure such as the roof or plumbing.

Your purchase offer and any resulting contract should be contingent upon experts inspecting the house and reporting that it is in good condition or can be repaired for a reasonable price. The contract should also allow you a reasonable time to arrange for all required inspections. A buyer usually pays for the cost of the inspections, but it is possible to negotiate with the seller to pay a portion. Inspections routinely include termite, electrical and plumbing, and roof. In addition, you may want a soil engineer to check the foundation, or a general contractor to do a full inspection. Depending on the property, you may want to arrange specialized inspections for hazards from floods, earthquakes, and other natural disasters, as well as environmental hazards like asbestos and lead.

The cost of these inspections can mount up, and in rare situations be as much as $1,000—so you need to be careful when you make an offer and not overspend on multiple inspections.

If the house is in good shape, you can proceed, knowing that you're getting what you paid for. If inspections reveal problems—such as an antiquated plumbing system or major termite problems—you can negotiate with the seller about who will pay for necessary repairs, or you can back out of the deal, assuming your contract is properly written to allow you to do so.

RESOURCE

Where to find local referrals to inspectors and useful FAQs about home inspections. Check out the American Society of Home Inspectors (ASHI) at www.ashi.com.

Escrow and Closing Costs

The final transfer of the house to the buyer is called the "closing." It occurs after both the seller and the buyer have met all the terms of the contract. (See "What Is a Deed?" below.) In buying and selling a house, paperwork and money must eventually change hands. This is when you have to finalize your intentions as to who is taking title, and how you are going to "nest" your ownership interests.

The practice is for the buyers to deliver their money and the sellers to deliver the house deed to a third person, called an escrow holder. As a matter of custom, in some areas, the buyer pays for this service, but in others, the seller pays or the cost is shared. Oftentimes you (the buyers) will also be paying in advance some of the ongoing house expenses, like insurance and transfer taxes and the prepayment of your property taxes, at closing. The escrow holder hangs on to everything until all inspections are complete, the papers are signed, and financing is arranged. Then, "escrow closes," which means the seller gets his or her money and the buyer becomes the official owner, subject to the lender's "security interest" in the property.

In some states, a lawyer must handle the real estate closing, unless you handle the transaction without professional help from a broker or agent.

What Is a Deed?

Before escrow closes on a new house, you'll need to choose how to take "title" (documented legal ownership). Title is evidenced by a deed recorded at the County Recorder's office or other land records office. A deed is the document that transfers ownership of real estate. It contains the names of the old and new owners and a legal description of the property, and is signed by the person transferring the property.

In many other states, attorneys typically are not involved in residential property sales, and a title or escrow company handles the entire closing process.

Check with your real estate broker or with your state department of real estate for advice on house closings.

Taking Title to Your New Home

When you buy a house with your partner, you must decide how you will own the property, or, as they say in the real estate business, how you will "take title." Since in this context "title" is a synonym for "ownership," your decision has huge and lasting consequences, particularly on taxes, dissolution, and estate planning issues. Assuming you are buying the house for personal and not business use, you have three basic choices:

- one person holds title as sole owner
- both of you hold title as "joint tenants," or
- both of you hold title as "tenants in common."

This section explains what each of these legal arrangements means and when each of them is appropriate. Later sections in this chapter provide contracts for different types of ownership (equal or unequal), and cover such basic issues as what happens to the house if you break up.

SEE AN EXPERT

Questions about taking title? Be sure to consult with an experienced real estate attorney.

Home Buying and the Marriage Question

Buying property will likely be an occasion for the two of you to talk about "the marriage question." We don't offer any relationship advice, but we do recommend that if marriage is on the horizon, this would be the right time to make that decision. We know that this process can be difficult for many couples, and so it may be impractical to resolve the marriage questions before you complete your house purchase. But because title and taxation issues both are profoundly different if you are married, changing your marital status after you buy the house can invite some complicated tax and ownership issues. And by the way, don't be tempted to tell the title officer you're married if you're not—it will only create confusion and possible problems down the road.

One Person's Name: Sole Owner

If a recorded deed contains only one name, that person is the legal owner and has full legal power to sell or will away the house or other real property, even if someone else has contributed to its purchase and holds a nonrecorded interest, even where the parties have signed a "co-ownership" contract.

Sometimes, a couple that intends to jointly co-own a house is tempted to put only one name on the deed to save on taxes, cope with one partner's bad credit, avoid creditors, or for some other reason. The tax savings can be attractive if one of your incomes is very high and the other's is very low, because it allows the high-income person to take all the house-related tax deductions—usually, this can be dealt with by allocating most or all of the deductible expenses to the higher-earning owner. Or, if one person's credit is terrible, it may seem like a good idea not to mention his or her interest in the property in order to get a loan (or to get a lower interest rate) to buy the house.

However, in most cases the risks inherent in putting a house that you intend to jointly own in one person's name far outweigh the benefits. If your partner is the only one named on the deed (and is therefore presumed to be sole owner), you may be out of luck if your partner sells the house and pockets the money, or dies and leaves it to someone else. Sure, you can sue your ex-partner in an attempt to recover the amount of your financial interest in the property, but this type of lawsuit is often difficult to win, as most states have a strong legal presumption that the person whose name appears on the deed is the owner. In any case, and even when there's a written contract between the two of you, a lawsuit designed to prove that a person whose name does not appear on the deed is a co-owner is likely to be expensive, stressful, and time-consuming.

If one person's credit will absolutely doom a loan application, it may be possible to take out the loan and purchase the property in one partner's name alone, and then add the second partner's name to the title immediately thereafter. But be very careful here: Make sure you actually follow through and add the partner's name officially, and be aware that in some places transfer taxes and fees may apply to the transfer. In some instances the lender may be entitled to "call in the loan" if you add someone to title like this, but in our experience this rarely happens as long as you stay current on the loan payments.

NOTE: In some states, including California, an owner can take title with a "transfer on death" provision. If you add someone as the transfer-on-death recipient, they aren't a current owner—and you can always cancel the transfer provision—but they will become the owner if you die while owning the property. If you want to protect your partner in case of your unexpected death, this provision might be an attractive alternative to a joint tenancy, will, or trust.

TIP

What if you decide not to name both owners on the deed? If you decide to list only one name on the deed, you may want to sign a separate contract that spells out the actual property interests of both parties. Before you do this, be sure to see a lawyer. Being an "off-title" owner can create a myriad of problems, especially with the tax authorities. The nonowner probably won't be able to deduct mortgage contributions or avoid the capital gains taxes on any profits earned if the two of you later sell the property. Or, creditors may claim that you are trying to conceal assets from them, which could lead to other problems. You should also talk with a lawyer about whether to record such an agreement with the County Recorder's office if you do sign one. In some places it can be very expensive to add someone to the title later on, especially if that person is not your legal spouse, so make sure you investigate before making a final decision. Similar tax and fee burdens apply when one of you buys into a house that your partner already owns. This is one of those situations where it's prudent to meet with a lawyer.

Joint Tenancy

If you take title as joint tenants, you share equal ownership of the property and each of you has the right to use the entire property. If one joint tenant dies, the other automatically becomes the owner of the deceased person's share, even if there's a will to the contrary. This is called the right of survivorship. In fact, some states require that after the words "joint tenants," you add the words "with right of survivorship" (hence the common abbreviations JTWROS or Jt Ten WROS).

> CAUTION
> **Check your state's required language.** If in doubt about the specific language you must use when taking title to a house, ask a title company, real estate broker, or attorney for the exact terminology required in your state.

An advantage of joint tenancy is that at the death of the first joint tenant, the property passes to the surviving joint tenant without the expense and trouble of probate proceedings.

Keep in mind, however, that just because you establish a joint tenancy does not mean it will last forever. If one joint tenant sells her share, the joint tenancy ends (in most states this is true even if the other joint tenant is unaware of the sale). The new owner and the other original owner become tenants in common (see "Tenants in Common," below). And in most states a joint tenant may end the joint tenancy at any time, again with the result that the owners become tenants in common with no right of survivorship.

Before taking title as joint tenants, be sure to consider the following issues.

Joint Tenancy Means Equal Shares

Joint tenancy is appropriate only when each joint tenant (in theory, there can be any number) owns the same percentage of the property. Thus, you and your partner can each own 50% of the house, or three people can each own one-third. But if you own 60% of a house and your partner owns 40%, joint tenancy won't work. In that case, you'll be tenants in common.

However, having one person provide most or even all of the down payment doesn't mean you can't be joint tenants. As long as you agree to "own" the house equally, joint tenancy will work fine. This can be accomplished if the person making the down payment gifts a half interest to the other or, more typically, if the more affluent partner agrees to lend the other partner his or her half of the down payment. If this is your plan, make sure that the loan is documented in a promissory note or a written agreement, as in some states a joint tenant has no right to a reimbursement unless the owners have a written agreement. With this arrangement, you own the house equally, but one partner will have to repay the loan out his or her 50% share of the proceeds of sale.

Risks of Joint Tenancy

Taking title to a house as joint tenants—whether it's a joint purchase or where one partner buys into his or her partner's house—can be an efficient way to provide for each partner's half to be transferred easily to the other partner upon a partner's death. But it carries with it some very real risks.

First, if the financial contributions are not truly equal, the equal ownership presumption of joint tenancy means that the greater contributor has made a gift to the lesser contributor. The value of this gift should be reported to the IRS, and while no tax is owed until the lifetime gifts exceed $5.49 million, the reporting requirements are a burden and eventually, for some couples, can become a tax liability. It can also result in a serious tax problem for high net worth individuals at time of death, since the value of the entire property is usually counted as part of the estate of the first partner to pass away. Of greatest impact, if the couple later splits, the lesser (or noncontributing) partner can claim a 50% ownership interest based on the language of the deed. If you really mean to add someone for survivorship purposes, it's far better to use a will, a trust, or a transfer-on-death deed (if your state allows it).

Second, if one partner has owned the house for a while or made a large down payment when it was purchased, transferring it into joint tenancy co-ownership also can create a tax reporting or tax payment liability. Remember, since joint tenancy means equal ownership, adding a partner to the title as joint tenant means you have just transferred a 50% interest to your partner.

Domestic Partnership and Title

In some cities, counties, and states, unmarried couples can register as domestic partners; some employers also provide benefits to registered domestic partners. Certain registries are only open to same-sex couples, based upon the philosophy that if you can marry legally, you don't need the domestic partner benefits. In any event, domestic partner registration won't have any impact on who holds title, nor on any claim a nonowner might have, based on contributions to a partner's property, unless you have registered in a marriage-equivalent state domestic partnership or civil union. The only effect it might have is to entitle you to an exemption from transfer taxes in some cities or counties at the time of dissolution. Check with your local County Recorder if this is an issue for you.

Third, since a joint tenancy deed doesn't meet the standards of a clearly articulated legal agreement, sometimes these transfers are challenged by relatives, who argue that their sibling or parent didn't really intend to bequeath their share of the property to their partner. A will or trust will be much more solid when it comes to these sorts of arrangements.

And lastly, using joint tenancy doesn't allow for any complex estate planning, such as letting your partner live in the house while he or she is alive, but then transferring it to your children upon your partner's death—that generally requires a living trust.

It may be just fine to take title initially as joint tenants—especially when you are each contributing the same to the purchase—but we encourage you to consult with a lawyer experienced in tax and estate planning laws before you let too much time go by. Usually there is no cost to changing the form of title later on, so long as you do it before any tax concerns arise, and of course, before you break up or either of you passes away!

See Chapter 9 for advice on wills and estate planning.

Tenants in Common

Perhaps the most common way for unmarried couples to take title to real property is as "tenants in common." Unlike a joint tenancy, a tenant in common may own an equal or an unequal share of the property, and has no automatic right to inherit the property when the other partner dies. When one tenant in common dies, his or her share of the jointly owned property is left to whomever is specified in a will or living trust or to legal heirs if he or she dies intestate (without a will or trust). This might well be his or her living together partner, but it could also be someone else. The crucial point that bears repeating is that if there's no will or trust, the deceased person's intestate heirs will inherit his or her share—and that does not include a living together partner.

If you choose to own the home as tenants in common but agree to sign wills stating that if one partner dies, the other will get the entire home, you still need to be careful. Your partner could change his or her will at any time to leave his or her share of the property to someone other than you. And there's no rule that says your partner must notify you of the change.

TIP

Living trusts are a way for tenants in common to avoid the cost and trouble of probate. See Chapter 9 for advice on transferring property through a living trust.

Tenants in common can legally own property in unequal shares—for example, one person could own 80%, and the other 20%. When ownership is unequal, both names are still listed on the deed as tenants in common. In most states, you can specify your ownership percentages on the deed or in a separate written agreement that you sign, and in some instances you may wish to record the document along with the deed at your County Recorder's office. You can also use a written agreement to provide for reimbursement of a down payment in lieu of unequal ownership and also include such a provision in your will or trust.

If you'd like your share of the home to go to someone other than your partner when you die, but want to make sure your partner has a place to live, you can own the home as tenants in common and include a life estate provision in the deed or include that provision in your will or trust documents. This means that upon your death, your partner can remain in the home until he or she dies. Then, your share of the home passes to your chosen heir.

> CAUTION
>
> **If ownership shares are unequal, put it in writing.** The law will normally presume 50-50 ownership when the deed to a piece of property says it is held by tenants in common or as joint tenants. If your ownership interests are unequal, put it in writing in the form of a contract, such as the one set out in "Contract for Unequal Ownership of a House," below.
>
> Two additional cautionary warnings: Even if you take title as joint tenants, in most states either partner can change the ownership to tenants-in-common, without the other's signature, thereby defeating the reciprocal inheritance provision. This rarely happens except in a nasty breakup situation, but it's something to pay attention to. Also, in theory, either partner can sell their tenant-in-common share of the property to a stranger, or even borrow against their separate share, though that rarely happens. One of the benefits of having a solid co-ownership agreement is you can prohibit such unwelcome transactions.

Changing Title

What happens if you take title in one legal format and later jointly agree you want to change it to another? For instance, because one of you is making a larger down payment, you might decide to take title as tenants in common. Several years later, after the birth of your child, you both decide it makes sense to change to joint tenants so as to avoid probate if one of you dies. This can be accomplished by purchasing a blank deed form and then making and recording a new deed granting the property "from Andrew West and Joanne Yu as Tenants in Common, to Andrew West and Joanne Yu as Joint Tenants With Right of Survivorship." You will also need to prepare and record a new deed if one partner is sole owner of a house and the other partner will become a co-owner (discussed below). Check with someone knowledgeable about real estate law to make sure you're using the proper deed and language and to determine whether this will trigger any tax liabilities.

RESOURCE

Resource for deeds in California. Californians who want to transfer title to California real estate should see *Deeds for California Real Estate*, by Mary Randolph (Nolo).

How House Ownership Agreements Relate to Property Agreements

The contracts in this chapter address the issues of home co-ownership. If your only legal concern is your home, shared or otherwise, then you will only need to complete one of these agreements. If you want to cover other assets you own, such as a car or furniture, you will also need to draft one of the property agreements in Chapter 3. Alternatively, you can combine the substantive sections of both agreements into one document, and then you only need to include one set of standard provisions regarding mediation and other technicalities. And, given the amount of money at stake in a co-owned property, this is one area where having a lawyer review the agreement probably makes sense—especially if one partner is putting in a lot more money than the other one, or if one partner is not going to be on the legal title.

Contracts for Couples Owning a Home Together

A house is a major economic asset—usually a couple's biggest. It follows that it's important to define your expectations and obligations promptly and clearly in writing. (This is in addition to taking title via a deed.) The rest of this chapter provides several different contracts for unmarried couples owning a home together. These contracts cover basic issues such as how you're sharing costs and ownership, what happens to the house if you break up or one of you dies, and how you intend to deal with disputes.

FORMS

Sample copies of the following forms are shown below:

- Contract for Equal Ownership of a House
- Contract for Unequal Ownership of a House
- Agreement for One Person to Move Into the Other's House and Become an Immediate Co-Owner, and
- Agreement for One Person to Move Into the Other's House and Become a Co-Owner Gradually.

The Nolo website has downloadable copies of these forms. See the appendix for the link to the forms in this book. Keep in mind that "title" refers to the names on the legal document that is recorded with the county. Having a private agreement is a good thing, but it doesn't fully protect the off-title contributor from an unauthorized sale or mortgaging of the property by the titled owner.

CAUTION

Get it in writing. Any unmarried couple that plans to jointly own a house or other real property should prepare a written contract. When it comes to an investment of this size, it's just plain nuts to try and wing it with pillow talk. If, later, your relationship becomes rocky, your memories of the details of a spoken agreement may differ. The unhappy result may be a lawsuit. As emphasized throughout this book, especially in Chapter 2, a written contract, particularly over something so expensive and important as a house, is the only way to protect yourself should you separate from your partner. Even if you are equal owners, having an agreement in place can make a dissolution far easier to manage.

Editing Contracts

One of our contracts for ownership of a house may be exactly what you need, but it's possible you may want to edit, add, or delete clauses. See "How to Edit or Modify a Living Together Agreement," in Chapter 3 for advice on editing contracts and agreements.

> **SEE AN EXPERT**
>
> **Some situations need a lawyer.** If your circumstances require something more complicated than the house ownership contracts included here, or if you want to make extensive changes on your own, get advice from a lawyer with experience in real estate—and if things are really complicated, you should be prepared to hire the lawyer to draft your agreement.

Notarizing and Recording a House Ownership Contract

After your contract is written, you may wish to record it at your County Recorder's office along with the deed. To do this in most states, you'll need to get your signatures notarized. Notarization means that a person authorized as a notary public certifies in writing that you're the person you claim to be. If you want to have your contract notarized, you and your partner must appear in front of the notary and show proof of your identity. The notary will watch each of you sign the document and then will complete an acknowledgment, including a notarial seal. You can often find a notary at a bank, lawyer's office, real estate office, or title insurance office, or at private post office businesses. Most charge under $20 to notarize a document.

Some couples, however, shouldn't or don't want to record their agreement—either for privacy reasons or because they don't want to bother recording every amendment they make in the future. And, some counties won't allow such documents to be recorded, though they may allow you to record a one-page "Memorandum" or "Abstract" of your agreement, summarizing the basic terms.

There's no clear right or wrong here, but for most couples, it's probably best not to bother with recordation, because it isn't necessary to make the contract legally valid, and most people prefer to keep their detailed agreements private. In either case, make sure you have a safe place to keep the agreement, like a safe deposit box or other secure location. Our suggestion is that you make duplicate signed originals, so each of you has one to save.

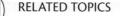 **RELATED TOPICS**

What happens to your house ownership contract if you get married? Basically, an agreement between unmarried couples will not be enforceable after marriage unless it was created shortly before the marriage in the anticipation of marriage and meets the standards of a premarital agreement. Instead, your state's marital property laws will apply. If marriage is in your future, be sure to read Chapter 2, which covers the impact of marriage on written living together agreements.

Contracts for Equal Ownership of a House

This section includes a contract for unmarried couples who want to share equal ownership of a house. The Contract for Equal Ownership of a House form is designed for two people who intend to share equally all house-related costs, including the down payment, purchase price, closing costs, insurance, taxes, repair and maintenance costs, and the like. Recognizing, however, that many unmarried couples want to share ownership equally even when they don't share equally in down payment and housing costs, this section also explains how to prepare a contract that reflects your particular situation.

Equal Ownership of a House—Each Partner Contributes One-Half of the Down Payment

This section describes choices you'll have to make when completing the Contract for Equal Ownership of a House, such as how to split housing costs, and explains standard language you'll see in the contract.

Contract for Equal Ownership of a House

michael Angelo and Helen Rifkin
make the following agreement to jointly purchase and own the house at 423
Bliss Street, Rockford, Illinois (hereafter house).

1. We will purchase the house for $ 380,000 (including closing costs).

2. We will take title as [*choose one*]:

   ☐ tenants in common, or

   ☒ joint tenants with right of survivorship.

3. We will each contribute one-half of the down payment and closing costs and pay one-half of the required payments for the mortgage, homeowners' insurance, property taxes, costs for needed repairs and routine maintenance, and [*fill in any additional costs or fees such as any fees required by a homeowners' association*] . Any improvements to the house costing more than $ 500 will be made by mutual consent with each of us agreeing to pay for half of all such improvements.

4. Should either of us decide to end the relationship and cease living together, one of the following will occur:

   (a) If one person wants to stay and the other wants to move on, the person staying will pay the person leaving fair market value (see Clause 5) for his or her share within 90 days. When payment is made, the person selling his or her share will deed the house to the person buying the house. The person buying the house will ensure that the selling partner's name is taken off the mortgage, but if the lender refuses to remove the selling partner's name from the mortgage, the buying partner will obtain a new loan in his or her name only and come up with the purchase price within 90 days. If the buying partner cannot obtain a new loan in his or her name only and come up with the purchase price within 90 days, the house shall be sold within 90 days of the demand for its sale by the departing owner. The costs of transfer and the new mortgage will be borne by the party keeping the house.

   (b) If both of us want to keep the house, we will try to reach a mutually satisfactory agreement for one to buy out the other. If by the end of two weeks we can't, the decision will be made as follows [*choose one*]:

Contract for Equal Ownership of a House (continued)

☒ (1) Right of First Offer. __Helen__

shall have the right of first offer. This means that __Helen__ may purchase __Michael's__

share of the house within 90 days for the fair market value of his/~~her~~ share (see Clause 5). If __Helen__ does not make full payment during this 90-day period, __Michael__

shall have an additional 90 days in which to buy out __Helen's__ share for its fair market value. When payment is made, the person leaving will deed the house to the person retaining it in his or her name alone. The person buying the house will ensure that the selling partner's name is taken off the mortgage. If the lender refuses to remove the selling partner's name from the mortgage, the buying partner will obtain a new loan in his or her name only. If neither person exercises his or her buyout right, or if the buying partner cannot obtain a new loan in his or her name only, the house shall be sold.

☐ (2) Coin Toss Method. A friend will be asked to flip a coin within 60 days of our decision to separate. The winner of the coin toss is entitled to buy out the loser's share, provided the winner pays the loser fair market value (see Clause 5) within 90 days. If full payment isn't made during this period, the loser of the coin toss will have an additional 90 days in which to buy out the winner's share of the property at fair market value (see Clause 5). When payment is made, the person leaving will deed the house to the person retaining it in his or her name alone. The person buying the house will ensure that the selling partner's name is taken off the mortgage. If the lender refuses to remove the selling partner's name from the mortgage, the buying partner will obtain a new loan in his or her name only. If the buying partner cannot obtain a new loan in his or her name only and come up with the purchase price within 90 days, the house shall be sold.

☐ (3) Other. _____

_____ .

(c) If neither of us wants to own the house or payment isn't made within 90 days, the house will be sold and the profits divided as follows: _____

__equally_____ .

Contract for Equal Ownership of a House (continued)

(d) We are both responsible for our share of the mortgage, insurance, and taxes until the house is sold or it changes ownership. If one of us moves out of the house before it is sold, the remaining person will make a good faith effort to find a tenant who will pay a fair market rent but will remain liable for his/her share of the expense. Assuming a tenant is found, the rental amount will be credited against the departing partner's payment for shared housing costs.

5. Should either of us decide to end the co-ownership relationship, we will do our best to agree on the fair market value of our house. However, if we can't agree, we will jointly choose and pay for the services of a licensed real estate appraiser to conduct an appraisal, and abide by the result. If we can't agree on an appraiser in the first place, each of us will independently retain and pay for the services of a licensed real estate appraiser. The fair market value of the house will be the average of the two appraisals. "Fair market value" for one person's share of the property is defined as an amount equal to the fair market value of the entire property, less the then-current mortgage amount, multiplied by that person's percentage ownership interest in the property.

6. Should either of us die, the survivor, if he or she has not become the owner of 100% of the deceased person's share through joint tenancy or a will, has the right to purchase the portion of the property given or left to someone else at the fair market value of that share (to be arrived at under the terms of Clause 5) within 200 days of the date of death.

7. If either of us is unable or unwilling to pay his or her agreed-upon share of the mortgage, taxes, or insurance payments in a timely manner, the other may make those payments. The extra payments will be treated as a personal loan to be paid back by the person on whose behalf they are made within six months, including __3__% interest per annum. If the loan isn't repaid in six months, the debtor must vacate the house and either sell his or her interest to the other party (in which case the buying partner must ensure that the selling partner's name is removed from the mortgage, as set forth in Clause 4) or agree to sell the entire property at fair market value which will be established by appraisal as set out in Clause 5.

8. This contract is binding on our heirs and our estates.

Contract for Equal Ownership of a House (continued)

9. Any dispute arising out of this agreement will be mediated by a third person mutually acceptable to both of us. The mediator's role will be to help us arrive at a solution, not to impose one on us. If good faith efforts to arrive at our own solution with the help of a mediator prove to be fruitless after two mediation sessions, either of us may make a written request to the other that the dispute be arbitrated. If such a request is made, our dispute will be submitted to arbitration under the rules of the American Arbitration Association, and one arbitrator will hear our dispute. The decision of the arbitrator will be binding on us and will be enforceable in any court that has jurisdiction over the controversy. By agreeing to arbitration, we each agree to give up the right to a jury trial.

Michael Angelo
Signature

December 15, 20xx
Date

Helen Rifkin
Signature

December 15, 20xx
Date

Clauses You Need to Complete

Clause 2 (Title). Here you specify how you are taking title (ownership)—as tenants in common or as joint tenants.

Clause 3 (Splitting Costs). This clause states that you will share equally in the down payment, purchase price, and all other housing costs, including maintenance and repair bills. To avoid disputes over money spent on home improvements, we recommend that improvements over a set dollar amount (such as $500—the amount is up to you) require mutual consent, with each partner paying half.

If you won't be sharing costs equally—for example, you're splitting the mortgage and other monthly housing costs two-thirds/one-third—simply edit the contract accordingly. If you're not sharing equally in the down payment or costs, and one person is lending the other money, see "Equal Ownership of a House—One Person Lends the Other Some or All of the Down Payment," below.

CAUTION

Keep track of all expenses. Even if your contract clearly spells out the costs that each partner will bear, you should keep records of your respective contributions as you make mortgage payments, repairs, and the like. That way, if you stray a bit from the original agreement (or even if you don't), you'll have written proof of who covered which expenses. This could be valuable if you later split up and disagree about who paid for what. And if worse comes to worst and you end up in court, these documents will also provide proof as to the exact amount of funds you each poured into the home. Judges in these types of cases typically look to the contributions each partner made in determining how the proceeds of the home sale will be divided. A joint checking account ledger can often serve the same purpose. If you use a joint account to pay all house bills, you can use an electronic format such as *Quicken* to keep track of expenses and contributions by each of you.

Clause 4 (Effect of Breakup on Home Ownership). The most complex clause in the Contract for Equal Ownership of a House deals with what happens if the two of you break up. This contract recognizes three possibilities:

- One of you wants to keep the house and the other doesn't.
- Both of you want the house.
- Neither of you wants the house.

Most likely, only one of you will want to stay or both of you will choose to move on. But if both of you want the house, problems are likely to develop. Clause 4 anticipates this possibility by providing several choices for deciding who gets the house should you split up and both partners want it:

4 (b)(1). Right of First Offer. You may want your contract to automatically give one of you the first right to buy out the other partner's share in the house at fair market value within 90 days. (This is different from a right of first refusal, where you get to match a third-party offer; we don't recommend the first refusal method, as it gets in the way of marketing the house on the open market.)

4 (b)(2). Coin Toss Method. You may opt for a coin toss to decide who gets to buy out the other. (The winner of a coin toss is entitled to buy out the loser's share at fair market value within 90 days.)

4 (b)(3). Other. You may come up with your own approach to decide the question of who owns the house if you both want it. For example, you could provide for the decision to be made with the help of a mediator, rather than the caprice of a coin toss, relying on a coin flip only if mediation fails.

CAUTION

If one partner does buy out the other, it is extremely important to change title to the home and mortgage documents to reflect the new ownership arrangement. Clause 4 specifies that the buying partner must execute the appropriate documents to do this. In addition, the partner selling a share of the home should ensure that his or her name is taken off the home loan. Otherwise, the selling partner will have no interest in the home, but will still be on the hook for the mortgage. Even if you and your partner agree in writing that the selling partner is not responsible for the mortgage, the original agreement with the lender remains unchanged. If the buying partner fails to make the mortgage payments, in some states the lender can seek payment from the selling partner. If this happens, the selling partner's only remedy is to sue the buying partner to force him or her to make the payments (or to reimburse the selling partner for any payments she has made). Such lawsuits are costly and time intensive. In addition, if the buying partner fails to make payments, the selling partner's credit rating will likely be damaged.

Unfortunately, most lenders will not agree to simply remove one partner's name from the loan documents (sometimes called a "release of coborrower"). Usually, in order to get the selling partner's name off the loan, the buying partner must obtain a new loan (refinance the home) in his or her name only. Clause 4 requires this of the partner buying the home. If the buying partner cannot qualify for a new loan, Clause 4 states that the home must be sold to a third party.

> **TIP**
> **Tax effects of a buyout.** Remember to pay attention to allocating any costs of transfer or taxes that might be triggered by a buyout. Usually the buying party pays those costs, which seems fair since the other party has to cover moving expenses.

Boilerplate Language

The Contract for Equal Ownership of a House provides standard "boilerplate" language for joint home ownership, including:

- how to determine the market value of the house should one of you need to buy out the other (Clause 5), and
- what happens to the property if one of you dies (Clause 6), or one of you is unable to pay your share of the expenses, such as monthly mortgage payments (Clause 7).

The contract also specifies that your agreement is binding on your heirs and estates (Clause 8) and provides for mediation should a dispute arise (Clause 9). For a detailed discussion of mediation and arbitration, see Chapter 10.

TIP

You can choose the interest rate for the partner paying the other partner's share. Clause 7 of the Contract for Equal Ownership of a House (which also shows up in some of the other contracts) provides that if one partner isn't able to make payments on the mortgage or expenses, the other partner can make those payments and the extra payments will be considered a loan from the paying partner to the nonpaying partner. The sample agreement shows that the loan comes with an interest rate of 3%, but you can choose whatever interest rate seems appropriate to you, as long as it's not usurious (completely unreasonable). We recommend using a rate that is close to the interest rate that a bank would pay on a savings account if the paying partner had kept his or her money in the bank, but you can use a higher one if you want it to serve as a deterrent to nonpayment. You also could provide that no interest will accrue at all, if you don't want your partner to have to pay interest just because he or she couldn't make the payment for a time.

Equal Ownership of a House—One Person Lends the Other Some or All of the Down Payment

You may wish to edit the Contract for Equal Ownership of a House agreement to deal with the common situation in which both members of a couple wish to own a house equally, but only one can come up with all the cash needed for the down payment. Assume Andrew, a successful artist, is able to sell a few paintings to come up with the full $50,000 down payment and closing costs for a little cottage with a mansard roof. Unfortunately, Alice, his partner, has no savings and can't contribute more than a few thousand dollars. However, Alice does have a good job, meaning she can afford to pay Andrew for a half interest in the house over time.

In this situation, a common approach is for Alice and Andrew to take title to the house as equal owners (either as joint tenants or tenants in common) with Andrew lending Alice her one-half of the down payment and Alice agreeing to repay him in affordable monthly installments. To accomplish this, Andrew and Alice should do two things:

1. rewrite Clauses 3 and 4 of the Contract for Equal Ownership of a House to reflect the unequal sharing of down payment costs, and

2. prepare a separate promissory note setting out the exact terms of the loan.

This section shows how to do these two things.

Substitute Language for Clauses 3 (Splitting Costs) and 4 (Effect of Breakup on Home Ownership)

Clause 3 of the Contract for Equal Ownership of a House specifies that you will share equally in the down payment costs. If you will not be paying equal amounts of the down payment, simply substitute the following for Clauses 3 and 4:

---

3. Andrew Dobbs [*name of person making the down payment*] will contribute all the down payment and closing costs for the house, amounting to $50,000 , with Alice Parker [*name of person borrowing money*] signing a promissory note to pay Andrew Dobbs $25,000 , plus simple interest of 5% over the next two years in equal monthly installments. Other than the down payment and closing costs, we will each pay one-half of the required payments for the mortgage, homeowners' insurance, property taxes, the costs for needed repairs and routine maintenance, and [*fill in any additional costs or fees such as any fees required by a homeowners' association*]. Any improvements to the house costing more than $500 will be made by mutual consent with each of us agreeing to pay half for all such improvements.

Clause 4 of the Contract for Equal Ownership of a House form lets you specify who gets the house should you split up. You may want to choose Clause 4(b)(1) and give the person making the down payment (in this case, Andrew) the right of first offer—at least until the time that the down payment loan has been repaid. It's a good idea (especially if you're the person borrowing the down payment money) to clarify what happens once the down payment loan has been repaid. Simply add language such as the following to Clause 4:

4. If our relationship ends after ____Alice Parker____ has fully repaid the loan as provided in the promissory note called for in Clause 3 of this agreement, the following will occur: ___*[specify 4(b)(1), 4(b)(2), or 4(b)(3)]*___ .

How to Prepare a Promissory Note

A promissory note is nothing more than legal jargon for a written promise to pay money to someone else. As with all legal documents, promissory notes often contain loads of needless hyped-up legalese. The note here is designed primarily to be used between family and friends, such as a close unmarried couple. You can use the Promissory Note included here for a down payment loan or any other loan between you and your partner.

The primary function of a promissory note is to serve as written evidence of the amount of a debt and the terms under which it will be repaid, including the repayment schedule (installments versus one lump sum payment) and interest rate (if any). To avoid disputes down the line, you should clearly spell out the terms of your agreement. Note: When one party makes a loan to the other one, the full repayment needs to be paid to the lending party—a payment to a third party (such as the mortgage lender) on behalf of both parties results in paying only 50% of the amount due to the lending party.

The Promissory Note shown below allows for repayment of the down payment in installments, rather than all at once, and it charges interest. Simply plug in the following information:

- names of the borrower and lender
- loan amount
- address where payment is to be made (such as your home address)
- interest rate (this should be between 2% and 5%, or somewhat less than the typical rate of return the lender would accrue for the same time period)
- monthly installment payment (you'll need to figure this out based on the loan amount, interest rate, and the number of months the borrower will take to repay the loan—see "Amortization Calculators: How to Get the Math Right," below), and

Promissory Note (Loan Repayable in Installments With Interest)

Name of Borrower: _Alice Parker_

Name of Lender: _Andrew Dobbs_

1. For value received, Borrower promises to pay to Lender the amount

   of _$25,000_

   at _10 Rose Street, Oakland, California,_

   at the rate of _3_ % per year from the date this note was signed until the
   date it is paid in full, no later than _October 1, 2023_ . Borrower will receive
   credits for prepayments, reducing the total amount of interest to be repaid.

2. Borrower agrees that this note shall be paid in installments, which include
   principal and interest, of not less than $ _277.55_ per month, due on the first
   day of each month, until such time as the principal and interest are paid in full.

3. If any installment payment due under this note is not received by Lender
   within _60_ days of its due date, the entire amount of unpaid principal shall
   become immediately due and payable at the option of Lender without prior
   notice to Borrower.

4. In the event Lender prevails in a lawsuit to collect on it, Borrower agrees
   to pay Lender's attorney fees in an amount the court finds to be just and
   reasonable.

Alice Parker   _November 1, 2013_
Signature   Date

Alice Parker
Printed name

- the number of days (such as 30 or 60) that the borrower has to pay each installment before the lender may require immediate and full payment of the loan balance. (Without this "acceleration" provision, a lender can't sue for loan installments not yet due, even if a borrower has missed many payments and has no intention to repay.)

What if you sell the house before the loan is repaid? Under the terms of the Promissory Note shown here, the borrower would still have the full amount of time (in our Alice-Andrew example, ten years from the start of the loan) to repay the loan. This may be years after the house is sold. In this situation, you may want to require that the complete balance of the loan be repaid before the borrower receives any proceeds from the house sale. If so, add this type of language to the end of Clause 2 in your promissory note:

> If our house at 10 Rose Street, Oakland, California, is sold before this loan and all interest due has been repaid, the Borrower will pay the Lender the remaining balance owed before receiving any proceeds from the house sale.
>
> If the proceeds are insufficient to cover this amount, the Borrower will pay back the loan from his or her personal funds within one year of the sale of the house.

Amortization Calculators: How to Get the Math Right

To compute the exact amount of monthly loan payments that include interest, all you need to know is the amount of the loan, the interest rate, and the repayment period. Then simply plug this information into an amortization calculator. Check out Nolo's free mortgage calculator at www.nolo.com. Check "Calculators" under "Free Legal Information."

 FORMS

The Nolo website includes a downloadable copy of the Promissory Note shown above. See the appendix for the link to this form.

TIP

There are many alternative ways to structure loan payments. You can prepare a promissory note with different terms (for example, installment payments without interest, or a lump sum payment with interest). The Nolo website (www.nolo.com) has a variety of promissory notes for sale.

Equal Ownership of a House—One Person Buys the House and the Other Fixes It Up

It's not uncommon for one person to contribute a greater portion, or even all, of the down payment, while the other agrees to contribute labor and/or materials to fix the place up, in exchange for equal ownership in the house.

> EXAMPLE: Bob and Evie plan to purchase a graceful but dilapidated Victorian. Evie has the cash for the down payment. Bob has no savings but used to work as a carpenter and has the expertise and time to renovate the house. Bob and Evie can each afford to make half the monthly mortgage, taxes, and upkeep expenses, and they want to own the place equally. After discussing different possibilities, they agree that Evie will contribute the entire $60,000 for the down payment and closing costs. Bob will match this amount by contributing $60,000 worth of materials and labor (at $50 an hour) to pay for his share. If Bob fails to do so or the couple separates in the next two years, Bob owes Evie 50% of the difference between what he has contributed and $60,000. And if the house is sold at a profit while Evie is still owed money (she has contributed more than Bob), she will take 100% of what she is owed off the top, with the remainder of the proceeds divided 50-50. Remember, since Evie contributed her down payment "to the house," Bob either needs to make an equal contribution or pay her 50% of the excess amount she contributed.

If Bob and Evie want to take title to the house as equal owners (either as joint tenants or tenants in common), they can use the Contract for Equal Ownership of a House. They would need to edit this contract to reflect the fact that Evie is making the full down payment and Bob will be paying off his share in labor and materials to fix up the house. To accomplish this, Bob and Evie should substitute a new Clause 3 of the Contract for Equal Ownership of a House to reflect their agreement.

3. _Evie_ [*name of person making the down payment*] will contribute all the down payment and closing costs for the house, amounting to _$60,000_ . _Bob_ [*name of person contributing labor and materials*] will contribute _$35,000_ for materials and _500_ hours of labor (valued at _$50_ per hour) over the 24 months immediately following the closing date, for a total contribution of _$60,000_ toward fixing up the house. _Bob_ will keep careful records of his contributions to be reviewed and initialed by _Evie_ on a monthly basis. If _Bob_ doesn't fulfill this obligation within two years, or should we separate before the end of two years, at the time of separation, _Bob_ owes _Evie_ the difference between what he contributed and _$60,000_ . Assuming money is owed, _Bob_ will sign a promissory note, agreeing to pay _Evie_ the outstanding balance plus _5%_ simple interest over a _12-month_ period in equal monthly installments. Other than the down payment and closing costs, we will each pay one-half of the required payments for the mortgage, homeowners' insurance, property taxes, and [*fill in any additional costs or fees such as any fees required by a homeowners' association*].

Clause 4 of the Contract for Equal Ownership of a House lets you specify who gets the house if you split up. You may want to choose Clause 4(b)(1) and give the person making the down payment (in this case, Evie) the right of first offer—at least until the time that the down payment loan has been repaid. It's a good idea to clarify what happens to Clause 4 once the down payment loan has been repaid (for example, after Bob has matched Evie's share of the down payment by the time and money he spends renovating the house). Simply add language such as the following to Clause 4:

If our relationship ends after _Bob_ has fulfilled his obligation to contribute _$60,000 in labor and materials_ as provided in Clause 3 of this agreement, the following will occur: [*specify 4(b)(1), 4(b)(2), or 4(b)(3)*].

Contract for Unequal Ownership of a House

This section includes a contract for unmarried couples who do not share equally in ownership of a house. Especially when one partner contributes substantially more to the down payment than the other, that person may want to own more than half of the property, rather than make a loan to the other owner. As with the Contract for Equal Ownership of a House, you can tailor this agreement to your own particular situation when it comes to issues such as sharing monthly housing costs and what happens to the house if you break up.

To complete the Contract for Unequal Ownership of a House form, follow the directions above, with the following exceptions:

Clause 2 (Title). The Contract for Unequal Ownership of a House assumes you will take title as tenants in common, the appropriate form for taking title when you have unequal shares of ownership in the house. In some states, you can put the percentages of ownership on the deed; even if you don't do so, the terms of your written agreement will be binding. Since you are unequal owners, you can't take title as joint tenants, as that presumes equal ownership. If you are contributing un-equally to the house purchase but you want to choose joint tenancy on the title, you will need to go with the equal ownership agreement, with a right of reimbursement for the excess contribution.

Clause 3 (Splitting Costs). The clause in this contract allows you to split costs, such as down payment and monthly mortgage payments, however you want.

> **EXAMPLE:** Kelly and Sam contribute different amounts to the down payment on a house (Kelly one-third and Sam two-thirds) and they decide to split ownership of the house the same way. To keep things simple, Sam will pay two-thirds of the monthly mortgage, taxes, and insurance payments. Because they use the house more or less equally, Sam and Kelly agree to divide utilities and other routine monthly expenses equally.

Contract for Unequal Ownership of a House

Sam Rutherford and _Kelly Franklin_ make the following agreement to jointly purchase and own the house at _9 Oak Road,_ _Austin, Texas_ (hereafter house):

1. We will purchase the house for $ _400,000_ (including closing costs).
2. We will take title as tenants in common with the following shares:

   Sam   _2/3_

   Kelly   _1/3_

3. _Sam_ will contribute _2/3_ and _Kelly_ will contribute _1/3_ of the down payment and closing costs. _Sam_ will pay _2/3_ and _Kelly_ will pay _1/3_ of the required payments for the mortgage, homeowners' insurance, property taxes, and [_fill in any additional costs or fees such as any fees required by a homeowners' association_]. All use-related expenses (including utilities and the cost of routine repairs) and maintenance will be paid equally. Any improvements to the house costing more than $ _500_ will be made by mutual consent with each of us agreeing to pay half, and each shall contribute equally to all such improvements. We agree to share use and occupancy of the house equally even though Sam owns a greater share of the house.

4. Should either of us decide to end the relationship and cease living together, one of the following will occur:

   (a) If one person wants to stay and the other wants to move on, the person staying will pay the person leaving fair market value (see Clause 5) for his or her share within 90 days. When payment is made, the person selling his or her share will deed the house to the person buying the house. The person buying the house will ensure that the selling partner's name is taken off the mortgage, and the buying party will cover all the costs of the new loan and the transfer of title. If the lender refuses to remove the selling partner's name from the mortgage, the buying partner will obtain a new loan in his or her name only. If the buying partner cannot obtain a new loan in his or her name only, or come up with the purchase price within 90 days, the house shall be sold within 90 days of the demand for its sale by the departing owner.

Contract for Unequal Ownership of a House (continued)

(b) If both of us want to keep the house, we will try to reach a mutually satisfactory agreement for one to buy out the other. If by the end of two weeks we can't, the decision will be made as follows [*choose one*]:

☒ (1) Right of First Offer. If both of us want to keep the house, __Sam__ will have the right of first offer. This means that __Sam__ may purchase __Kelly's__ share of the house within 90 days for the fair market value of ~~his~~/her share. (see Clause 5). If __Sam__ does not make full payment during this 90-day period, __Kelly__ will have an additional 90 days in which to buy out __Sam's__ share for the fair market value. When payment is made, the person leaving will deed the house to the person retaining it in his or her name alone. The person buying the house will ensure that the selling partner's name is taken off the mortgage. If the lender refuses to remove the selling partner's name from the mortgage, the buying partner will obtain a new loan in his or her name only. If neither person exercises his or her buyout right, or if the buying partner cannot obtain a new loan in his or her name only, the house shall be sold.

☐ (2) Coin Toss Method. A friend will be asked to flip a coin within 60 days of our decision to separate. The winner of the coin toss is entitled to buy out the loser's share, provided the winner pays the loser fair market value (see Clause 5) within 90 days. If full payment isn't made during this period, the loser of the coin toss will have an additional 90 days in which to buy out the winner's share of the property at fair market value (see Clause 5). When payment is made, the person leaving will deed the house to the person retaining it in his or her name alone. The person buying the house will ensure that the selling partner's name is taken off the mortgage—and will cover the costs of the new loan and the transfer costs. If the lender refuses to remove the selling partner's name from the mortgage, the buying partner will obtain a new loan in his or her name only, or come up with the purchase price within 90 days. If the buying partner cannot obtain a new loan in his or her name only, or come up with the purchase price within 90 days, the house will be sold.

Contract for Unequal Ownership of a House (continued)

☐ (3) Other. _____

_____.

(c) If neither of us wants to own the house or payment isn't made within 90 days, the house will be sold and the profits divided as follows: ___Sam: ²⁄₃___ and ___Kelly: ¹⁄₃___ .

(d) We are both responsible for our share of the mortgage, insurance, and taxes until the house is sold or it changes ownership. If one of us moves out of the house before it is sold, the remaining person will make a good faith effort to find a tenant who will pay a fair market rent. Assuming a tenant is found, the rental amount will be credited against the departing partner's payment for shared housing costs.

5. Should either of us decide to end the co-ownership relationship, we will do our best to agree on the fair market value of our house. However, if we can't agree, we will jointly choose and pay for the services of a licensed real estate appraiser to conduct an appraisal, and we will abide by the result. If we can't agree on an appraiser in the first place, each of us will independently retain and pay for the services of a licensed real estate appraiser. The fair market value of the house will be the average of the two appraisals. "Fair market value" for one person's share of the property is defined as an amount equal to the fair market value of the entire property, less the then-current mortgage amount, multiplied by that person's percentage ownership interest in the property.

6. Should either of us die, the survivor, if he or she has not become the owner of 100% of the deceased person's share through a will, has the right to purchase the portion of the property given or left to someone else at the fair market value of that share (to be arrived at under the terms of Clause 5) within 200 days of the date of death.

7. If either of us is unable or unwilling to pay his or her agreed-upon share of the mortgage, taxes, or insurance payments in a timely manner, the other may make those payments. These payments will be treated as a personal loan to be paid back by the person on whose behalf they are made within six months, including ___3___% interest per annum. If the loan isn't repaid in six months, the debtor must vacate the house and either sell his or her interest

Contract for Unequal Ownership of a House (continued)

(in which case the buying partner must ensure that the selling partner's name is removed from the mortgage, as set forth in Clause 4) or agree to sell the entire property at fair market value which will be established by appraisal, as set out in Clause 5.

8. This contract is binding on our heirs and our estates.

9. Any dispute arising out of this agreement will be mediated by a third person mutually acceptable to both of us. The mediator's role will be to help us arrive at a solution, not to impose one on us. If good faith efforts to arrive at our own solution with the help of a mediator prove to be fruitless after two mediation sessions, either of us may make a written request to the other that the dispute be arbitrated. If such a request is made, our dispute will be submitted to arbitration under the rules of the American Arbitration Association, and one arbitrator will hear our dispute. The decision of the arbitrator will be binding on us and will be enforceable in any court that has jurisdiction over the controversy. By agreeing to arbitration, we each agree to give up the right to a jury trial.

Sam Rutherford
Signature

February 2, 20xx
Date

Kelly Franklin
Signature

February 2, 20xx
Date

> ### Reflections on Contract Writing: Keep It Simple!
>
> Trying to divvy up ownership of a house with 100% accuracy can be more trouble than it's worth. We can't overemphasize that the best contracts are the simplest. For example, we recommend rounding off fractional ownership interests (25% and 75%, not 24.328% and 75.672%). And if one partner puts up a little extra cash or labor, or forks out a bit more money to make an emergency roof repair, either forget it or consider the extra contribution a personal loan and record it in a separate promissory note rather than repeatedly redrafting your ownership contract to adjust your respective ownership percentages a smidgen. As long as any separate promissory notes are paid off before or when the house is sold, this approach is safe and simple.

If one person has lent the other down payment money, be sure to read the discussion of "Equal Ownership of a House," above, especially the discussion of promissory notes. It's not easy to decide whether to use the loan approach or the unequal ownership concept. If the property goes way up in value, the unequal ownership structure will favor the owner with the greater share—but if the property values go down, the one making the larger contribution would be better served by the loan model. Because you don't know which direction values are heading, there is no right or wrong answer. Instead, pick the approach that most closely matches the way you think about your co-ownership arrangement.

Agreement for One Person to Move Into the Other's House and Become an Immediate Co-Owner

Sometimes one of the partners already owns a house when they decide to live together. Although occasionally the couple decides to sell their existing house(s) and buy one together, it is also common for one person to move in with the other into a house already owned by him or her. When this happens, issues of property ownership and how to deal with expenses inevitably arise.

In some cases, the person moving in simply agrees to pay half (or some other agreed-upon portion) of monthly expenses, (mortgage payments, insurance, taxes, and the like) as rent—putting off the decision to share ownership until both partners gain confidence that their relationship is likely to endure.

In other situations, the couple decides that the person moving in will become a co-owner by paying the original owner for half of the property's equity. This can be done in one lump sum or by paying the existing owner in monthly installments (under a separate promissory note). It's crucial that you be clear as to whether the nonowner is buying in or just being a tenant—for your own sake, as well as for applying the right tax rules.

The Agreement for One Person to Move Into the Other's House and Become an Immediate Co-Owner shown below can be used in either situation. To complete this contract, follow the directions in "Contract for Unequal Ownership of a House," above. It is very similar, except for the first few clauses, which spell out your agreement on the following:

Clause 2 (Fair Market Value of the House). You will need to agree upon the fair market value of the house. See Clause 9 for advice on determining this figure.

Clause 3 (Equity in the House). The current owner will need to determine how much equity he or she has in the house after you establish a fair market value of the property and adjust for the outstanding mortgage debt.

Clause 4 (Share of Ownership). The current owner can decide to sell whatever portion of ownership he or she wants.

Clause 6 (Payment for Share of Ownership). You may agree to either make full payment at the time of signing this agreement, or make monthly installments under a separate promissory note, such as the one in "How to Prepare a Promissory Note," above.

The rest of the Agreement for One Person to Move Into the Other's House and Become an Immediate Co-Owner (Clauses 8 through 13) mirrors Clauses 4 through 9 of the contracts shown above. If one person will be paying off the costs of the house in installment payments with a promissory note, be sure to read "Equal Ownership of a House—One Person Lends the Other All or Part of the Down Payment," above, for advice, including possible language changes to the contract. If a nonowner is going to contribute to his or her partner's residence and never become an owner of record, we strongly recommend having a written agreement clarifying whether or not the nonowner will receive any share of the appreciation, or will simply be considered a renter.

Agreement for One Person to Move Into the Other's House and Become an Immediate Co-Owner

_____Faye Curtis_____ and _____Fred Miller_____ agree as follows:

1. ___Faye Curtis___ now owns the house at ___10 Briar Cliff Drive,___ ___Atlanta, Georgia_____ (hereafter house).

2. The fair market value of the house is currently $___450,000___.

3. Equity in the house (fair market value less mortgage and other house-related indebtedness) is $___150,000___.

4. _____Faye Curtis_____ hereby sells ___½___ of the equity in the house to _____Fred Miller_____ for $_75,000_, retaining a _½_ interest in the house.

5. We will take title as [_choose one_]:

    ☒ tenants in common with the following shares:

    _____Faye Curtis_____   ½ _____

    _____Fred Miller_____   ½ _____

    or

    ☐ joint tenants with right of survivorship.

6. The buy-in payment is due as follows [_choose one_]:

    ☒ full payment of $___75,000___ is due upon signing of this agreement.

    ☐ beginning with the first of the month after this contract is signed _____ will make a payment in equal monthly installments, including simple interest of _____ per year, and this agreement will be recorded in a separate promissory note.

7. All future housing costs, including payments for the mortgage, homeowners' insurance, property taxes, and [_fill in any additional costs or fees such as any fees required by a homeowners' association_], will be split as follows: _equally_. All use-related expenses (including utilities and the cost of routine repairs) and maintenance will be split as follows: _equally_. Any improvements to the house costing more than $_500_ will be made by mutual consent with each of us agreeing to pay half, and each shall contribute equally to all such improvements.

Agreement for One Person to Move Into the Other's House and Become an Immediate Co-Owner (continued)

8. Should either of us decide to end the relationship and cease living together, one of the following will occur:

(a) If one person wants to stay and the other wants to move on, the person staying will pay the person leaving fair market value (see Clause 9) for his or her share within 90 days. When payment is made, the person selling his or her share will deed the house to the person buying the house. The person buying the house will ensure that the selling partner's name is taken off the mortgage, and will cover the costs of the new loan and the transfer of title. If the lender refuses to remove the selling partner's name from the mortgage, the buying partner will obtain a new loan in his or her name only. If the buying partner cannot obtain a new loan in his or her name only, or come up with the purchase price within 90 days, the house will be sold.

(b) If both of us want to keep the house, we will try to reach a mutually satisfactory agreement for one to buy out the other. If by the end of two weeks we can't, the decision will be made as follows [*choose one*]:

☒ (1) Right of First Offer. If both of us want to keep the house, __Faye__ shall have the right of first offer. This means that __Faye__ may purchase __Fred's__ share of the house within 90 days for its fair market value (see Clause 9). If __Faye__ does not make full payment during this 90-day period, __Fred__ shall have an additional 90 days in which to buy out __Faye's__ share for its fair market value. When payment is made, the person leaving will deed the house to the person retaining it in his or her name alone. The person buying the house will ensure that the selling partner's name is taken off the mortgage. If the lender refuses to remove the selling partner's name from the mortgage, the buying partner will obtain a new loan in his or her name only, and will cover the costs of the new loan and the transfer of title. If neither person exercises his or her buyout right, or if the buying partner cannot obtain a new loan in his or her name only, and come up with the purchase price within 90 days, the house shall be sold.

Agreement for One Person to Move Into the Other's House and Become an Immediate Co-Owner (continued)

☐ (2) Coin Toss Method. A friend will be asked to flip a coin within 60 days of our decision to separate. The winner of the coin toss is entitled to buy out the loser's share, provided the winner pays the loser fair market value (see Clause 9) within 90 days. If full payment isn't made during this period, the loser of the coin toss will have an additional 90 days in which to buy out the winner's share of the property at fair market value (see Clause 9). When payment is made, the person leaving will deed the house to the person retaining it in his or her name alone. The person buying the house will ensure that the selling partner's name is taken off the mortgage, and will cover the costs of the new loan and the transfer of title. If the lender refuses to remove the selling partner's name from the mortgage, the buying partner will obtain a new loan in his or her name only. If the buying partner cannot obtain a new loan in his or her name only, and come up with the purchase price within 90 days, the house shall be sold.

☐ (3) Other. _____

_____

_____ .

(c) If neither of us wants to own the house or payment on a buyout isn't made within 90 days, the house will be sold and the profits divided as follows:

_____ Faye: ½ and Fred: ½ _____ .

(d) We are both responsible for our share of the mortgage, insurance, and taxes until the house is sold or it changes ownership. If one of us moves out of the house before it is sold, the remaining person will make a good faith effort to find a tenant who will pay a fair market rent. Assuming a tenant is found, the rental amount will be credited against the departing partner's payment for shared housing costs.

9. Should either of us decide to end the relationship, we will do our best to agree on the fair market value of our house. However, if we can't agree, we will jointly choose and pay for the services of a licensed real estate appraiser to conduct an appraisal, and we will abide by the result. If we can't agree on an appraiser in the first place, each of us will independently retain and pay for the services of a licensed real estate appraiser. The fair market value of the house will be the average of the two appraisals. "Fair market value" for one person's

Agreement for One Person to Move Into the Other's House and Become an Immediate Co-Owner (continued)

share of the property is defined as an amount equal to the fair market value of the entire property, less the then-current mortgage amount, multiplied by that person's percentage ownership interest in the property.

10. Should either of us die, the survivor, if he or she has not become the owner of 100% of the deceased person's share through joint tenancy or a will, has the right to purchase the portion of the property given or left to someone else at the fair market value of that share (to be arrived at under the terms of Clause 9) within __100__ days of the date of death.

11. If either of us is unable or unwilling to pay his or her agreed-upon share of the mortgage, taxes, or insurance payments in a timely manner, the other may make those payments. These payments will be treated as a personal loan to be paid back by the person on whose behalf they are made within __6__ months, including __3__% interest per annum. If the loan isn't repaid in six months, the debtor must vacate the house and either sell his or her interest (in which case the buying partner must ensure that the selling partner's name is removed from the mortgage, as set forth in Clause 4) or agree to sell the entire property at fair market value, which will be established by appraisal as set out in Clause 9.

12. This contract is binding on our heirs and our estates.

13. Any dispute arising out of this agreement will be mediated by a third person mutually acceptable to both of us. The mediator's role will be to help us arrive at a solution, not to impose one on us. If good faith efforts to arrive at our own solution with the help of a mediator prove to be fruitless, either of us may make a written request to the other that the dispute be arbitrated. If such a request is made, our dispute will be submitted to arbitration under the rules of the American Arbitration Association, and one arbitrator will hear our dispute. The decision of the arbitrator will be binding on us and will be enforceable in any court that has jurisdiction over the controversy. By agreeing to arbitration, we each agree to give up the right to a jury trial.

Faye Curtis
Signature

March 9, 20xx
Date

Fred Miller
Signature

March 9, 20xx
Date

Check Out Legal and Tax Issues Before Transferring a Share of Your House

If you decide to sell a share of your house, consult with a tax accountant and real estate attorney so that you understand all the tax and legal issues involved. The rules for a partial buyout by an unmarried partner are a bit murky, so if a lot of equity is involved, check with an accountant or a tax attorney.

Check out the tax consequences. If you receive no money from the sale of an interest in your house in a particular year, there is normally no taxable gain or income to report from the sale; but it may be considered a gift, which can have long-term estate tax consequences for the donor. If you do receive money from the sale, you have to determine what percent is a return on your initial capital or subsequent capital investment (not taxed) and what percent is interest and profit (which may be subject to a tax if the house has a great deal of value). However, federal tax law (and the law in most states) now provides that if the house has been your residence, and you have been on title, for at least two of the last five years before the sale, the first $250,000 in capital gains received by each partner is not taxed. In some states, you also may have to pay a transfer tax or increased property taxes. For information on tax laws involving real estate transactions, visit the IRS website at www.irs.gov. IRS Publication 523 specifically covers tax issues when selling your house.

Beware of the Due on Sale Clause. If you sell a share of a house already subject to a mortgage or deed of trust, you may need lender approval under the terms of a "due on sale" clause. Most real estate mortgages contain a due on sale clause that requires that the borrower pay off the entire mortgage before selling the property, unless the lender approves the sale without full payment of the mortgage. The lender may not approve for a variety of reasons, especially if your fixed rate mortgage interest rate is below the current market rate, but many lenders do not enforce this clause at all. This may mean you'll need to pay off the existing mortgage and refinance. Or it may cause you to rethink the wisdom of the entire transaction. For example, you might decide not to change ownership at all, but instead use the other partner's money to purchase other assets that would remain in his or her name, but be used to benefit both partners.

CAUTION

Be sure to change title. Whenever you change ownership of a house or other real property, you need to prepare and record a new deed reflecting current title. Failing to do so can create a lot of problems—not just between the two of you, but also when it comes to filing tax returns or selling the place. Most significantly, an off-title "owner" probably won't be entitled to the favorable tax exemptions owner-occupants receive when they sell their residence for a profit.

Agreement for One Person to Move Into the Other's House and Become a Co-Owner Gradually

Where one member of a couple is more affluent than the other, the most realistic approach for many couples is to draft an agreement that allows the person moving in to become a co-owner gradually. Although there are a number of ways to do this, the most common is to provide that each month the person moving in will pay a portion—or, possibly, all—of the monthly mortgage cost in exchange for receiving a tiny equity share in the house. You can use the Agreement for One Person to Move Into the Other's House and Become a Co-Owner Gradually for this purpose. A sample is shown below.

There is no correct way to determine how much the gradual co-owner must pay before he or she becomes a half-owner of the home. Many factors come into play, making the calculation tricky. For example, the value of the home probably will fluctuate during the time period when payments are made. The more the original owner has already paid, the more the gradual co-owner will have to pay. Since both parties are living in the house, some portion of the monthly payment should be allocated for occupancy, not to the buy-in contribution. The length of the mortgage will factor in too. And finally, part of the gradual co-owner's payment will go toward interest, not principal—making the interest rate important as well.

Agreement for One Person to Move Into the Other's House and Become a Co-Owner Gradually

_____Alan Martin_____ and _____Alison Salinger_____ agree as follows:

1. __Alison__ owns the house at __57 Primrose Path, Omaha,__ __Nebraska__ (hereafter house), subject to a mortgage with the __Prairie National Bank__ in the amount of $ __200,000__ .

2. The fair market value of the house is currently $ __300,000__ .

3. __Alison's__ equity in the house (fair market value less mortgage or other house-related indebtedness) is $ __100,000__ .

4. Beginning with the date this contract is signed, __Alan__ will pay all monthly expenses for the mortgage, homeowners' insurance, property taxes, utilities, and necessary repairs and maintenance, estimated to be $ __2,500__ per month, and will continue to do so until his ~~or her~~ total payments equal $ __100,000__ or until we separate or agree to modify this agreement, after which the payments will be split equally. Of that $ __100,000__ , $ __50,000__ will be considered to meet __Alan's__ obligation to pay half of the expenses, while the other $ __50,000__ will be considered to be repayment to __Alison__ of half of the equity interest.

5. __Alan's__ share of the total net equity of the house shall be figured at the rate of __1%__ for every month that he ~~or she~~ pays all of the expenses as set out in Clause 4, based on __$1,000__ of the monthly payment contribution counted as the equity buy-in amount. For example, if __Alan__ pays all the expenses for two years, his ~~or her~~ interest in the house equity shall be __24__ %.

6. __Alison__ shall deed the house to __Alison Salinger and Alan Martin__ as "Tenants in Common" and record the deed and this contract, upon the signing of this agreement.

7. Should we separate prior to the time that __Alan__ contributes $ __100,000__ , __Alison__ shall have first right to remain in the house and buy out __Alan's__ equity share as determined by Clause 5. __Alan__ shall leave within 30 days of the decision to separate.

8. Once __Alan__ contributes $ __100,000__ , the house shall be owned equally by both of us, and all expenses for taxes, mortgage, insurance, and repairs shall be shared equally.

9. Should we separate after the time that ___Alan___ contributes $ ___100,000___ , one of the following will occur:

(a) If one person wants to stay and the other wants to move on, the person staying will pay the person leaving fair market value (see Clause 10) for his or her percentage share at the time, within 90 days. When payment is made, the person selling his or her share will deed the house to the person buying the house. The person buying the house will ensure that the selling partner's name is taken off the mortgage. If the lender refuses to remove the selling partner's name from the mortgage, the buying partner will obtain a new loan in his or her name only. If the buying partner cannot obtain a new loan in his or her name only, the house shall be sold.

(b) If both of us want to keep the house, we will try to reach a mutually satisfactory agreement for one to buy out the other. If by the end of two weeks we can't, the decision will be made as follows [*choose one*]:

☒ (1) Right of First Offer. If both of us want to keep the house, ___Alison___ shall have the right of first offer. This means that ___Alison___ may purchase ___Alan's___ share of the house within 90 days for its fair market value (see Clause 10). If ___Alison___ does not make full payment during this 90-day period, ___Alan___ shall have an additional 90 days in which to buy out ___Alison's___ share for its fair market value. When payment is made, the person leaving will deed the house to the person retaining it in his or her name alone. The person buying the house will ensure that the selling partner's name is taken off the mortgage. If the lender refuses to remove the selling partner's name from the mortgage, the buying partner will obtain a new loan in his or her name only. If neither person exercises his or her buyout right, or if the buying partner cannot obtain a new loan in his or her name only, the house shall be sold.

☐ (2) Coin Toss Method. A friend will be asked to flip a coin within 60 days of our decision to separate. The winner of the coin toss is entitled to buy out the loser's share, provided the winner pays the loser fair market value (see Clause 10) within 90 days. If full payment isn't made during this period, the loser of the coin toss will have an additional 90 days in which to buy out the winner's share of the property at fair market value (see Clause 10). When payment is made, the person leaving will deed the house to the person retaining it in his or her name alone. The person buying the house will ensure that the selling partner's name is taken off the mortgage. If the lender refuses to remove the selling partner's name from the mortgage, the buying partner will obtain a new loan in his or her name only. If the buying partner cannot obtain a new loan in his or her name only, the house shall be sold.

☐ (3) Other: _____

_____

_____ .

(c) If neither of us wants to own the house or payment on the buyout isn't made within 90 days, the house will be sold and the profits divided as follows: _Alison: ½ and Alan: ½_____ .

(d) We are both responsible for our share of the mortgage, insurance, and taxes until the house is sold or it changes ownership. If one of us moves out of the house before it is sold, the remaining person will make a good faith effort to find a tenant who will pay a fair market rent. Assuming a tenant is found, the rental amount will be credited against the departing partner's payment for shared housing costs.

10. Should either of us decide to end the relationship, we will do our best to agree on the fair market value of our house. However, if we can't agree, we will jointly choose and pay for the services of a licensed real estate appraiser to conduct an appraisal, and we will abide by the result. If we can't agree on an appraiser in the first place, each of us will independently retain and pay for the services of a licensed real estate appraiser. The fair market value of the house will be the average of the two appraisals. "Fair market value" for one person's share of the property is defined as an amount equal to the fair market value of the entire property, less the then-current mortgage amount, multiplied by that person's percentage ownership interest in the property.

11. Should either of us die, the survivor, if he or she has not become the owner of 100% of the deceased person's share through joint tenancy or a will, has the right to purchase the portion of the property given or left to someone else at the fair market value of that share (to be arrived at under the terms of Clause 10) within _200_ days of the date of death.

12. This contract is binding on our heirs and our estates.

13. Any dispute arising out of this agreement will be mediated by a third person mutually acceptable to both of us. The mediator's role will be to help us arrive at a solution, not to impose one on us. If good faith efforts to arrive at our own solution with the help of a mediator prove to be fruitless, either of us may make a written request to the other that the dispute be arbitrated. If such a request is made, our dispute will be submitted to arbitration under the rules of the

American Arbitration Association, and one arbitrator will hear our dispute. The decision of the arbitrator will be binding on us and will be enforceable in any court that has jurisdiction over the controversy. By agreeing to arbitration, we each agree to give up the right to a jury trial.

Alison Salinger   _May 7, 20xx_
Signature   Date

Alan Martin   _May 7, 20xx_
Signature   Date

There are several options to determine the amount the gradual co-owner must pay before owning a half interest in the home:

- Some couples ignore all of the above factors and decide that the new owner simply must pay an amount equal to the original owner's current equity, on top of the equal contribution to the regular monthly payments. You need to be clear about what is paid out to third parties (of which 50% is paid on behalf of the other owner), as opposed to payments made directly to the other owner, which constitute a 100% payment toward equity.

- Some couples decide that the gradual co-owner must pay more than the original owner's current equity, perhaps 25% or 50% more, based on an estimate of long-term appreciation. Couples that follow this approach do so on the theory that money already invested is worth more than money to be invested in the future. And, the fair market value of the house is likely to increase over time.

- Another approach is to consult an expert in real estate finance who is familiar with the local market, and get an opinion as to what would be a reasonable amount.

Starting a Family

Having a Child: Legal Obligations of Unmarried Parents 206

Naming the Baby and Getting a Birth Certificate 207

Naming the Father: Paternity 208

    Paternity Statements 210

    Sample Paternity Statement 211

Legitimacy of Children Born to Unmarried Parents 212

    Standards of Proof of Paternity in States Adopting the
        Uniform Parentage Act 213

    Standards of Proof of Paternity in States That Have Not Adopted
        the Uniform Parentage Act 214

Adopting a Child 217

    Overview of Adoptions 217

    Stepparent and Second-Parent Adoptions 218

Public and Private Benefits for a Child of Unmarried Parents 221

Inheritance Rights of a Child of Unmarried Parents 222

FORMS IN THIS CHAPTER
Chapter 7 includes instructions for and a sample of the Acknowledgment of Parenthood form, and the Nolo website includes a downloadable copy of this form. See the appendix for the link to the forms in this book.

At some point, you and your partner may decide that even though you aren't interested in getting married, you'd like to have a child. While there are no insurmountable legal problems in raising a child without being married, there are several issues to consider. This chapter covers some of the most common questions facing unmarried couples having children, including naming the baby, naming the father (paternity), adoptions, and inheritance rights of children of unmarried parents.

Because family law varies from state to state, be sure to check your state's laws on specific rules, such as adoption, paternity, and custody, and consult a family law specialist as needed.

RELATED TOPICS
Related topics in this book include:
- Custody, visitation, and support of children from a previous marriage: Chapter 8
- Issues involving children when an unmarried couple separates, including child support, visitation, and custody rights, and how to prepare a parenting agreement: Chapter 10
- How to research state and local laws on adoption, paternity, and unmarried couples: Chapter 11.

Having a Child: Legal Obligations of Unmarried Parents

Parents are legally responsible for their children, regardless of whether the parents are married to each other or not. Courts don't care why people have children. Whether you decide to have children after careful planning, checking the location of the planets, or just letting it happen is legally irrelevant. If a child arrives, both biological parents (married or unmarried) have a duty of support. And even if the father did not want the child, or split from his partner before the baby was born, he remains responsible for the child's support.

Naming the Baby and Getting a Birth Certificate

In most states, you may give your child any first, middle, and last name you like. Whether you are married or not, you don't have to give the baby the last name of either parent if you don't want to, and the child does not have to have the father's last name to be considered "legitimate."

The procedure for naming a baby is simple. A representative of the local health department or similar agency, or a hospital social worker, meets with the new mother in the hospital immediately after the birth and asks her the child's name and some questions about the mother's health and the father's name and occupation. The mother doesn't have to name the child at this time, though she will probably be urged to do so. The information the mother gives is typed on a form that she signs. The state then issues a birth certificate, which usually doesn't reveal whether or not the parents are married.

If the baby isn't born in a medical facility, the mother or the physician, midwife, or other person assisting in the delivery must notify health officials of the birth. Again, there's no legal requirement that the baby be named at this time, but it's common to do so.

In either case, if the mother did not name the baby or provide the father's identity, it is possible to update the birth certificate later to include that information. The state Department of Health or Bureau of Vital Statistics in every state will have procedures for adding the father's name to the child's birth certificate or amending the birth certificate to show the child's name. If you are going to be adding the father's name to a birth certificate, most states will require an unmarried father to sign an acknowledgment of paternity (see below for more detail on paternity issues).

RESOURCE

Resource on birth certificates. For information on your state's Department of Health (which will either handle vital statistics or refer you to the state Bureau of Vital Statistics), visit the website of the National Center for Health Statistics at www.cdc.gov/nchs.

Naming the Father: Paternity

Paternity simply means "the state of being a father." When an unmarried couple has a child, it's essential that the father's paternity be established as soon as possible after the baby is born. This protects the mother, the baby, and especially the father, by greatly reducing the possibility that a judge will deny the father custody or visitation of his child, or other rights to which fathers are legally entitled. It also helps ensure that the child will be eligible to receive benefits through the father, including health, survivors', disability, and life insurance benefits.

The best way to establish the father's paternity is by naming him on the birth certificate as described above. Under U.S. Department of Health and Human Services regulations, all states must offer unwed parents an opportunity to establish paternity by voluntarily signing an acknowledgment of paternity, either at the hospital or at a later time. In many states, as a result of political pressure to reduce the number of mothers on welfare by ensuring that there is someone else with an obligation to support the child, hospital personnel will make every effort to get the father to sign the acknowledgment.

CAUTION

Don't acknowledge paternity if you're not the father. Signing to acknowledge paternity is a very good idea if you are the father of the child, but if you're not the father, or if you are not sure, don't sign on the dotted line. If you sign a paternity statement, you'll be liable for child support and even for reimbursing the state for welfare payments made to the mother, until you can prove that you are not actually the child's father.

In some states, including California, the only way that an unmarried father's name can be placed on a child's birth certificate is if the father signs a voluntary declaration of paternity. If the father is not present at the hospital following the birth, the mother will not be able to list him as the father on the birth certificate in his absence—the father and mother will instead have to sign the voluntary declaration of paternity at a later time, and have the father's name added to the birth certificate later. A voluntary declaration of paternity signed by both parents has the same legal effect as a court order, so once it's signed and submitted to the appropriate agency, the father's paternal rights are firmly established. If you live in a state that requires a voluntary declaration of paternity before placing an unmarried father's name on a birth certificate, and you and your partner split up before the baby is born, you may have to bring a legal action to establish paternity if your ex-partner won't sign the voluntary declaration.

Don't Lie About the Child's Father

In states where the mother can state the name of the father even if he is not present, some women are tempted to write down a name other than the actual father's on the birth information form. This is most common when the mother no longer sees the biological father and is involved with someone whom she would prefer to have raise the child or who is financially better able to do so. Identifying a man as the baby's father when that man is not actually the father is a terrible idea. An unmarried couple's current relationship may not last forever and complicated legal questions of paternity and support can grow from listing the wrong person as the father of a child. In a well-known case (*In re Clausen*, 502 N.W.2d 649 (Mich. 1993)), the mother of Baby Jessica lied on her baby's birth certificate, saying that the father was her new boyfriend, and did not tell her ex-boyfriend that she had given birth to their child. When the mother and her new boyfriend gave the baby up for adoption, the ex-boyfriend found out and wanted to step in and reclaim Baby Jessica. A long legal battle ensued between the new adoptive parents and the biological parents, with Baby Jessica caught in the middle (the baby was eventually returned to her birth parents). To avoid such potential problems, it is always best to accurately state who the biological father is.

Paternity Statements

We would be surprised if you were able to get out of the hospital without naming the father on the birth certificate or signing a voluntary declaration of paternity, if you are both present for the birth and it's clear that your partner is the child's father. However, if for some reason you do not name the father on the birth certificate or sign a voluntary acknowledgment of paternity at the hospital, then it is essential that you prepare and sign an informal "paternity statement." If you have named the father on the birth certificate or signed a voluntary acknowledgment of paternity, you can still (in some circumstances) sign a paternity statement just to make your life easier. For example, if you lose the child's birth certificate and haven't yet ordered a new one, you might be able to use the paternity statement at the child's school or while traveling. It also serves as additional evidence of paternity should the mother ever contest the father's relationship with the child.

If the father signs an acknowledgment of paternity or a paternity statement sometime after the child's birth, his parental rights are normally still established as long as no dispute over custody or adoption arises in the interim. However, the U.S. Supreme Court has held that if a father waits until a custody dispute arises, it may be too late to establish full parental rights—unless the father has had an ongoing relationship with the child. (*Quilloin v. Walcott*, 434 U.S. 246 (1978).) For example, in one case, the Court denied a father's request to block a child's adoption —and, by so doing, cut off his parental rights—where he had no real relationship with his children and did not try to legitimate them until the adoption proceeding began. (*Lehr v. Robertson*, 463 U.S. 248 (1983).) In some states, only a father who has established paternity by coming forward promptly and demonstrating a full commitment to his parental responsibilities must be notified of adoption proceedings. (*In re Kelsey S.*, 823 P.2d 1216 (Cal. 1992).) And if he does learn of the proceedings, he may have no legal standing to object.

In many other states, there is a trend toward giving unmarried fathers more rights, especially where the father has promptly and consistently attempted to form a paternal relationship with a young child but was prevented from doing so by the mother's actions. For example, where the mother failed to tell the father of the birth of their child, but the father later discovers the birth and promptly makes a good faith effort to assume responsibility for the child, the courts generally will protect his rights, as in the Baby Jessica case. (*In re Clausen*, 502 N.W.2d 649 (Mich. 1993).)

Sample Paternity Statement

Assuming you haven't signed one in the hospital, or just want to do another one for the reasons described above, you can prepare a paternity statement yourself quite easily. We include a sample Acknowledgment of Parenthood, to be signed by both parents.

FORMS
The Nolo website includes a downloadable copy of the Acknowledgment of Parenthood form shown below. See the appendix for the link to this form.

Acknowledgment of Parenthood

Lazarus Sandling and _Rebecca Conlon_ hereby acknowledge that they are the biological parents of _Clementine Conlon Sandling_, born _January 1, 20xx_, in _New York City, New York_.

Lazarus Sandling and _Rebecca Conlon_ further state that they have welcomed _Clementine Conlon Sandling_ into their home and that it's their intention and belief that _Clementine_ is fully legitimate for all purposes, including the right to inherit from and through both parents.

Lazarus Sandling and _Rebecca Conlon_ further expressly acknowledge their duty to raise and support _Clementine Conlon Sandling_.

We declare under penalty of perjury that the information set forth in this document is true and correct.

Rebecca Conlon	_March 2, 20xx_
Signature	Date
Lazarus Sandling	_March 2, 20xx_
Signature	Date

[Notarize]

! CAUTION
State-issued forms are preferable to homemade paternity statements. As discussed above, all states have official forms on which a man can voluntarily acknowledge his paternity of a child. In some states, there is a time limit for signing these forms, but in others there is no time limit, and in many states, the father's signature on the forms acts as a substitute for a court order, officially establishing his parental relationship with the child. A homemade form will not accomplish the same thing, so before you create one, find out whether you can still sign a voluntary declaration of paternity with the state.

Simply fill in the father's name (and the mother's if you're using the Acknowledgment of Parenthood form), and the child's name, birth date, and place of birth in the appropriate sections.

Prepare two copies of the statement and have your signatures notarized on both copies. Notarization isn't required, but it's an excellent idea. In the event the father dies, the mother may have to present the paternity statement to various public agencies—and possibly life insurers and other private companies. Notarization proves that the father's signature wasn't forged after the father's death.

The mother and father should each keep a copy of the notarized paternity statement. Some states have set up procedures to file paternity statements with a state agency. For information on doing this, contact your state's Department of Health or Bureau of Vital Statistics. To find your state's Department of Health (which will either handle vital statistics or refer you to the state Bureau of Vital Statistics), visit the website of the National Center for Health Statistics at www.cdc.gov/nchs/w2w.

Legitimacy of Children Born to Unmarried Parents

Most states and the federal government have moved away from using the words "legitimate" and "illegitimate" in differentiating between children whose parents are married or not married. Some states have adopted the Uniform Parentage Act, which says that "the parent and child relationship extends equally to every child and to every parent, regardless of the marital status of the parents." Other states have modified versions of the Act in place, but either way, many states have now abandoned outdated notions of legitimacy.

Even in the states that have adopted this Act, however, it's still crucial to know who a child's parents are. This is because when it comes to inheritance, child support, custody, adoption, and many other areas of the law, the rights and duties of parents are clearly stated. (For an overview of these rights and duties, check out information on Nolo's website at www.nolo.com.) And don't think that a father's refusal to sign a paternity statement will get him off the hook for paying child support. If a father doesn't voluntarily sign a paternity statement, the state will go to court to establish that he is the father and collect child support.

TIP

Being named father on a birth certificate isn't always adequate proof to a court that the named man is the father. A lawsuit to have a man declared the father of a child is called a paternity or support action. It can be brought by either the mother or the father. Advances in blood and DNA tests make it possible to determine paternity with better than 98% accuracy, and to disprove it with 100% accuracy.

In *Trimble v. Gordon*, 430 U.S. 762 (1977), the Supreme Court held that states may set up different standards of proof necessary to establish paternity, as long as the standards are not completely arbitrary.

Standards of Proof of Paternity in States Adopting the Uniform Parentage Act

In the states that have adopted the Uniform Parentage Act, a man is presumed to be the father in any of the following circumstances:

Circumstance 1: He is married to the mother at the time the child is born, or was married to her within 300 days of the birth of the child. This means that, if the man dies or the couple divorces while the mother is pregnant, he is still presumed to be the father.

Circumstance 2: He and the mother, before the birth of the child, attempted to get married (obtained a license and had a ceremony) but the marriage wasn't valid because one person was still married to someone else, the clergyperson could not perform a marriage, or a similar reason, *and* the child was born during the attempted marriage or within 300 days after the termination of the marriage, be it by court order, death, or simple separation.

Circumstance 3: After the child's birth, the father and the mother have married (or gone through a ceremony in apparent compliance with law) although the marriage could later be annulled for some reason, and the man.

a. has acknowledged paternity in writing—for example, by signing a paternity statement

b. with his consent, is named the father on the child's birth certificate, or

c. pays child support under a written, voluntary promise or has been ordered to pay support by a court.

Circumstance 4: While the child is still a minor, the man (who is not married to the mother) receives the child into his home and openly holds out the child as his natural child.

These rules create presumptions. Legally, a presumption means that certain facts are presumed to produce a certain legal conclusion unless rebutted by strong evidence. For example, in Circumstance 4, if a man takes a child into his home and says he's the father—even though he never married the mother—he's presumed to be the father. This doesn't mean that he is—he or the mother might prove that though he received the child into his home and told everyone that he was the father, he wasn't. This can lead to a court fight involving blood tests to prove paternity.

Standards of Proof of Paternity in States That Have Not Adopted the Uniform Parentage Act

There are still quite a few states that haven't yet adopted the Uniform Parentage Act, and many of these still use the terms legitimate and illegitimate. But except for the use of the term illegitimate, the laws of these states relating to the rights of unmarried parents are usually similar to the provisions of the Uniform Parentage Act. This is because in a long line of court decisions, beginning with *Levy v. Louisiana*, 391 U.S. 68 (1968), the U.S. Supreme Court has struck down most state laws giving legitimate children more legal rights than illegitimate children.

Competing Presumptions

Some situations may present competing presumptions of fatherhood. For example, suppose a woman cohabiting with an unmarried partner is still married to another man. If a child is born during that time (while the marriage still exists), the husband is legally presumed to be the child's father. But if the unmarried partner acknowledges paternity by signing an acknowledgment of paternity and holding the child out as his own, he generally will *also* be presumed to be the child's father. When there are competing presumptions and both men want to be considered the child's father, it will be difficult to avoid a court proceeding to determine who the child's father is.

Biology is not necessarily destiny. In one California case, a man who was not the child's biological father still won a court battle of competing presumptions. (*Steven W. v. Matthew S.*, 33 Cal.App.4th 1108 (1995).) A similar result was reached in a Colorado case in which the court held that the best interests of the child must be considered in weighing competing presumptions of paternity. (*N.A.H. v. S.L.S.*, 9 P.3d 354 (2000).) In a case in Indiana, a woman was not allowed to challenge her ex-husband's paternity rights, even though genetic testing showed he was not the child's biological father, because she had been cohabiting with him when the child was conceived (before they got married) and she had consistently identified him as the father, including in court documents relating to their divorce. (*Ohning v. Driskill*, 739 N.E.2d 161 (2000).) On the other hand, a Maine court upheld an order declaring a man was *not* the father of a child born to his ex-wife during the marriage, because both parties knew the husband was not the biological father. (*Stitham v. Henderson*, 768 A.2d 598 (2001).)

Abandonment of a Child

The right to be considered a full legal parent can be lost if a parent fails to exercise parental responsibilities. The law calls this "abandonment." In most states, abandonment is defined as a period of time (often two years) in which a parent who does not have physical custody fails to contact and—if the parent has the ability—to support a child. Some states have shortened this time period to one year. If you have no money and don't have the ability to support your child, you won't be considered to have abandoned your child as long as you visit regularly. The key is that if you are not the parent with custody, you must stay involved with your child to the best of your ability.

An absent parent who has not assumed any parental obligations for several years faces an uphill battle if the other parent files an abandonment action or there's a custody fight. However, the absent parent is still entitled to be notified and have a hearing on a custody challenge. (*Stanley v. Illinois*, 405 U.S. 645 (1972).) It is important to note that if a parent has relinquished the opportunity to develop a relationship with the child, and has only a biological link to the child, courts may not take the claim for custody very seriously. Obviously, if a parent without custody has made repeated attempts to contact a child and has been prevented from doing so by the other parent, a court would be willing to give the case more consideration. If you have not been regularly visiting and supporting your child, you should go to court to assert your rights as soon as possible. A parent who is out of contact with a child is extremely vulnerable to having parental rights terminated in an abandonment proceeding.

In most states that still label children illegitimate, it's possible to change the label from illegitimate to legitimate if any of the following things apply:

- The parents marry each other. (Children born during a marriage that is later annulled remain legitimate.)
- The father signs a paternity statement or voluntary declaration of paternity acknowledging in writing, under penalty of perjury,

that the child is his. If the state has a registry for children born of unmarried parents, it is also a good idea to file the paternity statement with your state's Bureau of Vital Statistics.

- The father welcomes the child into his home or holds himself out as the father.
- The parents go to court and have a judge rule that the man is the father. This can usually be done by joint petition—where the parents go to court together in a nonadversary proceeding.

 RELATED TOPICS
To find your state law on legitimacy, check your state code (Chapter 11 tells you how). Look in the index under "Children," subheading "Legitimate."

Adopting a Child

In addition to, or instead of, having your own biological child, you and your partner may want to adopt a child. Adoption is a court procedure by which an adult legally becomes the parent of someone who is not his or her biological child. Adoption creates a parent-child relationship recognized for all purposes—including child support obligations, inheritance rights, and custody. The birthparents' legal relationship to the child is terminated, unless the adoption is a stepparent or a so-called "second-parent" adoption, in which case only the parent without custody loses parental rights.

Overview of Adoptions

If an unmarried couple jointly adopts a child, or if one partner legally adopts the biological child of the other, both parents are legal parents. This means both have equal legal responsibilities to raise and support the child. If the couple separates, each has the right to petition a court for custody of (or visitation with) the child, and each has an obligation to provide child support.

Adoption is primarily governed by state law. As a general rule, any adult who is found to be a "fit parent" may adopt a child as long as the child is free for adoption, meaning that appropriate consents have been given. It is legal for single people to adopt children in many states. Unmarried couples may adopt jointly, and unmarried people may adopt through a procedure known as a single-parent adoption. You'll need to check your state laws to see what rules apply in your particular situation. Some states frown on adoption by unmarried people, but most allow it.

Adoption agencies are allowed to create their own rules about who can adopt and under what circumstances, as long as they don't run afoul of state law. While there are often no specific legal prohibitions against unmarried couples adopting children, you may find that adoption agencies are biased against unmarried couples, or make it more difficult for unmarried couples to adopt. You should be prepared to explain why you haven't married and to make a good case for your fitness as a parent. In general, you should expect to do extra work to prove that your home is a stable and healthy environment for raising children. A local social service agency will conduct a home study, interview both partners, and then report to the court, which must approve adoptions. You may have a longer wait for a child, or you may have to broaden your ideas about the age and type of child you want to adopt.

SEE AN EXPERT

Get a good family law attorney if you want to adopt. Social service and government agencies often discriminate against unmarried couples, and adoption proceedings can often be complex (particularly if it's a private adoption), so you'll need to get some legal advice before you and your partner try to adopt. For an overview of legal issues involving adoptions, including different options, such as agency and private adoptions, see the Adoption, Guardianship & Parenting topic on Nolo's website at www.nolo.com.

Stepparent and Second-Parent Adoptions

In a stepparent adoption, a parent marries someone other than his or her child's other parent, and the new spouse adopts the child. When the adopting couple is married, the adoption is usually readily approved.

These adoptions usually don't cost much and may not require a home study by a social worker. The equivalent process for unmarried couples is called "second-parent adoption." When the adopting couple is unmarried, the cost may be higher and a social worker home study is almost always required. In addition, a number of states still frown upon second-parent adoptions when the couple is unmarried. If you are considering one of these adoptions, you'd be wise to consult with a local family law attorney to get an evaluation of your rights. Keep in mind that if you don't adopt your partner's biological child, you risk losing access to the child if you and your partner separate. (Separation issues are discussed in Chapter 10 of this book.)

When Can a Stepparent or Second Parent Adopt?

A child cannot be adopted without the consent of both parents, unless one parent has failed to establish a parent-child relationship with the child or has abandoned the child.

If the noncustodial parent is the father, the social service agency will determine whether his consent is needed before a stepparent or second-parent adoption can take place. A father who signs a paternity statement, provides support (if he can), and maintains a relationship with his child, can probably prevent the child from being adopted by someone else. In addition—especially if the child is a baby and the father has had little opportunity to support or visit the child—or has been prevented from doing so by the mother—he may be able to prevent the stepparent or second-parent adoption and petition the court to obtain visitation.

If the noncustodial parent is the mother, the social service agency will have to obtain her consent or recommend that her parental rights be terminated. Unmarried mothers without custody must pay support if they can and visit the child—or face losing the child to a stepparent or second-parent adoption.

Remember, once a person formally adopts a child—whether through a stepparent adoption or second-parent adoption—that person has all the legal rights and responsibilities of a biological parent, including the right to make decisions about the child's welfare and the responsibility to provide financial support.

Examples of Stepparent and Second-Parent Adoptions

Here are a few examples of stepparent and second-parent adoptions. These scenarios involve an unmarried couple, Linda and Frank, who have a baby, Mollie.

EXAMPLE 1: Frank takes off before his and Linda's baby Mollie is born. He doesn't send support or contact Linda or the baby for three years, despite having the opportunity to do so. At this point, Linda marries Herman who wants to adopt Mollie. Linda's consent is necessary for this adoption, but Frank's probably isn't. Under the laws and procedures in force in most states, the adoption agency will normally make an effort to notify Frank. If he shows up, he must be given a hearing, but his opposition to the adoption won't count for much. The fact that Frank abandoned Mollie will probably prevent him from successfully opposing the adoption by Linda's new husband.

EXAMPLE 2: This time Linda and Frank live together for several years after Mollie is born. When they split up, Linda keeps Mollie, and later marries Herman. Frank holds Mollie out to the world as his child, visits her, and pays support to Linda. He never signs a paternity statement, however. Whether Herman can adopt Mollie without Frank's consent depends on state law. If the state has adopted the Uniform Parentage Act, Frank's consent is necessary because he has legitimated Mollie by welcoming her into his home and acknowledging that he's her father. In other states, the fact that Frank has continued to support and visit Mollie will count strongly in his favor; Frank would be in an even stronger legal position to prevent the adoption if he had signed a statement acknowledging paternity soon after Mollie was born, or even when he and Linda separated. In a state where a voluntary declaration of paternity is the equivalent of a court order, Frank's legal standing will allow him to block the adoption.

EXAMPLE 3: Same situation as Example 2, except that when Mollie is born, Frank signs a paternity statement. Every state will require Frank's consent before allowing Herman to adopt Mollie, unless Frank later abandons Mollie.

EXAMPLE 4: This time, before Linda and Frank split up, Frank signs a paternity statement, but never contacts Mollie again. If he refuses to consent to Herman's adopting her or can't be found, a court will decide whether Frank has forfeited his parental rights by abandoning Mollie. An effort will be made to notify Frank of the hearing.

EXAMPLE 5: This time, Frank keeps Mollie after he and Linda split up. Frank marries Susan, who wants to adopt Mollie. Linda must consent to the adoption. If she refuses, there must be a hearing to terminate Linda's parental rights, and she must be given a chance to oppose. If Linda hasn't supported or contacted Mollie for a long time, it's likely she will lose her parental rights.

Public and Private Benefits for a Child of Unmarried Parents

If a parent becomes disabled or dies, the person's biological or legal child may be entitled to receive income, such as from Social Security, government or pension benefits, or possibly a private insurance company (life insurance). In the past, benefits derived through the father were often unavailable to or reduced for "illegitimate" children—children born "out of wedlock." For example, Social Security regulations used to grant more benefits to the legitimate child of a deceased, retired, or disabled father than to an illegitimate child.

However, the U.S. Supreme Court has long since ruled that treating children differently on this basis is unconstitutional. It no longer makes any difference whether a child is "legitimate" or "illegitimate" for purposes of receiving Social Security and similar government benefits.

When it comes to private benefits, children of unmarried couples are similarly protected in most instances. For example, if you name your children as the beneficiaries of a life insurance policy, they will receive the policy proceeds if you die while the policy is in effect, whether you're married to their other parent or not.

Even though the legal rights of children born outside of marriage have greatly improved, that's not a reason for a father to fail to take steps to further protect them. The best way to do this is to sign a paternity or parenthood statement right away when your child is born. If you die, and you have failed to sign such a statement or otherwise clearly form a parent-child relationship with your child, Social Security or other federal, state, or private benefits may be denied your child because there's no proof that you were the father.

Inheritance Rights of a Child of Unmarried Parents

You can leave your property to anyone you want in a will, trust, joint ownership device, or other estate planning device. (Chapter 9 explains how.) In short, you don't have to sign a paternity statement or raise a child to leave the child property. But to be sure your child is provided for after your death, you do need to affirmatively leave property to your child in your will or by use of a trust. This is because if a parent of an illegitimate child dies without a will, most states do not protect the child's right of inheritance as strongly as if the child were born to married parents or otherwise legally legitimated. For example, in some states, in the absence of a will or trust, the child can fully inherit from the mother but not from an unmarried father. Even in states that allow illegitimate children to inherit from a father in the absence of a will, the time in which the child can make a claim against the father's estate may be limited.

In the case of *Trimble v. Gordon*, 430 U.S. 762 (1977), the Supreme Court made it clear that a father's signing a paternity statement will normally be adequate to fully protect the inheritance rights of children born out of wedlock if there's no will. If your state rules allow a father to acknowledge paternity for the purpose of inheritance in a way other than a paternity statement, that will also be sufficient. For example, in some states, in the absence of a will, a child can inherit if the father admitted paternity prior to his death or if paternity was determined by a court. But obviously, a child's legal right to go to court to try and claim a share of an estate is not nearly as advantageous as being left property under the terms of a will. Or to put this point bluntly, if you want a child to inherit regardless of the child's legitimacy under your state's laws, accomplish this by leaving the child property in your will or other estate planning device. Chapter 9 explains how and why unmarried couples should prepare to protect each other and their children.

You and Your Ex-Spouse and Children From a Prior Relationship

Getting a Divorce While Living With Someone Else 225

    Grounds for Divorce..226

    Effect of Fault on Division of Marital Property...230

    Effect of Fault on Alimony..230

Living Together and Impact on Custody of Children From
    a Prior Marriage 231

    Types of Custody..232

    Best Interests of the Child..233

    Anatomy of a Contested Custody Case 235

    How to Create a Custody Agreement 236

Visitation With Children From a Prior Marriage...238

Child Support for Children From a Prior Marriage 239

The Effect of Living Together on Alimony and Child Support
    From a Prior Marriage 241

    Alimony..241

    Child Support 243

I f you have been married in the past or are currently married to someone other than the person you live with, you may encounter special legal problems. This is especially true if you have children or receive alimony (called maintenance or spousal support in some states), and you and your ex-spouse did not part on good terms.

This chapter covers key issues you may face if you are living with someone while going through a divorce (or if you've already divorced), including the impact of your living with someone on division of marital property, alimony, and child custody and support.

SKIP AHEAD
You can skip this chapter if neither you nor your partner has ever been married or had children outside of your current relationship.

CAUTION
If a nasty divorce threatens, think twice before living with a new partner—especially if children are involved. If you and your spouse aren't divorcing amicably, read this chapter carefully, research your state's law, and consult with a good family law attorney. If you conclude that you may lose property, alimony, or custody by living with your new partner, consider putting off living together until your divorce is final. This is especially true if cohabitation is illegal in your state. Also, remember that on a practical and emotional level, the fact that you are living with a new partner may anger a former spouse, who may look for ways to retaliate.

Finally, keep in mind that if you've already been divorced and granted alimony, living with someone may affect your right to continue receiving alimony. Because alimony laws differ from state to state and change often, it's essential to check the current legal rules of your state.

RELATED TOPICS
Related topics covered in this book include:
- Having or adopting a child with an unmarried partner: Chapter 7
- Issues involving custody and support of children when you separate from an unmarried partner: Chapter 10
- How to find and work with a lawyer and research family law in your state: Chapter 11.

RESOURCE

For an overview of divorce and family law, see the Divorce & Family Law topic on Nolo's website at www.nolo.com. Also, Nolo has several useful books on the subject of divorce, including *Nolo's Essential Guide to Divorce*, by Emily Doskow, *Divorce and Money*, by attorneys Violet Woodhouse and Lina Guillen, and *Divorce Without Court: A Guide to Mediation and Collaborative Law*, by Katherine E. Stoner.

Getting a Divorce While Living With Someone Else

In every state, some type of "no-fault" divorce is available. "No fault" means that the divorce isn't based on someone being at fault for ending the marriage. The spouse suing for divorce does not need to accuse the other of wrongdoing. Instead, the person requesting the divorce must only state one of two things:

- that the spouses no longer get along and they want to go their separate ways (in legalese, the couple is incompatible, has irreconcilable differences, or there's been an irretrievable or irremediable breakdown of the marriage), or
- that the couple has already separated and has been living apart by mutual consent for a certain period of time.

Does this mean that if you leave your spouse and live with someone else, this can't be used against you in the divorce? Not necessarily. Although every state has no-fault divorce, over 30 states have also kept their traditional fault-based divorces (based on adultery, mental cruelty, desertion, and the like) as well. This means that in many states a spouse can, at least in some circumstances, request a fault-based divorce and show that you mistreated him or her. As explained below, this may have serious effects on how marital property is divided after divorce and whether you receive alimony (and how much). Also, no matter what type of divorce is obtained, "fault" may be raised in a property or support negotiation or in a child custody or visitation hearing.

TIP

Regardless of your state's laws, you and your spouse can divide your property however you want. Even in states where one person's fault can have a bearing on division of property or alimony, this need not make a difference to you and your spouse. Many people get civilized divorces in states where fault-based divorces are possible. They make custody, support, and property decisions in a spirit of compromise, not based on who hurt whom. If you and your spouse are separating amicably, you needn't worry about the effect of living with someone else. But in case memories grow short, consider writing down your understanding as to property, support, and custody decisions. We provide a sample cooperative custody agreement later in this chapter. This type of agreement isn't technically enforceable in court, especially as it relates to children. A court must look at all the factors when considering the "best interests of the child." But if you end up in a court fight, a judge may seriously consider the agreement if it is fair to everyone involved.

Grounds for Divorce

The "Grounds for Divorce" chart below lists the legal reasons a spouse must give to request a divorce in each state. This section explains how to read the notations on the chart.

Fault Divorce

Traditionally, in order for a couple to obtain a divorce, one spouse had to prove that the other spouse was legally at fault. The "innocent" spouse was then granted the divorce from the "guilty" spouse. The "guilty" spouse would usually have to pay a substantial amount of alimony (or receive less than he or she would otherwise be entitled to) or give up marital property to which he or she was otherwise entitled.

Today about two-thirds of the states still allow a spouse to allege fault in obtaining a divorce, on grounds such as:

- adultery—sexual relations by a married person with someone other than the person's spouse
- mental cruelty—any act of inflicting unnecessary emotional pain, and
- desertion—voluntary abandonment of someone by a spouse without the abandoned spouse's consent.

Grounds for Divorce

Here is a state-by-state listing of the legal reasons a spouse must give to request a divorce. For an explanation of the headings (Fault, No-Fault, etc.), see "Grounds for Divorce," above.

	Fault Grounds	No-Fault Grounds	Separation	Length of Separation*
Alabama	✓	✓	✓	2 years
Alaska	✓	✓		
Arizona		✓		
Arkansas	✓		✓	18 months
California		✓		
Colorado		✓		
Connecticut	✓	✓	✓	18 months
Delaware	✓	✓	✓	6 months
District of Columbia			✓	6 months
Florida		✓		
Georgia	✓	✓		
Hawaii		✓	✓	2 years
Idaho	✓	✓	✓	5 years
Illinois		✓	✓	6 months
Indiana	✓	✓		
Iowa		✓		
Kansas	✓	✓		
Kentucky		✓		
Louisiana	✓		✓	1 year
Maine	✓	✓		
Maryland	✓		✓	12 months
Massachusetts	✓	✓		
Michigan		✓		

* If the separation is not by mutual consent or if there are children involved, the period of time may be different than what is shown here.

	Fault Grounds	No-Fault Grounds	Separation	Length of Separation
Grounds for Divorce (continued)				
Minnesota		✓		
Mississippi	✓	✓		
Missouri	✓	✓	✓	1 year
Montana		✓	✓	180 days
Nebraska		✓		
Nevada	✓	✓	✓	1 year
New Hampshire	✓	✓		
New Jersey	✓	✓	✓	18 months
New Mexico	✓	✓		
New York	✓	✓	✓	1 year
North Carolina	✓		✓	1 year
North Dakota	✓	✓		
Ohio	✓	✓	✓	1 year
Oklahoma	✓	✓		
Oregon		✓		
Pennsylvania	✓	✓	✓	1 year
Rhode Island	✓	✓	✓	3 years
South Carolina	✓		✓	1 year
South Dakota	✓	✓		
Tennessee	✓	✓	✓	2 years
Texas	✓	✓	✓	3 years
Utah	✓	✓	✓	3 years
Vermont	✓		✓	6 months
Virginia	✓		✓	1 year
Washington		✓		
West Virginia	✓	✓	✓	1 year
Wisconsin		✓	✓	12 months
Wyoming	✓	✓		

In some states, alimony and property division are not linked to fault. For example, although a fault divorce is still available in Illinois, alimony is awarded and property divided regardless of fault. Conversely, although fault divorces have been eliminated in Florida, adultery can be a factor in determining alimony.

No-Fault Divorce

Any divorce where the spouse suing for divorce does not have to accuse the other of wrongdoing is a no-fault divorce. You can simply claim incompatibility, irreconcilable differences, or irretrievable or irremediable breakdown of the marriage, rather than blaming your spouse. If this is the only check on the chart, you are in a pure no-fault state.

Separation

For divorces based on the fact that the spouses have already separated, we include the time that you must be apart (Length of Separation column on the "Grounds for Divorce" chart). This may be as short as six months (Vermont) or as long as five years (Idaho). If the separation is not by mutual consent or if there are children involved, the period of time may be different than what is shown here.

What Does All This "Fault" and "No-Fault" Language Really Mean?

If your state still has fault divorce, and your spouse is angry because you've moved in with your current love interest, your spouse may drag your living situation (which is technically adultery) into court. Also, even if your state has no-fault divorces, this doesn't mean that living with someone new won't affect your divorce in terms of the division of marital property and payment of alimony.

Covenant Marriage and Divorce

In a few states, couples can enter into a "Covenant Marriage," which is basically designed to make divorcing more difficult. Before seeking a divorce, couples must seek marital counseling, and the spouse seeking the divorce must prove fault—by proving either that the parties have been separated for a specified period of time, or that the other spouse committed adultery, committed a felony, or physically or sexually abused a child of one of the parties. Currently, Arizona, Arkansas, and Louisiana have covenant divorce.

Effect of Fault on Division of Marital Property

In most states, property acquired during marriage (except for gifts and inheritance) is divided more or less equally between husband and wife at divorce.

In some states with fault divorces, living with someone new (adultery) may result in your being awarded less of the marital property (such as real estate, furniture, cars, and stocks) than you would have otherwise received. And even in a few states that have no-fault divorces, adultery can still be considered when it comes to dividing your marital property, with a judge empowered to award more to the innocent spouse or the spouse who is not living with someone. On the other hand, some states allow divorces based on one spouse's adultery, but adultery cannot be used to keep that spouse from getting his or her share of the marital property.

Effect of Fault on Alimony

Alimony (sometimes called spousal support or maintenance) is the money paid by one ex-spouse to the other for support under the terms of a court order or settlement agreement following a divorce. Alimony is not the same thing as child support (discussed in "Child Support for Children From a Prior Marriage," below).

Alimony was necessary in most divorces a generation or two ago— when men typically went off to work, leaving mother and children at home. Today, with so many women working, alimony is granted less frequently (or for shorter periods) and isn't even requested in some cases. Typically, if no alimony is awarded at the time of divorce, a spouse can't seek alimony at a later time.

When couples have been married for many years, alimony is still commonly granted, especially if one spouse has had primary responsibility for raising the children and has been out of the workplace or working only part time. Alimony may also be granted in a situation in which both spouses work, but one enjoys a significantly higher income than the other.

Living with an unmarried partner may affect your right to receive alimony in some states. In many states, a spouse who is considered guilty of adultery may either be barred from receiving alimony altogether or receive less than a full share of alimony. Ironically, some of these states have done away with adultery as a basis for divorce. Also, this is not a universal rule. Some states with fault divorces don't allow adultery to influence property division. Some states do not reduce or terminate alimony on the basis of adultery. But almost all states may reduce alimony payments if the recipient cohabits—especially if this reduces that person's need for support. Finally, several states are silent on the issue of fault consideration and alimony.

Living Together and Impact on Custody of Children From a Prior Marriage

If you and your former spouse agree on custody, the court will normally ratify your agreement without considering the details of how you lead your life. For instance, a judge won't know (or necessarily ask) whether one of you is living with another person unless your ex brings it to the judge's attention.

If you and your spouse are battling over custody, however, the traditional advice is to not live with a new partner and to be discreet in your sexual activity, at least until the court makes a decision. This advice applies to both fault and no-fault divorces, as a parent's living arrangement is always admissible in a custody dispute on the theory that a court needs as much information as possible to determine "the best interests of the child."

As you'll notice, we use the word "traditional" to describe the "no sex, no living with anyone" advice. This is because many states now have more relaxed legal attitudes toward living together. While we can't say that most judges are enthusiastic about granting custody to a parent who is part of an unmarried couple, judges will not necessarily deny custody to a parent solely because the parent lives with someone else, especially when the new relationship is stable and nurturing. Therefore, the decision to live or not live with someone (other than a platonic roommate) while fighting over custody should be decided situation by situation, state by state. Especially if your former spouse is likely to make an issue of it, you should consult with a family law attorney to find out about local practices and prejudices.

Types of Custody

There are two types of custody in most states—physical and legal. Physical custody is the right to have the child live with you. Legal custody is the right to make important decisions about the child's upbringing—for example, regarding schooling and medical care.

Custody should not be confused with child support. Every parent has an obligation to support his or her children. When one parent has physical custody and the other has visitation rights, the parent with visitation rights is usually ordered to pay some child support to the other parent, who is usually deemed to be meeting his or her obligations through the custody itself.

Custody may also be sole or joint. Joint legal custody means that the parents plan jointly for their children's future, as they did before the divorce. Joint physical custody is typically worked out by the parents, taking into consideration things like the parents' and children's schedules and desires, the quality of schools, relationships with friends, and so on. Joint custody doesn't mean that the children must spend six months of each year or half of every week with each parent. In fact, in many states, a judge may award joint legal custody at the same time one parent is named as the primary caretaker of the child and one house as the primary home for the child.

For parents who communicate well and are equally dedicated to raising their children, joint custody can be an ideal situation. In fact, in some states, courts are required to order joint custody unless there is some unusual circumstance. By balancing the power and decision making, both parents are more likely to provide financial support for and maintain close relationships with their children. A potential drawback to joint custody is the possibility that arguments will drag on forever because neither parent has final say. However, family counseling (sometimes called "divorce" or "separation" counseling) can go a long way toward avoiding or working through such problems.

Best Interests of the Child

In all states, child custody and visitation issues are decided according to "the best interests of the child." This means that the judge who hears the case will consider all evidence before deciding who will provide the better home. Although mothers are more often granted physical custody than are fathers, particularly for young children, there is no longer an automatic preference in favor of women. Today, many men win physical custody of their children.

Frequently asked questions about custody and visitation include:

- *If I live with a man, can my children be taken from me?*
- *If my husband is an alcoholic (or a recently recovering alcoholic), will he be able to get custody of (or visitation with) the children?*
- *I was once arrested for possession of marijuana; does this mean I can't get custody?*
- *My income comes from Social Security disability and other public programs, while my husband has a well-paying job. Does this mean he'll get custody of the kids?*
- *My son is nine years old and wants to live with me; will the court let him?*
- *Is it possible for a father to get custody of young children?*

The answer to all of those questions is, "It depends." No matter what your next-door neighbor, best friend, or brother-in-law tells you, the law doesn't say that adultery, smoking marijuana, or even being involved in antisocial conduct means you can't win, or will lose, custody. In addition, the fact that one parent's income is much larger than the other's isn't necessarily a reason the court will use to award the more affluent parent custody.

The point is that many factors—not just whether or not you're living with someone else—are related to what is in a child's best interest. The court's decision will normally favor the parent who will best maintain stability in the child's life. The way each parent lives can be an important factor when a court decides custody issues. In any given case, the judge may consider one person's lifestyle to be more in the best interest of the child than the other's.

In a few states, a judge can use a parent's cohabitation to deny custody. For example, an Arkansas court stated "a mother's ongoing relationship was immoral, failed to set a proper example for the children, and resulted in harm to the children." (*Nix v. Nix*, 706 S.W.2d 403 (Ark. 1986).) Courts in a few other states have similarly disapproved of cohabitation and have forced a change in custody, especially where the children were aware of their custodial parents' intimate conduct.

In general, however, the bottom line is that the judge, as a human being, will apply his or her own standards and prejudices when deciding which parent gets custody. Some judges don't like unmarried persons living together, even though society no longer considers living together the "no-no" it was 30 years ago.

RESOURCE

Comprehensive guide to child custody. *Nolo's Essential Guide to Child Custody & Support*, by Emily Doskow, provides solid information on custody, including the various types and custody trial procedures.

Custody Issues If You Have Been Divorced for Some Time

Now suppose you have been divorced for some time and have custody of your children. You want to move in with a new partner, but want to be sure this won't give your former spouse legal grounds to challenge your custody of your children.

The question of child custody can always be reexamined by the court. If a judge finds that it's in the best interest of your children to change the custody of your kids to the other parent, then the judge can order this. State law varies as to whether a judge can consider your living with someone to be a negative factor in deciding whether or not custody arrangements should be modified.

Anatomy of a Contested Custody Case

In many places, fighting over custody is no longer as simple as going into court with your arguments at the ready. Now, parents with custody disputes usually must attend court-ordered mediation sessions to try to work out a parenting plan, before they'll be allowed to see a judge. In some places, the mediator will make a report to the judge with a recommendation of how custody should be decided. In others, the mediator simply works with the parents, but doesn't report to the court afterwards.

Some courts may also order an evaluation of the family, which might be performed by a social worker employed by the county or by a private social worker or therapist with training in child custody evaluation. A child custody evaluation will include interviews with both parents and the children, background checks, and sometimes psychological testing.

Once all the mediation and evaluations are completed, you'll then have your day in court. The judge isn't compelled to follow the recommendations of the mediator or evaluator, but as a practical matter most do. If the social worker or mediator recommends that you get custody, you've won more than half the battle. If not, you're at a serious disadvantage, but you can still proceed to the trial, and you may ask the social worker or mediator to come to court to be cross-examined about the report. This is especially important if the report contains factual inaccuracies.

At the trial, the judge may ask your children where they want to live. Some judges ask only older children; other judges never ask any children. Most judges will pay little—if any—attention to the opinion of a child under seven, but will probably respect the wishes of a teenager if the chosen parent is otherwise suitable. Judges also tend to keep brothers and sisters together unless there is a strong reason not to.

> ! CAUTION
>
> **A judge has the power to deny custody to both parents.** During a divorce proceeding, a judge need not award custody of the children to either the mother or the father if he or she finds them unfit. Instead, the judge can award custody to a relative, a friend, or even the local juvenile court.

How to Create a Custody Agreement

Even though you may never want to speak to your former spouse or partner again, it is vital for you both to sit down and decide how you will continue to raise your children. Because the two of you know your children best, forming a parenting agreement together makes the most sense. Also, it will save you from the risk of a drawn-out court battle.

A very basic custody agreement, Sample Cooperative Custody Agreement, is shown below. It is common for custody agreements to be much more detailed, covering when parents will spend time with the children, how to handle holidays, vacations, and birthdays, the role of each parent in the children's education, health care and more. This agreement may serve as a placeholder while you work out the details of a more thorough one.

While some parents can make agreements on their own without outside help, many others turn to mediators or family law attorneys to help them resolve one or more problem areas.

Negotiation

Negotiating a custody agreement that is fair to both you and your former spouse makes great sense. While it may seem impossible, try to put aside your anger and hostility to create a parenting plan that puts your children's best interests first. Choose a setting that is neutral and prepare yourself by writing a list of all the important factors you want to discuss regarding the custody of your children. Obviously, this will include your children's living arrangements, education, medical care, and emotional needs. Listen to all the requests your ex makes and be willing to compromise. If you strongly disagree on a particular issue, set it aside and concentrate on the things you can work out. Often, if a spirit of compromise develops over the course of your negotiations, it will extend to solving even your most difficult problems.

Mediation

If you and the other parent can't arrive at a good agreement yourselves, your next step is to enlist the help of a neutral third party who is skilled in the area of child custody. Family mediators are trained to handle

Sample Cooperative Custody Agreement

Sean and Barbara Washington agree to the following:

1. We have decided to go our separate ways and no longer plan to live together.

2. Our children John Washington, age 5, and Richard Washington, age 3, will reside with Barbara Washington, and Sean will spend as much time as possible with the children.

3. Sean will provide a reasonable amount of support to Barbara each month, taking into consideration his salary and the needs of the children. Initially, this will be $800 per month per child.

4. As neither of us plans to marry again soon, it's understood and accepted that both of us will very likely have personal friendships that may involve sex and that either or both of us may decide to live with someone of the same or opposite sex.

5. We will proceed to get a divorce as amicably as possible and neither of us will try to influence the court by raising the fact that the other is having a relationship or living with a third person.

6. Any dispute arising out of this contract will be mediated by a third person mutually acceptable to both of us. The mediator's role will be to help us arrive at a solution, not to impose one on us. If good faith efforts to arrive at our own solution to all issues in dispute with the help of a mediator prove to be fruitless after two mediation sessions, either of us may make a written request to the other that the dispute be arbitrated. If such a request is made and agreed to, our dispute will be submitted to arbitration under the rules of the American Arbitration Association, and one arbitrator will hear our dispute. The decision of the arbitrator will be binding on us and will be enforceable in any court that has jurisdiction over the controversy. If mediation fails and an arbitrator cannot hear the subject matter of our dispute, we will submit our controversy to a court that has jurisdiction to make a binding decision.

Barbara Washington
Signature

October 19, 20xx
Date

Sean Washington
Signature

October 19, 20xx
Date

difficult custody and visitation issues. While a mediator will not make a decision for you, they are adept at guiding parents to arrive at their own plan. Many states mandate the use of a mediator to try to solve custody disputes and some even provide mediators at low cost.

 RELATED TOPICS
More information on mediation and child custody. Chapter 10 covers the subject of mediation. You'll also find an in-depth discussion of family mediation and many detailed suggestions about how to draft a child custody and visitation plan and workable parenting agreements in the book *Building a Parenting Agreement That Works: Child Custody Agreements Step by Step,* by Mimi Lyster Zemmelman (Nolo).

Visitation With Children From a Prior Marriage

If a court grants you (or your former spouse) custody of the children, the other parent (or you) will be given the right to visit, unless the court believes that the noncustodial parent's physical presence would be detrimental to the children. As with custody, decisions about visitation are also made based on the "best interests" of the children. If you and your ex-spouse can communicate enough to agree on a visitation schedule, the court will probably grant "reasonable visitation rights" and leave it to you to work out the details as to when, where, and how visitation will take place.

If, however, you and your ex-spouse cannot agree on visitation, the court will define the visitation rights for you. The court might say, for example, that "Barbara Washington shall have the right to visit with the children every Saturday from 10:00 a.m. to 5:00 p.m., plus three weeks during the summer months, the weeks to be agreed upon by the parties"; or "Sean Washington shall have the right of visitation on the first weekend of every month from 6:00 p.m. on Friday to 6:00 p.m. on Sunday provided he picks the children up from, and returns them to, Barbara Washington's home."

Sometimes, courts impose restrictions on visitation beyond times and places, such as requiring 24-hour notice of visitation; prohibiting the noncustodial parent from removing the child from the county, state, or, in rare cases, the child's own home; prohibiting the noncustodial parent from drinking alcohol while with the children; or where there's evidence of abuse, requiring another adult to be present during the visit.

In addition, courts in a few states may prohibit a parent from visiting the children in the presence of the person that parent lives with, or prohibit the children from spending the night with a parent whose new partner is present in the house. If the custodial parent has a new relationship, most courts will continue to allow visitation as long as the living together situation doesn't have an adverse effect on the child. Louisiana is one state that still prohibits visitation when the parent's live-in lover is present in their home, even when the couple is discreet, because such visits might undermine "the children's respect for the family institution." (*Lasseigne v. Lasseigne*, 434 So.2d 1240 (La. 1983).) Court decisions like this are far from the rule, however, and if you've been given such an order, speak to an attorney regarding your obligations, your rights, and a possible appeal. But in the meantime, understand that it's not wise to violate a court order.

Child Support for Children From a Prior Marriage

In every state, parents are required to support their children, whether or not the parents were married when the child was born. The federal Child Support Enforcement Act (42 U.S.C. § 651) requires every state to adopt a formula setting a minimum amount of child support depending on the financial resources of the parents, the needs of the children, and other factors, such as the amount of time the child spends with each parent. The effect of this law is that child support—or at least a minimum amount of child support—is set more or less automatically by plugging parents' income and expense information into a computer program. The law has resulted in higher child support awards than in the past, and has decreased litigation, because there's less to fight about. Your state's formula may be available from court clerks' offices or the local support division of the district attorney's office (which enforces child support orders). In some states there are also support calculation programs available online for a moderate fee.

RESOURCE

State guidelines and information on child support rules. The National Child Support Enforcement Association (www.ncsea.org) has contact information for every state child support enforcement agency. Also, *Nolo's Essential Guide to Child Custody & Support*, by Emily Doskow, provides comprehensive details on how child support is determined and how to negotiate support.

CAUTION

Failure to support is a crime. If you have custody of your children and live with someone else, your ex-spouse is still required to support the children. Your ex may be angry at your new living arrangement and tempted to try to get out of paying child support by quitting his or her job or refusing to look for work. However, the court will probably structure payments based on your ex's ability, not inclination, to work. Refusing to support your children when you have the ability to do so is a crime in all states. People who repeatedly fail to take their child support obligations seriously may spend a short time behind bars and may be denied professional licenses or passports.

If the person you live with is not your children's parent, then that person has no obligation to support your children. The amount of child support your ex-spouse is ordered to pay usually isn't affected by the fact that you live with someone else. However, if your new partner provides shelter or buys food, clothing, or other items for you, your ex-spouse may petition the court to reduce his or her child support obligation. It will be your ex-spouse's responsibility to show that your new partner pays many of the children's expenses, freeing up most of your income. If your ex-spouse can prove this, a court may rule that you have more income available to support your children, and reduce your child support.

In most states, judges have at least some discretion to deviate from the guideline child support formula if the amount is unjust or inappropriate, based on factors such as the financial resources of the custodial parent and child-related expenses.

> **TIP**
>
> **If you receive child support and live with your partner or new spouse, consider signing an agreement to keep all of your earnings and property separate.** That way, you stand a better chance of not losing your support payments. Courts in some states have held that joint income could not be considered in making a child support award when the custodial parent and new partner had such an agreement.

Be aware that states are buckling down in collecting child support. All states have laws to grab the wages of a parent who falls behind in child support. A wage attachment means that an amount to cover the child support is taken out of a paycheck and paid directly to the custodial parent or a government agency. With the help of the federal government, states are cooperating to collect child support from parents who move to another part of the country. In short, paying child support is not only morally good, but it can also keep you out of jail.

The Effect of Living Together on Alimony and Child Support From a Prior Marriage

Once your divorce is final and alimony and child support decisions are made, either by the court or through your own agreement with your ex, can they be changed? Once again, it depends.

Alimony

If alimony is granted for an extended period, it normally terminates if the receiving spouse remarries, unless there's an agreement or court order to the contrary entered at the time of the divorce. However, judges in some states, in some circumstances, have the discretion to continue alimony even after the spouse receiving it remarries—unless your written settlement agreement specifies that payment will stop if one of you remarries.

What happens if the alimony recipient starts living with a partner, rather than remarrying? Alimony may still be terminated or reduced, depending on where you live and the circumstances:

- Most states will authorize reduction or termination of alimony upon cohabitation only if the cohabitation significantly decreases the recipient's need for support.
- Other states will terminate alimony regardless of whether the recipient's economic need is diminished by cohabiting.
- In still other states, alimony will not be affected should the spouse who receives it begin living with someone.

The definition of "cohabitation" may vary widely:

- A court in Illinois recently held that a former spouse could be deemed as cohabiting with another person on a "resident, continuing conjugal basis" although her boyfriend lived in a separate residence. What this jargon amounts to is that even though her boyfriend always spent the night at his own apartment, the court felt that the fact that he spent most of his time in her apartment and ate meals there was enough to qualify him as cohabiting with her and, as a result, terminated her alimony. (*In re Marriage of Herrin,* 262 Ill.App.3d 573 (1994).)
- Some states, like New York, require that the alimony recipient must not only live with someone (cohabit), but also "hold him or herself out as the spouse" of the person she lives with before alimony is terminated (alimony recipients rarely do this, so alimony is seldom cut off).
- Arkansas has a different approach, and requires that the alimony recipient not only live with, but also have children with, the new partner, before alimony will be terminated.
- California and Tennessee both presume that the recipient's need for support has been reduced once he or she starts cohabiting. In other words, if you move in with a new partner, unless you can prove to a judge that you still need the same amount of alimony, it will be reduced or terminated.

In those states that do not have laws or court decisions that specifically address the impact cohabitation might have on alimony, it is difficult to predict how a judge will rule. Regardless of state law, if you and your ex-spouse have made an agreement that support or alimony won't be affected if the person who receives it begins living together with someone new, your agreement will stand. And bear in mind that the person requesting a change in alimony or support payments is the one who must prove that an ex-spouse's economic situation has changed significantly.

Child Support

Child support may only be changed by court approval following a formal request for modification of child support. If you're a noncustodial parent and you live with someone—perhaps even support that person and his or her children—will the amount of child support you pay be reduced? Because you have no legal duty to support your new partner and new partner's children, a judge won't reduce your support obligation. Your primary duty is to your own children, not your friend's. At the same time, if your living expenses are reduced because you share them with another person, a judge may deviate from the child support formula because a greater amount of your income has been freed up.

Wills and Estate Planning

What Happens If You Don't Do Any Estate Planning?...........................246

Typical Estate Plans...247

Figuring Out What You Own: Taking Inventory...........................249

An Introduction to Wills..252

　What Wills Do..252

　Who Can Make a Valid Will?..252

　Preparing a Basic Will...254

Avoiding Probate..258

　Revocable Living Trusts...259

　Payable-on-Death Bank Accounts...260

　Transfer-on-Death Beneficiaries for Securities, Retirement Accounts,
　　and Other Assets...261

　Joint Tenancy..261

　Life Insurance...262

　Simplified Probate Procedures for Small Estates......................263

Estate and Gift Taxes..264

　Will Your Estate Owe Federal Taxes?...264

　How the Federal Gift and Estate Tax Works.............................265

　Estate Tax Breaks for Married Couples......................................265

　State Estate Tax...266

　Avoiding or Reducing Estate Taxes..267

Balancing the Needs of Your Partner and Your Children..............268

　How a Property Control Trust Works..269

　Imposing Restrictions on How Trust Property Is Used.............270

Funerals and Other Final Arrangements..272

Many of us avoid the subject of death whenever possible. We don't plan for what will happen to our property, who will care for our minor children, or even whether we'll be buried or cremated.

Unfortunately, this invites disaster for unmarried couples. State inheritance laws are designed to pass property only to spouses and blood relatives. So if you die without making legally binding arrangements for your partner to inherit your property, it will usually go to your closest relatives—not your partner.

This chapter explains what you need to do now to ensure that your property goes to the people you want to inherit it. It also explains how you can structure these arrangements with an eye toward sparing your survivors the hassle and expense of probate.

> **TIP**
>
> **Planning for incapacity.** In addition to planning for your death, you should also take steps to protect yourself, your partner, and your assets in the event that you ever become unable to make your own medical or financial decisions because of injury or serious illness. The best way to ensure that your affairs will be managed as you wish is to prepare a health care directive and a durable power of attorney for finances. (See "Making Medical and Financial Decisions for Your Partner" in Chapter 4.)

What Happens If You Don't Do Any Estate Planning?

Without a will or other legal means (for example, a living trust) for transferring property at your death, a surviving partner will inherit nothing unless you have a legally recognized common law marriage, or a registered domestic partnership or civil union in a state that allows it. Instead, close blood relatives will inherit everything.

If you die without a will, state "intestate succession" law determines who inherits your assets. The exact rules vary from state to state, but a typical intestate succession law provides that if you're unmarried:

- If you have children, your property is divided equally among them. If you have a deceased child who had children (your grandchildren), these grandchildren divide the deceased child's share.
- If you leave no children or grandchildren, all of your property goes to your parents equally.
- Next in line are your brothers and sisters, who share equally unless any have died leaving children, in which case the nieces and nephews split your deceased sibling's share.
- If you leave no children, grandchildren, parents, or siblings, your nephews and nieces share your estate equally unless you have grandnephews and grandnieces whose parents have died, who receive their deceased parents' share.
- If you have none of the relatives listed above, your estate passes to your grandparents. If they're not alive, their children (your uncles and aunts) take equally. If any of these relatives have died, their share goes to their children.
- If you have none of these relatives, your property goes to the state.

To learn about your state's intestate succession laws, visit www.nolo. com./legal-encyclopedia/intestate-succession.

Typical Estate Plans

An estate plan doesn't have to be complicated. Many couples need only a few documents:

- wills
- beneficiary designations for retirement accounts, life insurance, and bank and investment accounts, and
- living wills and powers of attorney for finances and health care (discussed in Chapter 4).

You may want a trust, or to do some more planning to avoid probate, reduce estate taxes, or put restrictions on how property will be used after your death. But for many people, the basics are fine.

> EXAMPLE 1: John and Liz, an unmarried couple, have two young sons, Alex and William. John's 14-year-old daughter from an earlier relationship, Abby, also lives with them. John and Liz aren't married, but John has always acknowledged paternity of all three children. Abby's mother hasn't been heard from in many years.
>
> John and Liz both make wills, leaving their assets to each other. In their wills, they each name John's sister Gwen (after getting her approval) as personal guardian for Alex and Will. John's will names Liz as personal guardian for Abby, with Gwen as alternate guardian. John and Liz also name each other as beneficiaries of their retirement plans, on forms provided by the plans' managers.
>
> John and Liz each have a few thousand dollars saved up and a little equity in their jointly owned house, but it doesn't amount to much. To provide cash to take care of their children if they should die while the children are still minors, they each buy a ten-year term life insurance policy to pay $200,000 if one of them dies ($400,000 if they both do). Each names the other as primary beneficiary and names the children as alternate beneficiaries. In their wills, they leave all their property to each other, with the children as alternate beneficiaries. If the kids inherit while they're still minors, Gwen will manage the money for them as a "custodian" (discussed below).
>
> EXAMPLE 2: Elaine and Richard, who both have grown children from previous marriages, are living together with no plans to marry. Both have enough to live on independently, and they haven't combined their finances. They do own their house together. To make an estate plan, they:
> - Make wills. Each leaves the other some assets, and leaves some directly to their children.

- Create a living trust for Richard, who has a lot of assets and wants to spare his family the expense of probate after his death (discussed later in the chapter).
- Update their beneficiary designations. They look over the paperwork for their retirement plans and investment accounts, and name beneficiaries to inherit these assets.
- Make living wills and powers of attorney (see Chapter 4). After discussing their end-of-life health care wishes, each gives the other authority to make those decisions on the other's behalf if it's ever necessary. Elaine gives her son a financial power of attorney, giving him authority over her assets if she ever becomes unable to manage them herself.
- Put their house in a trust, providing that when one of them dies, the survivor will have the right to live in it for life. When the survivor dies, the house will be sold and the proceeds split among all their children.

Figuring Out What You Own: Taking Inventory

Before making a will or doing other estate planning, you need to know what property is yours. If you've lived with your partner for a long time, your property may be so mixed up with your partner's that you can't tell who owns what. If you and your partner want to leave all of your property to the survivor, who owns what doesn't matter as much. But if not, sit down and make an agreement defining property ownership.

You can use a property ownership agreement like the one shown below, or one of the living together agreements in Chapter 3, with one very important exception: An agreement like this *cannot* change ownership of real estate or any item (a car, for example) with a title document. For those assets, you must change the deed or title slip to show the ownership arrangement you want.

Sample Property Ownership Agreement

Tomas Finnegan and Keija Adams agree as follows:

1. We have been living together for ten years, and during that time much of our property has been mixed together so that it isn't completely clear who owns what.

2. The purpose of this agreement is to categorize all of our real and personal property owned on January 10, 20xx, as set out below. Property purchased after that date will be owned by the person who buys it, unless we decide differently as set forth in agreements made at the time of purchase or later.

3. From the date of this agreement, all property listed in Category 1 belongs solely and absolutely to Tomas, all property listed in Category 2 belongs solely and absolutely to Keija, and all property listed in Category 3 belongs to both in the shares noted.

Category 1: Tomas

1. 20xx Ford Mustang
2. G.E. washer & dryer
3. 100 shares of stock in Melt-in-Your-Mouth Popcorn, Inc.

Category 2: Keija

1. 20xx Yamaha motorcycle
2. BMX stereo & related stereo equipment
3. Restaurant Workers Credit Union account

Category 3: Tomas and Keija

1. House at 2547 Jones Street, St. Louis, MO, owned in joint tenancy.

Tomas Finnegan | _January 10, 20xx_
Signature | Date

Keija Adam | _January 10, 20xx_
Signature | Date

What If You Had an Oral Agreement?

What if you and your partner had an agreement that you would own everything 50-50, but it wasn't in writing? If your partner dies owning assets in his or her name and doesn't leave them to you in a will, then the people who would inherit from your partner under state law—close relatives—might think that they should inherit everything. If you can't work something out, then to get a portion of your deceased partner's property, you would have to bring a lawsuit and prove that you and your partner had an oral or implied contract to share property ownership.

The outcome of such a lawsuit is uncertain at best. But a court might rule in your favor if:

- You worked in the home and your partner earned the money, but agreed orally to share everything.
- You worked in the home, your partner earned the money, and there was an implied contract between you, under which you expected to share in the fruits of your labor.
- You and your partner bought items jointly and agreed that they belonged to both of you.

You may succeed, especially if friends and relatives step forward and testify that they knew about your understanding.

As a surviving partner left without any inheritance from a deceased partner, you might also prevail in court by proving that basic fairness demands that you be treated as a partial owner of the property. In other words, you worked hard to buy or create the property, so you should get at least part of it. For example, you might show that you and your partner jointly contributed to the purchase of a piece of real estate, but for some reason the property was put only in your deceased partner's name.

An Introduction to Wills

A will is a document in which you specify who inherits your assets when you die. It is easy to make a simple, valid will, and you can leave your property to anyone you wish, including the person you live with. You can change or revoke your will whenever you like; you're not stuck with it once you make it. Discussing your will with your partner may be a good idea, but there is no legal requirement that you do so.

What Wills Do

In a will, you can:

- Leave anything you own solely (money, stock, clothes, cars, real estate, and so on) to any person or institution you choose.
- Forgive debts owed to you.
- Name your executor (personal representative)—that is, the person who will wind up your affairs after your death.
- Nominate a personal guardian for your minor children, in case you and the other parent someday aren't available to raise them.
- Set up simple trusts for children, to delay when they get inherited property outright.
- Disinherit anyone you want (except a legal spouse).
- Leave assets that you don't specifically list in your will or don't yet own, such as a house you later inherit or money you win in the lottery years after making your will. There's no way, other than a will, to choose who inherits such property.

Who Can Make a Valid Will?

Any adult of "sound mind" can make a valid will. To be of sound mind for purposes of making a will, you need to be aware of:

- what a will does and that you are making one
- which people you would normally be expected to provide for, such as your children, and
- what you own.

Disinheritance

- You can leave your assets to whomever you wish.
- If, however, you are married, your spouse might have a claim to some of your property. A surviving spouse who is unhappy with what he or she inherits from you can claim a share of your estate. How large a share depends on state law.
- Generally, children cannot claim any of your estate. However, if you wish to leave nothing to a child (or a child of a deceased child), you should mention the child in your will. If you don't, the child might, if it looked like you inadvertently overlooked him or her, be able to claim a portion of your estate. Usually, only a child born after you made your will can make such a claim.

You must also be able to decide how to leave your property, and you cannot be under someone else's control to the extent that your document expresses their wishes, not yours.

CAUTION

Will contests are rare. But if you own valuable property and are afraid that relatives who object to your relationship will challenge your will, take steps to leave evidence that you were of sound mind and not under undue influence when you signed it. Talk to a lawyer about how to head off problems.

You and your partner should each make your own will. Some couples are interested in making a joint will, leaving each person's property and specifying what happens to the property when the second person dies, but it's not a good idea. Such a will takes away the freedom of the survivor to dispose of property as he or she wishes, and may not be valid in some states.

If you want to put restrictions on the surviving partner's control over property after your death, a better alternative is to establish a trust that spells out the restrictions. For example, you could use a trust to leave your house to your partner for life, with it going to your children from a former marriage when your partner dies. (See "Balancing the Needs of Your Partner and Children," below.)

Preparing a Basic Will

It's easy to prepare a will using software, an online service, or a book with good instructions. (Some of Nolo's will-making resources are listed below.) Many people do it themselves, without a lawyer. If you do it yourself but are unsure about certain aspects, you can always take the document to a lawyer and get your questions answered.

What about just writing out your wishes by hand? Handwritten, unwitnessed wills, called "holographic" wills, are legal in about half the states. To be valid, a holographic will must be written, and signed entirely in the handwriting of the person making the will. Some states require that it also be dated. Regardless of your state's rule, it's better to print out your will and sign it in front of witnesses. Courts treat holographic wills somewhat suspiciously, because they are far easier to forge than are witnessed wills.

Will-Making Resources From Nolo

A will isn't a complicated document; it's easy to make your own valid will with these resources from Nolo, all valid in every state but Louisiana. In addition, you can find lots of free information on making a will and planning your estate on Nolo's website at www.nolo.com.

- *Quicken WillMaker Plus*, Nolo's comprehensive estate planning software, lets you create a will, health care directive, durable power of attorney for finances, final arrangements letter, and more.
- At Nolo.com, you can make your will quickly and easily online.
- The *Quick & Legal Will Book*, by Denis Clifford, shows you how to make a basic, legal will quickly and easily. Includes sample wills and downloadable forms.

Naming a Personal Guardian for Your Children

If you have minor children, nominate a personal guardian for them in your will. Naming a guardian provides for the unlikely possibility that neither parent will be able to raise the children.

If your relationship with the other parent is strained, you may not want that person to raise your kids if something happens to you. You may believe that someone else—for example, your current partner—would be the best guardian for your child. You can name that person as the guardian, but if the other legal parent challenges your choice in court, he or she will almost certainly prevail unless it can be proved that the other parent:

- has never assumed—or tried to assume—the role of parent in the first place (for example, a father who never signed a statement acknowledging paternity or otherwise acted like a parent)
- has abandoned the child, or
- is unfit as a parent.

It's difficult to prove unfitness unless there are serious problems such as child abuse, substance abuse, or mental illness. The fact that you don't like or respect the other parent is never enough, by itself. If you honestly believe that the other parent is incapable of properly caring for your child or simply won't assume the responsibility, state your reasons in writing. Nolo's *Quicken WillMaker* software shows you how.

When you decide on a guardian, be sure the person you name is willing and able to do the job. If your child's other parent is still alive, you should, if possible, agree on whom to nominate. And it's best not to name a couple as personal guardians, even if you expect both would act as guardians. It raises potential conflicts, especially if the couple splits up.

If a guardian is ever necessary, the court must appoint one; the judge will appoint the person you named in your will unless he or she is convinced that it is not in the child's best interest. If there are no conflicts about who should be guardian, the process is usually straightforward.

Naming Someone to Manage a Child's Inheritance

If you leave property to your children, you must think about who will manage it if you die while your children are young. It's usually wise to name the same person as both personal guardian and manager of your children's money. But if there's a good reason, you can name different people to care for your children and manage their finances. Make sure your choices are compatible with each other—they will have to work together.

If you don't arrange for someone to manage the property, the court will do it for you if necessary. These court procedures are time-consuming and costly and could produce a result you wouldn't like. Here are several ways to appoint the manager you prefer:

- **Leave property to your children's other parent.** This is an excellent approach if you have a close-knit family and the other parent is a competent financial manager. Especially if moderate amounts are involved, it often doesn't make sense to create a more elaborate plan.
- **Use the Uniform Transfers to Minors Act (UTMA).** In all states except South Carolina you can use a law called the UTMA to name a custodian to manage property you leave to your minor children for the child's benefit until the children reach an age between 18 and 25, depending on your state's laws. The UTMA works particularly well if you're leaving smaller amounts of money that won't need long-term management.
- **Create a child's trust.** For large amounts or long-term management, consider establishing a simple child's trust in your will or living trust. The person you name as trustee of the trust manages the money for your child and doles it out for education, health, and other needs under the terms of the trust. The child's trust ends at whatever age you designate, and any remaining money is turned over to your child outright at that time.

Children With Special Needs

If you have a child who will likely need help for his or her whole life, don't just leave that child a share of your estate—if you do, it could jeopardize essential government benefits, like access to health care through Medicaid. You may want to set up what's called a special needs or supplementary trust, which is designed to preserve eligibility for benefits. See *Special Needs Trusts: Protect Your Child's Financial Future*, by Attorneys Kevin Urbatsch and Michele Fuller-Urbatsch (Nolo), for information on how to set up such a trust.

Naming an Executor

In your will, you name someone to serve as your executor (called a personal representative in some states). Your executor is responsible for handling your property after you die. Your executor should be someone you trust and can rely on, and who will likely be available at the time of your death. You should name at least one alternate executor in case your first choice dies before you, declines to serve, or is unable to serve when you die. Your executor can be a person who inherits under your will. So if you plan to leave your partner the bulk of your estate, it's also fine (and common) to name him or her as executor.

If you name an out-of-state executor, the court may require a bond (a kind of insurance policy that protects the estate from loss) or impose other requirements. If you want to name an out-of-state executor, check your state's laws to see whether your state places any restrictions on your choice. (These laws are summarized in *The Executor's Guide*, by Mary Randolph (Nolo), and in the articles "Restrictions on Out-of-State Executors on Nolo.com.)

Changing or Revoking Your Will

At some point, you may want to change your will. For example, say your friend Maria dies, and the book collection you were going to leave her you now want to leave to Martha.

When you should change your will is a matter of common sense. It's usually time to do it when your family undergoes a significant change, such as the birth of a child or the ending of your partnership. You may also want to change your will if your property ownership situation changes in a major way—for example, if you buy a house or receive a good-sized inheritance. When you do wish to make a change, you can't just cross out a provision in your will or handwrite a change in the margin. Changes must be made formally.

It usually makes good sense to revoke your will and make a new one, rather than changing the old one. You can add a "codicil" to make minor changes or additions to your current will, but doing so is usually just as much trouble as making a whole new will, because a codicil must be signed, dated, and witnessed just like a will.

The best way to revoke a will is to write a new one, expressly stating that you are revoking all previous wills. Alternatively, you can tear up the old one, but this isn't as reliable—there may be copies floating around, which people could try to follow later if they don't know you intended to revoke the old will. If you destroy your will, do it in front of witnesses. Otherwise, after you die, it may be difficult to determine whether you really intended to destroy it.

Avoiding Probate

Probate is a court proceeding during which your will is filed, assets gathered, debts and taxes paid, and property distributed to your beneficiaries. The process is time-consuming and expensive. Although the cost of probate (attorney fees, court filing fees, and often, appraisal fees) varies, depending on your state and the type of property you own, it can amount to up to 5% of your estate. These fees are taken out of your property and reduce the amount received by your beneficiaries. In contrast, if property is transferred outside of probate, you eliminate fees. And beneficiaries get their property as much as nine months to a year sooner than they would if your estate were probated.

Do You Need to Avoid Probate?

If your property is of modest value (less than $150,000), planning to avoid probate probably won't result in enough savings to be worth the trouble. Even if you own considerable property, if you are reasonably young and in good health it still often makes sense to limit estate planning to writing a simple will. When you're older, you can engage in more sophisticated planning. After all, probate-avoidance planning doesn't save you any money until your death and, if done too soon, must be redone.

If you wish to avoid probate, there are well-established methods of transferring property that do so. These include:

- holding property in a revocable living trust
- naming payable-on-death beneficiaries for bank accounts, U.S. government securities, retirement accounts, and, in most states, stocks and bonds
- holding title to your car in transfer-on-death form (in states where this is allowed)
- recording a transfer-on-death deed for real estate (in states where this is allowed)
- owning property in joint tenancy, and
- buying life insurance to provide quick cash for survivors.

Each method has advantages and drawbacks, discussed briefly below.

Revocable Living Trusts

A basic revocable living trust does essentially the same job as a will—that is, leaving your property to the beneficiaries you name—with the major plus of avoiding probate. Living trusts are the most comprehensive way for members of an unmarried couple to avoid probate. They are very flexible. You can transfer all your property by living trust, or if appropriate, use one to transfer only some assets, leaving the rest by other methods.

The document that creates the trust is normally just a few pages long; in it, you name yourself as trustee (the person in charge of trust property) and say who is to inherit what. You also name a successor trustee—the person who will distribute the trust property to your beneficiaries after you die. The successor trustee (who can be a trust beneficiary) is also usually empowered to manage the trust if you become incapacitated.

Then—and this step is crucial—you must legally transfer property to yourself in your capacity as trustee. The trust document can control property only if it is owned in the trustee's name.

These trusts are called "living" because they're created while you are alive (sometimes they're called "inter vivos" trusts by folks who can't give up Latin). And they're called "revocable" because you can revoke or change them at any time, for any reason, before you die. While you live, you still effectively own all the property you hold in your living trust and you can do whatever you want with it: sell it, spend it, or give it away.

There are no serious drawbacks or risks involved in creating or maintaining a living trust. You don't need to obtain a taxpayer ID number for the trust or maintain separate trust tax records. All transactions involving trust assets are reported on your personal income tax return. After you die, your successor trustee simply obtains the property from whoever holds it, and transfers it to your beneficiaries. No probate court proceeding is required.

EXAMPLE: Robert creates a living trust and names his partner, Kate, as successor trustee. In the trust, Robert leaves several small items to friends and names Kate as the beneficiary of his main assets, a house and an apartment building. Robert executes and records deeds transferring title to those buildings to himself in his capacity as trustee. When Robert dies, Kate, as successor trustee, distributes the small gifts to Robert's friends and executes deeds transferring the house and apartment building to herself. No probate is needed.

CAUTION

Even with a living trust, you still need a will. If you make a living trust, you should also have a will to deal with property acquired shortly before death or not otherwise covered by the trust, and to name a personal guardian for any minor children.

Payable-on-Death Bank Accounts

A payable-on-death (POD), bank account, sometimes called an "informal trust," is a bank account that avoids probate. On a simple form provided by the bank, you name the person or people you want to receive the money when you die. During your life, you retain full and exclusive control over the account—you can withdraw funds in the account, make deposits, or close the account. At your death, the account passes to the beneficiary without probate.

There are no drawbacks to a POD bank account, except that most financial institutions will not allow you to name an alternate beneficiary in case your first choice predeceases you (something you can do with a living trust). Most banks have standard forms allowing you to create a POD account by either opening a new account or placing a beneficiary designation on an existing account. Bank fees for POD accounts are normally no higher than the fees for other types of accounts.

Transfer-on-Death Beneficiaries for Securities, Retirement Accounts, and Other Assets

You are allowed to name a pay-on-death beneficiary for several other types of assets. Your beneficiary will inherit the property after you die, with no need for probate. These investments include:

- U.S. government securities (bonds, notes, and bills)
- money in IRAs, Keoghs, and 401(k) retirement plans
- stocks, bonds, and other marketable securities in states that have adopted the Uniform Transfers on Death Security Registration Act (all states except Louisiana and Texas)
- vehicles (allowed only in some states), and
- real estate, with a transfer-on-death deed (available in some states).

Joint Tenancy

Joint tenancy is a form of shared property ownership that can be used for both real estate and personal property. What sets joint tenancy apart from most other forms of joint ownership is its "right of survivorship" feature—when one joint tenant dies, his or her share automatically passes to the surviving joint tenant. If there is more than one survivor, each acquires an equal share of the deceased's interest. Indeed, you can't leave a share of joint tenancy property to anyone except the other joint tenant. Any attempt to do so by using a will or living trust is invalid.

Joint tenancy is an excellent probate-avoidance device for property you and your partner acquire equally together, assuming you each want your share to pass to the other at your death. Because in almost all states joint tenants must own equal shares, it usually won't work if one person owns a larger share than the other. Joint tenancy ownership can be created in property owned solely by one person if the owner transfers title to both partners "as joint tenants with right of survivorship" (or similar language required in some states).

In contrast, establishing a joint tenancy by transferring one partner's separately owned property simply to avoid probate is often a poor idea. Here's why:

- **You're giving away property.** If you make someone else a joint tenant of property that you now own yourself, you give up half ownership of the property. The new owner has rights that you can't take back. For example, the new owner can sell or mortgage his or her share—or lose it to creditors.

- **You may have to file a gift tax return.** If the value of the interest you give to a new co-owner (except your spouse) exceeds $14,000 in one year, you must file a gift tax return with the IRS. No tax is actually due, however, until you give away a large amount (currently, more than $5.49 million) in taxable gifts. There's one big exception: If two or more people open a bank account in joint tenancy, but one person puts all or most of the money in, no gift tax is assessed against that person. But when a joint tenant who has contributed little or nothing to the account withdraws money from it, this may be considered a taxable gift.

- **The IRS often treats the first partner to die as the owner of 100% of the property (until the surviving partner can prove otherwise).** This can create significant tax problems for a high-asset estate.

Life Insurance

If you have few assets but children who depend on you for support, consider buying a moderate amount of term life insurance to cover your children until they're on their own. Because term life insurance pays benefits only if you die during the covered period, it's far cheaper than other types of life insurance.

Life insurance proceeds are paid directly to the policy beneficiary without going through probate. The only exception is if the proceeds are payable to your estate, in which case they are subject to probate. For this reason, it's usually a poor idea to name your estate as beneficiary, unless the estate will have large obligations for debts or taxes and there are no other liquid assets available to pay them.

Simplified Probate Procedures for Small Estates

Almost every state now offers shortcuts through probate—or a way around it completely—for "small estates." Each state defines that term differently. Many large estates, worth hundreds of thousands of dollars, also benefit from these laws by qualifying for special transfer procedures that speed property to inheritors.

There are two basic kinds of probate shortcuts for small estates:

- **Claiming property with affidavits—no court required.** If the total value of all the assets you leave behind is less than a certain amount, the people who inherit your personal property—that's anything except real estate—may be able to skip probate entirely. The exact amount depends on state law, and varies hugely. Some states allow up to $100,000 or $150,000. If the estate qualifies, an inheritor can prepare a short document stating that he or she is entitled to certain items of property under a will or state law. This paper, signed under oath, is called an affidavit. When the person or institution holding the property—for example, a bank where the deceased person had an account—receives the affidavit and a copy of the death certificate, it releases the money or other property.
- **Simplified court procedures.** Another option for small estates (again, as defined by state law) is a quicker, simpler version of probate. The probate court is still involved, but it exerts far less control over the settling of the estate. In many states, these procedures are straightforward enough to handle without a lawyer, so they save money as well as time.

You can find the details of these procedures in *8 Ways to Avoid Probate,* by Mary Randolph (Nolo).

Estate and Gift Taxes

Many people fear that "death taxes" will eat into whatever inheritance they leave their family or friends. But the truth is that only the very richest families in America have enough inherited wealth to justify concern about federal estate tax. More than 99% of estates do NOT owe federal gift and estate tax. More estates—but still a tiny percentage—owe state estate tax.

Estate taxes are imposed whether or not assets go through probate at your death; probate avoidance has no effect on tax avoidance. If, however, your estate is large enough to be subject to estate taxes (discussed below in "Will Your Estate Owe Federal Taxes?"), a lawyer will be happy to show you ways to reduce or avoid them.

Will Your Estate Owe Federal Taxes?

For deaths in 2017, federal estate taxes will be assessed only if you leave more than $5.49 million in taxable assets. (This amount increases each year with inflation.) Don't have that much? You, like 99% of the country, can quit worrying about federal estate tax.

If you think you might bump up against the $5.49 million exemption amount, estimate the value of your taxable estate. Start by taking the value of everything you own, and then subtract the value of property that's exempt from tax. The result is your taxable estate.

Here, you can make a very rough estimate of what your taxable estate might be worth at your death.

Gross value of everything you own (including your share of jointly owned property) at your death	$ _____
Taxable gifts you make during life	+ _____
What you owe on that property	– _____
Property left to your spouse	– _____
Property left to tax-exempt charities	– _____
Various deductions for funeral expenses, etc.	– _____
Taxable estate	= $ _____

How the Federal Gift and Estate Tax Works

The federal estate tax is part of the unified federal "gift and estate tax." Basically, you can give away (during your life) and leave (at your death) up to $5.49 million without owing tax. But if your taxable gifts plus your taxable estate together add up to more than $5.49 million, tax will be due. The top rate is 40%.

What are taxable gifts? Most lifetime gifts aren't taxable. For 2017, gifts of up to $14,000 per recipient are not taxable. In addition, gifts to spouses, donations to tax-exempt charities, and direct payments for someone's medical or educational expenses also aren't taxable.

> **EXAMPLE:** While Tamar is alive, she makes taxable gifts totaling $900,000. At her death in 2017, she leaves an additional $2 million. Her estate does not owe any gift and estate tax, because her taxable gifts plus her taxable estate don't add up to more than $5.49 million, the exempt amount for the year of her death.

Estate Tax Breaks for Married Couples

Married couples get two big breaks when it comes to the federal gift and estate tax. These breaks can provide powerful incentives for very wealthy couples to consider marriage.

First, all property given or left to a spouse, as long as that spouse is a U.S. citizen, is exempt from the gift and estate tax. (You can give your noncitizen spouse up to $143,000/year free of gift tax, but all money inherited from you is subject to the estate tax if the estate is big enough.)

> **EXAMPLE:** Toshiro and Yuko have lived happily together for 13 years. During that time, their small electrical supply business has grown into a regional supplier worth about $12 million. If either partner dies, his or her one-half share will be subject to a hefty estate tax (at least under current tax law). To pay a huge tax bill, the survivor might even have to sell the business. But if Toshiro and Yuko marry, all property inherited by the surviving spouse will be exempt from estate tax.

Second, spouses can share their individual estate tax exemptions. This "portability" rule gives married couples a $10.24 million exemption (under current law), split between them in any way that provides the greatest tax benefit. For example, say a man dies and leaves $4 million to his widow; no estate tax is owed because property left to a spouse is tax-free. The widow then dies, leaving $7 million (her own $3 million plus the $4 million she inherited from her husband) to their children. Her estate won't owe any estate tax, even though the estate is over the exemption amount, because the estate can use $1.5 million of the husband's unused exemption.

State Estate Tax

Some states impose an estate tax (on the estate, before property is distributed to inheritors) or an inheritance tax (on people who inherit).

State estate tax. Only 15 states collect their own estate tax. These taxes don't normally take a large bite out of an estate; however, some states do have an exemption amount that is lower than the federal exemption. If you live in one of those states, your estate may owe state estate tax, even if it doesn't owe federal estate tax. To learn more about state estate taxes, go to www.nolo.com/legal-encyclopedia/state-estate-taxes.

Inheritance tax. This tax is paid by the people who inherit property and is based on the value of what they inherit. In many states with inheritance taxes, your partner will pay more inheritance tax than if you left the same property to a spouse or blood relative. This is because the inheritance tax rate, or the amount of property that is exempt from inheritance tax, is often based on the relationship of the deceased to the beneficiary. Commonly, property left to a spouse is exempt from tax. Minor children get a big exemption, too, and pay a low rate. Unrelated individuals (called "strangers" by some statutes) who inherit from you get the lowest exemption and pay the highest rate.

You can get a copy of your state rules from your state tax office. Also, there are summaries of state inheritance tax rules in *The Executor's Guide*, by Mary Randolph (Nolo), and you can learn more about state inheritance tax at www.nolo.com/legal-encyclopedia/state-inheritance-taxes.html.

States With Their Own Estate Tax		States With Their Own Inheritance Tax
Connecticut	Minnesota	Iowa
Delaware*	New Jersey	Kentucky
District of Columbia	New York	Maryland
Hawaii	Oregon	Nebraska
Illinois	Rhode Island	New Jersey
Maine	Vermont	Pennsylvania
Maryland	Washington	
Massachusetts		
* Estate tax repealed as of July 1, 2018.		

TIP

Know where you reside. Figuring out where you legally reside isn't always simple. If your voting records, driver's license, car registration, bank accounts, and other key documents all contain one address, that's the state of your residence. If you divide your time between more than one state, however, and it's not be clear where you reside, pick the state with no, or a lower, estate or inheritance tax and make sure all key records support your choice. If you're wealthy, get legal advice on this issue.

Avoiding or Reducing Estate Taxes

Lawyers have developed many schemes the rich can use to escape or reduce estate taxes. Some legal tactics include:

Make nontaxable gifts. Currently, gifts of up to $14,000 per person per year are not subject to gift tax; you can make an unlimited number of gifts as long as they don't exceed $14,000 per recipient per year. (This number is indexed for inflation and goes up periodically, in increments of $1,000.) You can also make nontaxable gifts of any amount to tax-exempt charities or to pay someone's medical or educational expense. A sustained program of gift-giving can significantly reduce the value of your estate.

Give away life insurance policies. Making a gift of a life insurance policy while you're alive can significantly reduce federal estate taxes. The reason is that when you give away a policy before death, it is valued, for federal estate and gift tax purposes, at a far lower dollar value than the amount it will pay off at death. By contrast, if you own the policy on your life when you die, all proceeds paid to your beneficiaries are included in your taxable estate.

Set up tax-saving trusts. There are several kinds of trusts (QTIPs, GRATs, QDOTs, charitable trusts, and more) that can defer or reduce the amount of estate tax your family will eventually have to pay. Consult an experienced tax attorney or tax accountant.

 RESOURCE
More information. To learn about options for people with large estates, see *Plan Your Estate*, by Denis Clifford (Nolo).

Balancing the Needs of Your Partner and Your Children

If you or your partner has children from prior marriages or relationships, special issues may emerge when it comes to estate planning. You may feel conflicted about how to leave your property in a way that's fair to all your loved ones. If you die first, your surviving partner may need additional income or the use of your property to live comfortably. On the other hand, you probably want to leave something to your children from a former relationship. Things get even more complicated if the children themselves feel entitled to inherit your property and become resentful if they believe they will lose it to your partner. If your partner and your children don't get along, the situation gets even dicier.

Fortunately, there is an estate planning solution to deal (at least partially) with the problem of possible conflicts over property: a property control trust. You'll need a lawyer to draw up this kind of trust.

How a Property Control Trust Works

A property control trust lets the surviving partner use all or just some of the trust property (or income from that property) for the rest of his or her life. When the survivor dies, the property goes to the children.

A property control trust restricts the rights of the surviving partner to use the property placed in the trust. The surviving partner is usually called the "life beneficiary" of the trust. His or her rights to use trust property, receive trust income, or spend trust principal are as limited as the person who establishes the trust (the grantor) determines they should be. Restricting the surviving partner's rights protects the trust principal, so that much of it remains when the surviving partner dies. Then, the trust property goes outright to the grantor's children from a prior marriage or to other beneficiaries the grantor named.

EXAMPLE 1: Grant and Helga, each in their late 60s, decide to live together. Grant has two children, ages 36 and 24, one from each of his two marriages. Helga has one child, age 39. Grant has an estate worth roughly $375,000; Helga's is worth $230,000. Both partners receive Social Security income and, in addition, Helga has a small pension. Neither has enough saved to be truly financially independent should the other die first. Each creates a property control trust and puts most of his or her property in it. Each trust provides that the surviving partner will have income from the trust for life, but no right to spend the trust principal. This way, they've each ensured that their estate will remain intact, to be received by their child or children after the surviving partner dies.

EXAMPLE 2: Lisi and Greg begin living together in their late 50s. Lisi has a child from an earlier marriage; Greg has two children from prior marriages. Lisi owns property worth $400,000. Greg owns property worth $310,000. They decide to buy a condo that costs $320,000. Each contributes half the down payment, and they share the mortgage payment equally.

Each partner decides to create a property control trust. Under the terms of each trust, the other partner, as life beneficiary, has the rights to:

- remain in the condo for life
- receive the income from other property placed in the trust, and
- spend trust principal only for medical costs that can't be paid from other resources.

Each partner names the final beneficiaries for his or her trust. Lisi decides that her final beneficiary will be her daughter. Greg, who is on good terms with his children and is also close to Lisi's daughter, names all three as his final beneficiaries, to share trust property.

Property control trusts are no guarantee that family conflicts and tensions will be eliminated or even reduced. But they can achieve some sensible control over a surviving partner's assets, and give you the comfort that you've done your best to provide for both your partner and your children.

Imposing Restrictions on How Trust Property Is Used

With a property control trust, you can impose a wide variety of restrictions on your partner's rights to use the trust property. For instance, you may give your partner the right to receive income from the trust, with no right to spend the trust principal. Or, although it's common to name the life beneficiary as the person to manage the trust (called the successor trustee), you could name someone else as the successor trustee. By doing this, presumably there's less chance that your partner will take too much of the trust principal.

Here are some of the controls that can be placed on a surviving partner's right to control trust property:

- The survivor can live in a house owned, or partially owned, by the trust, but can't sell it.
- The survivor can live in a house owned, or partially owned, by the trust, and can sell it only for the purpose of buying another residence, and then only with the approval of all trust beneficiaries.
- The survivor can live in a house owned, or partially owned, by the trust, but cannot sell it or rent it. If the survivor moves into a nursing home or assisted living facility and stays there for more than 90 consecutive days, the house must be turned over to the trust's final beneficiaries.
- The survivor is not the trustee, and will be paid trust income only as the trustee determines it is necessary for medical care or basic needs.

- The survivor is cotrustee with one of the final beneficiaries. Any decision regarding trust income or property, including distribution of income to the surviving partner, requires approval of both trustees. (Clearly, if you include this kind of provision, there must be good will between the cotrustees.)
- The survivor may drive a valuable car owned by the trust (as long as it's adequately insured), but can sell it only with consent of at least one final beneficiary.

The survivor must follow specific directions set out in the trust document, down to how he or she can use many items of trust property and how to care for valuable antiques.

All rights of the surviving partner to the trust property end if he or she marries or moves in with another living together partner.

EXAMPLE: Leticia, in her 70s, lives with Ben, also in his 70s. Leticia has been married twice, and has one grown child from each marriage. Her estate consists of her house worth $275,000 (all equity) and investments of $580,000. Ben owns much less, about $40,000 in savings and a modest pension plus Social Security.

Leticia wants her property to eventually go equally to her two children —but if she predeceases Ben, she doesn't want him thrown out on the street. To be sure this doesn't happen, she creates a trust to control her property, appointing the older of her two children as trustee. She arranges for her house and savings to go into the trust.

Ben is given the right to remain in the house for his life. However, if he leaves it for more than four consecutive months, whether to move to some tropical paradise or a nursing home, the house can be sold or rented if the trustee decides that's desirable.

Ben also has lifetime use of all furnishings and possessions in the house, with the same stipulation as above, and is to receive income of $5,000 per year from the investments in the trust. If the income from these investments is less than $5,000, Ben receives that lesser amount. If the income exceeds $5,000, the trustee has the power to give Ben more if he determines Ben needs it for basic needs, such as health care.

SEE AN EXPERT

If you are interested in a property control trust, talk to a lawyer. But first, we recommend that you read *Plan Your Estate*, by Denis Clifford (Nolo). It contains excellent material on how to use trusts in subsequent relationships.

Funerals and Other Final Arrangements

Many people make burial or cremation plans informally, trusting their loved ones to take care of the details after death. This works fine if you're confident your plans will be carried out. Sometimes, however, families ignore the deceased person's wishes and substitute their own, especially if they dislike the person you live with. This is possible because, in some states, only blood relatives have a say in making funeral plans.

If you're concerned about that possibility—or you just want to help your survivors by giving them some guidance during what is sure to be a hard time—you can:

- **Make the practical arrangements yourself.** Get a burial plot or arrange for cremation, and plan your funeral or memorial ceremony.
- **Leave a letter of instruction in a place where it will be available immediately at your death.** This is better than putting instructions in your will, which may not be read for several days. Readily available instructions will be a great aid to family and friends.

EXAMPLE: "I wish to be buried in the Green Meadow Cemetery in Lancastershire, Massachusetts, in plot number 4321B, which is reserved and paid for [or which will be paid for by my burial insurance through Carpenters Union 18]. I wish no elaborate ceremony and wish my remains to be prepared for burial by the Fraternal Brothers Burial Society under the contract that I have signed with them. Any decisions not already made, or necessitated by circumstances that I cannot now foresee, I entrust to my friend of many years, Lucinda Whitehorse."

RESOURCE

Help with final arrangements. Nolo offers two excellent resources to help you decide on final arrangements—from burial or cremation to memorial ceremonies—and leave instructions for loved ones. Nolo's *Quicken WillMaker Plus* software lets you prepare a final arrangements letter that makes your wishes clear. Or, if you prefer to use a workbook, *Get It Together*, by Melanie Cullen and Shae Irving (Nolo), provides a complete system to help you organize all your important paperwork and personal information, including final arrangements, for your survivors.

Nolo Estate Planning Books

- *Estate Planning Basics*, by Denis Clifford, is an overview of the estate planning process. It provides concise, easy-to-understand explanations of the major components of estate planning, including wills, living trusts and other probate-avoidance methods, estate taxes, property control trusts, and planning for someone to handle your medical and financial decisions if you are incapacitated.
- *Plan Your Estate*, by Denis Clifford, covers every significant aspect of estate planning. It is especially valuable for people with larger estates and discusses sophisticated techniques for reducing taxes.
- *Make Your Own Living Trust*, by Denis Clifford, provides a thorough explanation of this popular probate-avoidance device. It covers how a living trust works, how to create one, how to transfer property to the trust, and what happens when the trust maker dies. Comes with forms and all the information and instructions necessary to make a living trust and a basic will.
- *8 Ways to Avoid Probate*, by Mary Randolph, is a concise but detailed rundown of the many ways to avoid probate, including joint tenancy, pay-on-death bank accounts, and beneficiary designations for securities, vehicles, and real estate.
- *The Executor's Guide*, by Mary Randolph, will lead you through the process of settling your partner's estate if your partner has died and you are the executor of the estate. If you're the trustee of a living trust, check out *The Trustee's Legal Companion*, by Liza Hanks and Carol Elias Zolla.

Moving On—When Unmarried Couples Separate

Rules of the Unmarried Dissolution 278

    Divorce Laws 278

    Ownership of Property and Debts 279

    Courts Handling Disputes 279

    Alimony 279

    Child Custody and Support 280

The Process of Separation 280

    Prebreakup Tasks 281

    Immediate Breakup Issues 282

Ten Steps to Resolving Your Conflicts 289

Mediation, Arbitration, and Other Ways to Resolve Disputes 293

    Informal Negotiation Through Third Parties 294

    Mediation 294

    Arbitration 296

    How to Make an Agreement to Use Mediation and Arbitration 298

Lawyers and Lawsuits: Going to Court 301

    Typical Legal Claims in an Unmarried Dissolution 301

    Basic Rules for Going to Court 302

Solutions for Typical Property Division Problems 303

Tenants: Who Gets the Rental? 304

Homeowners: Dividing the House 305

    Who Owns the House? 306

    If One Partner Will Sell to the Other 307

    If Both Partners Will Sell the Property to a Third Party 311

    Dividing Other Real Estate 312

Foreclosure Divorce: Dealing With the Underwater House 312

Other Financial Assets and Liabilities 314

Putting It All Together: Preparing a Settlement Agreement........................... 316

Children: Custody, Visitation, and Support... 316

Your Rights Under the Law 319

Parenting Agreements 324

FORMS IN THIS CHAPTER

Chapter 10 includes instructions for and samples of the following forms:

- Short-Term Agreement Regarding Separation and Housing
- Agreement to Protect Property During a Breakup
- Agreement to Mediate and Arbitrate
- Home Buyout Agreement (One Co-Owner Sells to the Other)

The Nolo website includes downloadable copies of these forms. See the appendix for the link to the forms in this book.

In addition, this chapter includes several sample agreements: Sample Settlement Agreement, Sample Parenting Agreement (Both Parents Are Legal Parents), and Sample Parenting Agreement (Only One Parent Is a Legal Parent).

Despite your best intentions—just as is true for your married counterparts—statistics suggest that your relationship may not last forever. The anger and sense of loss that so often accompany a separation cannot be overcome by any law or counsel; emotional crises are best addressed through the help of friends, family, and therapists.

On the legal front, however, breaking up can be a lot easier for unmarried couples than going through a divorce. As long as you and your ex can agree on how to divide up your assets, there is no need to involve lawyers or the court system. Even if children are involved, in most states you have the opportunity to figure out the terms of your separation in private, according to whatever arrangements the two of you agree on.

But, if you and your ex are unable to resolve your disputes in an amicable fashion, you may end up in court. This can often be very difficult, because the codified divorce procedures that apply to married couples do not apply to unmarried folks.

This chapter will help you tackle the business of breaking up and minimize the likelihood of an ugly court battle. It covers:

- the laws that affect your separation
- the various stages of a breakup and the procedures and tasks involved with separating, such as dividing joint assets
- alternative dispute resolution methods, such as mediation, collaboration, and arbitration, and how these methods can help resolve conflicts, such as property disputes, faster, less expensively, and usually more fairly than a court fight
- basic guidelines for litigating your dispute in court, if it comes to that
- legal rules that cover property-related disputes
- how to prepare a settlement agreement, and
- custody issues facing separating parents.

SEE AN EXPERT

Expert advice may be necessary. When substantial assets or children are involved, consult an experienced attorney or financial adviser before agreeing about major issues of custody, property settlement, or support.

Why Living Together Agreements Are So Important If You Separate

Repeatedly throughout this book, we urge unmarried couples to prepare written agreements covering your property, your home, and other important issues. Properly written living together agreements are legally enforceable in court. Most important, a written living together agreement can minimize the potential of even going to court. The agreements in this book provide the basic framework for dividing property, deciding who lives where, and who gets what, and handling disputes out of court through mediation and arbitration.

Without a written agreement, separation will be more difficult, particularly if you have lived together a long time, or a lot of money or property is involved and your split is not amicable. In this case, you'll definitely want to consult an attorney or financial adviser.

Rules of the Unmarried Dissolution

While the specific rules differ slightly from state to state, the basic legal principles that regulate the property rights of unmarried couples differ from those governing married couples. Here's how.

Divorce Laws

Laws governing married couples who divorce (generally labeled marital or family law) do not apply to unmarried couples who separate—with the exception of unmarried couples living in a state that recognizes common law marriage (see Chapter 2) who qualify under their state rules, or those who have registered as domestic partners in those states that offer marriage-equivalent registration for opposite-sex couples.

The one exception is Washington State, which applies a presumption that family law rules are applicable to nonmarital dissolutions—with the opportunity for either partner to demonstrate why such rules should not apply in their particular case.

Ownership of Property and Debts

Each unmarried partner is presumed to own his or her own property and debts unless you've deliberately combined your assets (such as opening a joint account or putting both names on a deed to your home). This differs from married couples, for whom any debt or asset acquired by either spouse during marriage will usually be considered jointly owned in the event of a dissolution—unless the parties signed a prenuptial agreement modifying these rules.

The legal presumption of separate property ownership of the assets of unmarried partners can generally be overcome by a written agreement to share assets; in many states a proven oral or implied-from-the-circumstances agreement to share assets can also be enforced by the courts (although this can be extremely difficult if there is no written contract).

Where it's established that an unmarried couple's assets are jointly owned (for example, when both names are on a deed), the assets are presumed to be owned in equal 50-50 shares unless there is proof of a different agreement or, in some instances, where one partner clearly made a greater contribution and can prove it.

Courts Handling Disputes

The property aspects of your dispute will generally be handled by the ordinary "business" section of your state's civil courts, just as though you were going through a business dissolution. This means in most places you aren't entitled to any special mediation services or expedited hearings, which are common in divorce court, unless you have child custody or child support conflicts (these will most often be handled by the family law division of your local court). Interestingly, it also means that you are entitled to have a jury rule on your disputes, which is rarely the case with married couples.

Alimony

In most states, the standard rule is that neither unmarried partner is entitled to receive any alimony-type of support after a breakup unless there is proof of a clear agreement to provide postseparation support; in some states this must be a written agreement. The fact that one of you supported the other one during your relationship or that you signed wills providing for each other upon death generally is irrelevant to a claim for support unless you can prove that a contract to provide support after separation existed. For married couples, on the other hand, if either party has been financially dependent on the other, or if one person earns significantly more than the other after the breakup, the judge can order the higher earner to pay alimony (spousal support or maintenance) to the lower earner.

Interestingly, several years ago a report by the American Law Institute, an influential organization of lawyers, judges, and legal scholars, recommended sweeping changes in family law, including extending alimony-like payments to unmarried couples living together who split up after a long time. Few if any states are considering instituting any of these proposals, however, and we don't expect that to change, especially now that same-sex marriage is legal. In California and a few other states, state-registered civil union or domestic partners will be entitled to sue for alimony from their partners—but the law covers only same-sex couples and opposite-sex couples in which one partner is over 62.

Child Custody and Support

If you are jointly raising children and you are both legal parents, your marital status is irrelevant and normally you have the opportunity to work out a joint custody and support agreement without court intervention. And if you end up in court, the issues of custody, visitation, and child support will be handled just as they are for married couples. If only one of you is the legal parent (because the other parent did not adopt the child), in most states the nonlegal parent will have no right to future custody or visitation of the child, and will have no duty to support the child.

The Process of Separation

Now that you know the basic rules, you are ready to navigate the potentially troubled waters of dissolving your relationship. This section covers the chronological steps most unmarried couples follow after their decision to separate. The more you are able to keep the emotional dramas separate from the practical aspects of separation, the more likely you are to reach a fair and amicable settlement (easier said than done, we know).

> TIP
>
> **Consider the children.** If you have children, bend over backwards to reach amicable and realistic decisions about their custody and care. Remember, children are the truly needy members of your family, and they should come first. Getting the help of an experienced family mediator is often essential. There's more about kids below.

Prebreakup Tasks

If you are the one who is initiating the dissolution or you sense that the sky is about to fall, it is highly sensible to take preseparation precautions —especially if the breakup is not mutual. Here is a list of the tasks that may apply to your situation:

Review any living together, house ownership, or property agreements you have. In the best case scenario, you already have a written agreement that covers the division of property and separation issues. If so, read it carefully, and determine what must be done, including mediation (if necessary), in accordance with that agreement.

Organize financial documents and records. Locate the critical documents of your joint financial lives, make copies, and store them in a safe place. This includes joint bank and brokerage accounts, property deeds, business records, insurance policies, credit card information, tax returns, title certificates for cars, leases, investment records, promissory notes, and wills.

Protect physical and virtual assets. Secure valuable items of personal property, such as precious art or irreplaceable family heirlooms, if you believe your partner may try to sell or take them. Change your passwords on your email and bank accounts so that you can maintain privacy in the management of your affairs during and after separation.

> EXAMPLE: Jon and Marie are constantly fighting. Marie is worried that Jon, who has lost his job, may simply leave, taking with him all their valuables. To prevent this, she asks a trusted mutual friend to hold their artwork and her family silver. Then, she sends the oriental rugs out for cleaning and arranges to have them stored temporarily at the cleaners. Finally, she locks other valuables in a storage locker and gives the only set of keys to a neighbor she trusts completely.

Make an exit plan. Start thinking about who is going to live where. If you have a friend or close relative you can easily stay with for a while, make some tentative arrangements. Be careful, however, that you don't vacate your residence to such an extent that your partner could claim you've abandoned all rights of possession of your property. Continue to pay your share of the expenses, even if you aren't living there, until you and your partner agree otherwise in writing. And, continue to pick up your mail and check on the condition of the property, especially if you co-own the property.

Research the law. Find out how the law in your state handles the key elements of unmarried dissolutions. Start by reading "Rules of the Unmarried Dissolution," above, if you haven't already. If you have children or significant assets (especially if you have not signed written agreements), you may need to do more research or consult a lawyer. Chapter 11 shows how to do so.

Minimize spending. Avoid any new financial ventures with your partner, such as putting large sums of money into his or her business or into a joint bank account, agreeing to jointly incur a big debt such as a major renovation, or taking out a new line of credit on your house. If you have a significant amount of money in a joint account or a high limit on a joint credit card, consider closing these accounts or reducing their size. But in doing so, be sure you act fairly, in a manner that assures your partner that you are not trying to take anything that may belong to him or her.

If you are concerned about domestic violence, take steps to protect yourself. (See "If Your Partner Turns Violent," below.)

Immediate Breakup Issues

Once the bad news has been declared, or if you are undergoing an interim "trial" separation, each of you will face a series of practical, as well as emotional, challenges. While every dissolution presents its own list of property-related issues, here are a few simple guidelines that should help you manage the separation:

Immediately close all joint credit cards and bank accounts. If you have joint financial assets (for example, a joint brokerage account) you don't want to risk losing, immediately put them in a blocked account that requires both signatures for a withdrawal. If you haven't done so already,

If Your Partner Turns Violent

If your partner has been physically abusive in the past or you suspect your partner may become violent as you're separating, take steps to protect yourself.

While you're still living together, have a departure plan and place to go on short notice. Alert a friend or neighbor of the possibility that you may show up without warning. To facilitate a quick exit (if necessary), keep a set of keys and some cash either on your person or with a friend.

If your partner has moved out, change all the locks and consider buying an alarm system; get a new (unlisted) phone number and a private email account. Change the passwords on all your important accounts, especially your bank accounts.

Call the police if you feel threatened or have been a victim of violence. This is important for your physical safety, but will also be useful evidence if you want to obtain a temporary restraining order (TRO)—a decree issued by a court that requires the perpetrator to stop abusing you. The TRO may require, for example, that your ex stay away from your home and place of work. The order will also prohibit further acts of violence. Make sure your neighbors and coworkers know about the restraining order (and what your ex looks like) so they can call the police if he shows up at your home or office.

It's often a simple process to obtain a TRO. You can pick up the necessary forms at any police department, crisis intervention center, domestic violence organization, or, often, at the courthouse. While a TRO isn't a guarantee of safety, in most instances it can be very effective.

Once a court issues a temporary restraining order, a copy will be delivered to the batterer ordering him (or her) to stay away from you. A date will be set for the batterer to appear in court at which time a judge will decide whether to issue a permanent restraining order.

For more information, see Domestic Violence in the Divorce and Family Law section of Nolo's website at www .nolo.com. For referrals to local domestic violence resources, contact a local police department, crisis intervention center, social service organization, or battered women's shelter. Other useful resources are the National Domestic Violence Hotline (800-799-7233 or www.thehotline. org) and the National Coalition Against Domestic Violence (www.ncadv.org).

go back and read Chapter 4, which covers basic debt and credit issues involving unmarried couples. Also, "Solutions for Typical Property Division Problems," below, discusses how to deal with joint bank accounts, joint credit accounts, and other assets and liabilities. Change the passwords on your personal accounts.

Pay the bills. Make a list of the bills it is essential to pay, such as home insurance, utilities, and the car and mortgage payments. Create arrangements (together if possible) to keep these bills current. If money is tight, decide jointly which bills can be postponed.

Preserve your digital privacy. Increasingly these days we are seeing people acting in a hostile manner to disrupt their partner's electronic privacy. This can happen in many different ways—snooping into a partner's private emails, withdrawing funds from the other's account, blocking the partner's access to their own information, or deleting important documents from the other's files. It's crucial that you change your passwords promptly, to minimize the potential damage that an angry ex-partner can cause.

> **TIP**
>
> **A friend can help keep essential bills current.** If communication between you and your ex has completely broken down, ask a trusted friend to collect the necessary money from both of you and pay the most important bills. By following this approach you may still lose your mate, but you won't lose your house, find yourself uninsured, or end up (literally) in the dark. Alternatively, set up automatic deposits into the joint account, and auto-payments of the essential bills from the joint account.

Figure out who is going to live where in the short term and write up an agreement on how you are going to handle the costs and logistics of your decision. If you jointly own a house and one of you has agreed to move out, make it clear that a temporary departure is not a permanent abandonment of the residence. Also, decide whether the temporarily absent partner should pay any portion of the mortgage or insurance costs. If you are renters, you may need to decide whose name is going to stay on the lease and who is entitled to a return of the security deposit and how the combined rental expenses are going to be allocated. You may have already addressed these issues, such as who gets to keep the house or apartment, when you moved in together, using one of the agreements in Chapter 5 (renters) or Chapter 6 (homeowners). If not, go back and reread these chapters. Also, see "Solutions for Typical Property Division Problems," below, which covers housing issues for tenants and homeowners when separating.

You can use the Short-Term Agreement Regarding Separation and Housing shown below as a template for preparing an agreement to handle your interim housing affairs. If you wish, you can add or substitute other clauses, such as a more detailed mediation and arbitration clause, from the agreements in Chapters 5 and 6.

FORMS
The Nolo website includes a downloadable copy of the Short-Term Agreement Regarding Separation and Housing shown below. See the appendix for the link to this form.

Make some reasonable, practical decisions about the furniture and personal possessions. You may have already addressed these issues (what property is separate, what is jointly owned, who gets to keep what if you break up) in one of the property agreements included in Chapter 3. Whether or not you have a written agreement, don't feel compelled to sort everything out the moment you break up. Unless an object was clearly purchased by one person alone and was never gifted to the other partner, deciding who gets what may not be so simple. Valuable items, such as precious art or irreplaceable family heirlooms, should be handled with some thought. If one of you fears that the other may take or sell your personal belongings, it may be a good idea to put your possessions into a limited-entry storage locker for a few months or have a friend store them for you. (If you're really concerned, you might do this as one of your prebreakup tasks.) If you want to be a real stickler, prepare an Agreement to Protect Property During a Breakup, such as the sample shown below.

Short-Term Agreement Regarding Separation and Housing

___Sally Herendeen___ and ___Scott Spencer___ agree as follows:

1. We have agreed to live apart, effective___July 1, 20xx___.

2. ___Sally___ will remain in our apartment at ___145 Spruce Street, Cleveland, Ohio___ and ___Scott___ agrees to move out no later than ___July 14, 20xx___. If ___Scott___ elects to leave any of his ~~or her~~ personal belongings behind, he ~~or she~~ will remove them no later than ___August 1, 20xx___, at his ~~or her~~ expense, giving ___Sally___ ___three days___ prior notice of time of pickup. Any of ___Scott's___ personal belongings that he ~~or she~~ does not remove prior to ___August 1___ may be retained or disposed of by ___Sally___, unless we jointly agree in writing to another plan.

3. Any household expenses incurred prior to___July 1, 20xx___ will be split between us, following our usual allocation. Any household expenses incurred after ___July 1, 20xx___ will be the sole responsibility of ___Sally___, even if ___Scott___ remains until ___July 15___.

4. Housing costs after that date will be split as follows [*complete (a) or (b) depending on whether you rent or own your home together*]:

   ☐ (a) Renters

   ___Sally___ will be solely responsible for any and all rent due on or after ___July 1, 20xx___. The security deposit in the sum of $ ___1,000___ will be retained by___Sally___, in exchange for the agreement to pay the utility bills, telephone bills, and insurance incurred on or after___July 1, 20xx___. Scott will pay his own rental expenses.

   ☐ (b) Homeowners

   Bills and expenses. Effective ___[date]___, since ___[name]___ will be living in the residence, he or she will pay all monthly bills, including mortgage payments, insurance, utilities, and day-to-day maintenance costs (to unplug a toilet, for example). Property taxes and all necessary major repairs (to fix a leak in the roof or replace the furnace, for example) will be split by us equally. So long as we both continue to pay our share of these major expenses, we both shall be entitled to half of any increase in property values between ___[date]___ and the time the house is sold.

House ownership. We both agree to make a good faith effort to promptly resolve the issue of which of us will continue to own the residence long-term (or whether it will be sold). _[name]_ agreement to vacate the residence at this time shall not be interpreted as a waiver of his or her claim to an equal share of the equity, either through a buyout or a market sale. Unless an agreement is reached by __[date]__ or we agree jointly in writing to extend this agreement, the property shall be listed for sale on __[date]__ and, after paying off the mortgage and other house-related debts, the proceeds of sale shall be split equally between us.

5. Any disputes arising out of this agreement will be submitted first to mediation. We both agree to meet in good faith with a mediator for no fewer than _____ meetings in a month's time, with expenses to be shared equally. If any disputes remain unresolved after the mediation, the disputes will be submitted to binding arbitration, with the costs of the arbitration split equally between us. By agreeing to arbitration, we each agree to give up the right to a jury trial.

Sally Herendeen   _July 1, 20xx_
Signature   Date

Scott Spencer   _July 1, 20xx_
Signature   Date

📄 FORMS

The Nolo website includes a downloadable copy of the Agreement to Protect Property During a Breakup shown below. See the appendix for the link to this form.

Agreement to Protect Property During a Breakup

___Sally Herendeen___ and ___Scott Spencer___ agree as follows:

1. We disagree over who has the right to retain the following items of personal property: ___three oriental rugs, two Peggy Hopper serigraphs, and china set___.

2. In order to resolve this dispute, we have agreed to place these items in storage at the ___AAA Storage Locker in Cleveland, Ohio___. ___Scott___ will pay the monthly cost of storage, and our friend ___Suzanna Freed___ will retain the only key. Neither of us will attempt to gain access to this locker or remove any items from it until we have resolved this dispute.

3. If we are unable to resolve this dispute within ___three months___ of today, we will attempt to resolve the dispute in mediation, meeting with a mediator chosen by ___Suzanna___ and approved by both of us. If mediation does not result in a settlement, after two mediation sessions we will submit the dispute to binding arbitration, with the arbitrator chosen by ___Suzanna___ and approved by both of us.

4. Upon settlement of the dispute or receipt of the arbitrator's decision ___Suzanna___ will open the locker and we will each take the items awarded to us or as agreed upon by us.

Sally Herendeen	_July 1, 20xx_
Signature	Date
Scott Spencer	_July 1, 20xx_
Signature	Date

Deal with pets. Don't let your own emotional turmoil put your pets' well-being at risk. Unless your dog or cat clearly belongs to one person, follow a "best interests of the pet" approach, and attempt to agree on a living arrangement that is really in the animal's best interests. If one of you is getting custody of your pet, you should either make a financial adjustment (to allow the other party to buy an equivalent new pet) or agree on regular visitation. If significant medical bills for your pet are anticipated, try to work out a fair allocation of these as well. Be sensible here!

Try to assess whether there are longer-term disputes, and if so acknowledge to each other that it is okay to disagree for the time being. If you can both admit that there are conflicts that must be resolved a little later (and, as discussed below, agree on mediation as a method to resolve them), you will feel far more at ease—and less desperate to sort everything out the day you leave.

Ten Steps to Resolving Your Conflicts

After you've actually separated and each of you has reached some degree of emotional and physical stability, you should find it much easier to resolve any remaining areas of conflict. While each breakup comes with its unique disputes, there are a few general rules and procedures that you will probably want to follow.

It often helps to begin by conceptualizing the dissolution process as a series of tasks best handled over time (not as one impossibly large basket of jumbled tasks). True, even when approached sequentially, several of the component tasks may still seem daunting. But as long as you have confidence that you are making progress along a fairly predictable path, you are likely to feel less angry or discouraged. And remember, along with the freedom of not being married comes the responsibility of managing one's breakup without the burdensome legal rules of divorce.

Here, then, are the major paths (and some alternative steps) you can follow to resolve disputes:

1. The first big step is to make a clear list of the remaining issues each of you believes need to be resolved—from who owns what furniture to who gets to keep the apartment.

> **TIP**
>
> **Never argue over what to argue over.** At this beginning stage, any item that is on either partner's list should be treated as a problem that needs to be resolved. There will be plenty of time to eliminate seemingly trivial issues later.

2. The easiest and most direct way to resolve your conflicts is to negotiate with each other directly. See "The Power of Talk," below.

3. Decide which of several available procedures you are going to use to attempt to resolve the disputes you can't work out without help (for example, mediation or arbitration). Once you agree on the method you'll use to resolve your disputes, put your plans in writing and sign the document so you can move on to tackle the substantive issues. The Agreement to Mediate and Arbitrate form, shown below, can get you started.

4. Take stock of the emotional barriers that may prevent resolution (maybe you blame your ex for the breakup), and try as hard as you can to overcome them or at least put them to the side while you are focusing on the practical tasks. In addition to mediation, this may require formal separation counseling or meeting at a "safe place" with a trusted mutual friend or spiritual counselor who can help you calm your anger.

5. Figure out a realistic pace and timetable for resolving your substantive disputes. Commit to a schedule of meetings, phone calls, or emails, and then make a conscious effort to keep the ball rolling.

6. Attempt to limit your discussions to practical items such as who will get to keep certain property. Focus on finding solutions, not

allocating blame. Don't view your meetings as an opportunity to try to resolve the emotional rifts of your dissolution (any separation counseling should take place at another time). This is especially true in email communication—stick to the essential factual issues and leave your emotional rants to another day (and in another arena).

7. Educate and empower yourselves to handle property disputes rationally and competently. For example, for house-related disputes you may need to get an appraisal or learn the exact process of transferring title. For automobile disputes, you will want to determine the car's actual sales value and obtain a form from the state for transferring ownership. For couples with major assets (especially those that have increased in value), a visit to a tax consultant or financial adviser may be necessary.

The Power of Talk

Whether you choose to meet face to face or to communicate in writing, by phone, or by email, direct negotiation is likely to be the cheapest and quickest approach if—and only if—you are both able to follow these simple rules:

- Schedule face-to-face discussions ahead of time, being careful to pick a location and method that ensures privacy, concentration, and a calm interchange. Don't talk about heavy topics in the middle of the workday or when one of you is tired or stressed.
- Do your homework in advance (for example, arrange to have your house appraised before you meet), and don't be afraid to postpone a discussion if you need more information. But don't delay for more than a few days—or cancel meetings without a good reason—or your former partner is likely to jump to the conclusion that you are stalling.
- Keep good notes of your discussions, and promptly write down and sign any agreements you reach, even if you use a coffee-stained paper napkin to record the agreement.

SEE AN EXPERT

Check out the possible tax implications of your separation. Separating couples are often tempted to value assets and divide them 50-50 (or according to some other percentage that they agree is fair). But before you do this, consider the tax consequences. If your assets have appreciated (for example, the value of your stock in XYZ Corp. has tripled), the person who gets the asset may have to pay tax on it when sold. This can result in an unfair distribution between the partners because the other partner doesn't bear the tax burden. Also, if one partner transfers an asset to the other partner, the partner making the transfer may be subject to gift tax and the recipient may be subject to capital gains tax—taxes that married couples transferring assets don't face. In some states, significant tax penalties are imposed whenever real estate interests are transferred between unmarried partners.

The bottom line: Before splitting assets, get tax advice from an expert. For an overview of the issues involved when splitting assets that have appreciated, see *Divorce and Money*, by Violet Woodhouse (Nolo). Though geared toward divorcing couples, this book provides valuable advice for unmarried couples as well.

8. Figure out your starting negotiating position. Don't just focus on what you want or believe that you deserve: you also need to evaluate the likely outcomes for each area of dispute in the context of what it could cost to mount a serious court battle; for example, you may decide that accepting 40% instead of 50% of the amount in dispute makes more sense than engaging in protracted litigation. Once you determine your own bottom line, it's usually best to keep it to yourself—at least for a while. It's often unwise to offer too big a compromise too soon—unless your ex is really willing to settle all disputes quickly and reasonably. Better to ask for something closer to what you'd like to receive, and then be prepared to offer a series of small concessions, hoping your partner will begin to do the same, allowing you to work together to find common ground.

9. Assuming you agree on at least some things, start by writing them down. Then, as you work out the rest of the issues in dispute, add these to your "agreed-upon" list so that you gradually build

a comprehensive agreement. If your agreement is fairly short, a simple exchange of letters or emails is perfectly legal, as long as it is clear at the end of the day what you both agreed to.

Once you have settled a number of issues, prepare a written settlement agreement, such as the one shown below in "Putting It All Together: Preparing a Settlement Agreement."

10. Last, but certainly not least, you need to conscientiously implement your agreement. This means promptly completing and signing all the paperwork required to record and carry out its provisions. For items such as furniture and art objects, it may simply be a matter of hiring a mover. For financial accounts, a joint letter to the bank or the stock broker will usually be sufficient. For real estate transfers, a more formal set of tasks awaits you, as discussed below.

Mediation, Arbitration, and Other Ways to Resolve Disputes

Some couples can do all the heavy lifting of separating their lives themselves with no help from outsiders, while others may need to use one or two formal dispute resolution methods at different stages of their separation. It should go almost without saying that the more jointly owned property you have, the longer it can take to pull everything apart—particularly if you're starting from scratch and you have no written agreement spelling out ownership issues.

If either of you has trouble staying focused on the practical issues involved in your breakup or you can't avoid gut-wrenching psychodramas, you will probably need to ask a neutral third party—or sometimes two neutral parties—to moderate and structure your conversation, or work with an attorney who can serve as your advocate. This can be done in several different ways. The major factors to consider in choosing the right approach are:

- cost
- time (avoiding long delays)
- available dispute-resolution resources, and
- the need for special expertise (for example, dividing ownership of a good-sized business).

This section discusses alternatives to traditional court proceedings, such as mediation and arbitration. These are commonly known as alternative dispute resolution or ADR.

Informal Negotiation Through Third Parties

If either of you believes it's too emotionally difficult to negotiate directly with each other, each of you can select an advocate or representative who will then talk to each other without either of you being present. The advocates can exchange letters, emails, or phone calls or meet face to face. This kind of shuttle diplomacy is basically what lawyers do, but there is nothing wrong with having a trusted (and clearheaded) friend, real estate broker, or accountant play this role. Of course, all key decisions must eventually be made, or at least ratified, by you and your former partner. While turning negotiations over to representatives can be a slow process, it can work very well when your dispute centers on just a few practical issues (for example, the value of a business or real estate). But be sensitive to the fact that, especially if you hire lawyers to do this task, you want peacemakers, not warriors, and you need to watch the clock (as otherwise your legal fees can mount up fast).

Another approach is to hire lawyers who work collaboratively. Oftentimes they will schedule negotiating meetings with both of you present, so you can participate as well. This can facilitate a much quicker and more considerate resolution of disputed issues.

Mediation

Mediation is a nonadversarial process where a neutral person (a mediator) helps you settle your differences. Mediation is often used to help separating couples work out problems concerning division of property and issues involving children.

With mediation, the two of you get together to talk face to face about your disagreements, with a neutral mediator working to help you find realistic solutions. Sometimes the mediator will meet separately with each party and convey the positions back and forth. No one has the power to impose a solution—rather, you must work out your own agreement voluntarily. Unlike a judge, the mediator's role is to help you and your partner find common ground. When this happens, both parties usually feel like their dispute was resolved fairly, and a good foundation is laid for future cooperation. This approach is especially important if you have children. In addition, mediation often costs less than either an arbitration or court proceeding and, unlike going to court, is conducted in private.

Each of you can come into the mediation solo, or you can each bring an advocate along—either a friend or an attorney, depending on how complex your disagreements are. You also may want to bring along an advocate if your ex has better negotiation skills or more financial savvy. Make sure you let the mediator and your ex know in advance that you are bringing an advocate to the mediation session.

Mediation—which allows disputants to express personal and emotional issues, but eventually focus on practical ones—can produce great results, and it almost always moves more quickly than a protracted exchange of written communications. The key is to have a good mediator and to allow enough time to air your conflicts and find solutions. In this context, a series of shorter mediation sessions works best for some people, while half-day or even daylong sessions may be very useful if complicated property ownership issues must be resolved.

If your partner is refusing to try mediation, you might try to emphasize that agreeing to mediation is not an agreement to any particular outcome. It doesn't even guarantee that an agreement will be reached, although mediation is very often successful. Your partner should simply understand that mediation is the cheapest and quickest—and most humane—way to resolve conflicts.

Make sure to select a mediator you both have confidence in (and that you believe is neutral)—someone with the background and experience necessary to help you settle the issues in your case. The needs of a couple trying to resolve a dispute about real estate will differ from those of a couple fighting over the car and a few household possessions or from a couple grappling with custody issues. The mediator need not be an attorney, though it is often helpful to use a lawyer mediator if there are complex legal or property issues to be resolved. Custody issues are generally resolved with the help of a therapist or social worker mediators.

Even though the mediator is not providing you with legal advice, it's useful to be working with someone who is familiar with issues you are grappling with. To find a good mediator, get references from people you trust—friends, relatives, colleagues, or a trusted attorney. Depending on your situation, you may want to contact a community agency that offers mediation, usually by trained volunteers. Private practice attorney or therapist mediators are another option.

Remember to document any settlement you reach in a clear written agreement. Most mediators will help you draft the settlement agreement, or will do it themselves.

Once you have your agreement in writing, your contract is enforceable in court just like any other binding agreement.

RESOURCE

Mediation requires advance preparation and thought. From jointly agreeing on a good mediator, through planning your mediation strategy (for example, understanding your bottom line), to writing up the final agreement, you need to understand exactly what is happening and why. Information about mediation is available online from Nolo's website at www.nolo.com, under the heading "Small Claims Court and Lawsuits." An excellent source of more thorough information is *Mediate, Don't Litigate*, by Peter Lovenheim and Lisa Guerin, available as an e-book at www.nolo.com. Also, *Divorce Without Court: A Guide to Mediation & Collaborative Divorce*, by Katherine Stoner (Nolo), provides excellent advice on mediation that applies to unmarried couples as well as a married couple going through a divorce. While the legal aspects of your breakup will not be the same as those faced by married people, many of the emotional, practical, and financial issues are the same. Finally, if you have children, be sure to see *Building a Parenting Agreement That Works: Child Custody Agreements Step by Step*, by Mimi Lyster Zemmelman (Nolo). This book includes valuable advice on how mediation can help resolve custody and visitation disputes.

Arbitration

If mediation fails to resolve a dispute, arbitration often is the next best choice. Arbitration is best understood as a kind of private trial, but one that is quicker, less formal, and almost always cheaper than courtroom litigation. You sign an agreement to submit your dispute to a neutral decision maker (called an "arbitrator"), and agree to abide by the arbitrator's decision. Normally, arbitration awards are binding and not appealable. In order to make arbitration effective, you will need to reach agreement on the following before the arbitration hearing:

- **Set a timeline.** Agree on a rough timetable for bringing the disputes to a conclusion. Even though the precise date of the arbitration hearing can't be set until you select your arbitrator, try to get a clear sense of how many weeks or possibly months this process is going to take.

- **Select the arbitrator.** You can delegate the process of selecting an arbitrator to a friend or an attorney or your mediator if you have met with one, use a local arbitration agency business that will propose a list of arbitrators (with each party having the right to strike those who seem unfair or unqualified), or jointly pick a person. If you don't know much about a proposed arbitrator, check the person's references and level of expertise in handling your type of dispute.

- **Set the rules.** Sign a written agreement stating that you will abide by the arbitrator's decision, and agree to waive any rights to appeal. In most states, arbitration agreements can be enforced through the local courts, so you have a practical and cost-effective remedy if your ex doesn't comply with the arbitrator's order.

- **Decide on advocates.** Decide whether you can each bring an attorney or advocate with you to the arbitration hearing. Most folks prefer to retain the right to bring an attorney or an advocate to the hearing, even if they decide not to do so at the last minute. If you are easily intimidated by your ex or have trouble expressing yourself in a stressful situation, having an advocate will help. But if you are able to represent your position effectively and want to avoid the expense and adversarial climate that can result from bringing a lawyer, consider handling the hearing on your own. And even if you attend the hearing on your own, consider meeting with an attorney in advance to help you get prepared to present your case.

- **Agree on the issues in dispute.** Before you go into arbitration, if at all possible, make a shared list of the principal issues that need to be resolved. Acknowledge that new issues may arise later, but try to be as specific as you can about what it is you are fighting over, so both of you come prepared to discuss those issues.
- **Conduct your investigation.** Decide whether either of you needs to conduct any investigation or obtain copies of documents or other information before the hearing. For example, if only one of you has access to the real estate, financial, or business-related documents, you may need to agree to full disclosure of all key information as part of your agreement to arbitrate.
- **Decide who pays.** The arbitrator will charge by the hour, and typically each party foots half the bill. Often it's best for each side to pay their own fees, but this may not be the case if one party feels particularly aggrieved or has a lower income. An alternative is to empower the arbitrator to award attorneys' fees or arbitration costs to the prevailing party at the conclusion of the hearing.

How to Make an Agreement to Use Mediation and Arbitration

After you have decided what procedures the two of you are going to use to resolve your conflicts, you should prepare an agreement setting out how you want to move forward and what disputes you will be resolving. A sample Agreement to Mediate and Arbitrate is shown below. You can tailor it to your own situation.

FORMS
The Nolo website includes a downloadable copy of the Agreement to Mediate and Arbitrate shown below. See the appendix for the link to this form.

Agreement to Mediate and Arbitrate

_____Eric Stall_____ and _____Kate Pulis_____ agree as follows:

1. We have agreed to submit the following disputes to mediation, and if mediation is unsuccessful, to arbitration:

   a. Ownership of our residence in Orlando, Florida, including the disposition of the residence and our mutual claims for reimbursement for contributions made to the purchase and upkeep of the residence

   b. Ownership of our one automobile (2008 Toyota Corolla), including disposition of the automobile and our mutual claims for reimbursement for contributions made to its purchase and upkeep

   c. Kate's claim for reimbursement for money paid to City College in connection with Eric's education, and

   d. Eric's claim for a partial ownership interest in Kate's accounting business

   _____ .

2. We agree to discuss these areas of dispute in mediation, as follows:

   a. We will try to select a mediator jointly, and if no mediator is selected by _____April 1, 20xx_____ , each one of us will nominate one friend, and the two of them shall select the mediator.

   b. We shall meet no fewer than _____three_____ times to mediate, within _____6 weeks_____ of the selection of a mediator, with all costs of mediation split equally between us. The mediator will determine the time and place of each meeting. Each session will be at least two hours long.

   c. Until we reach an agreement, any compromise offers or proposals presented by either of us shall be confidential and, if mediation fails, will not to be disclosed to anyone else or used in any subsequent arbitration or court proceeding.

   d. If an agreement is reached, it shall be set out in writing and signed by both of us. If either of us fails to abide by it and an attorney is needed to enforce its terms in court, the prevailing party shall have the right to reimbursement of attorney's fees.

3. If after we mediate on ___three___ occasions no settlement is reached and we elect not to schedule any more mediation sessions, either of us may require arbitration by sending a written arbitration request to the other. If this occurs:

   a. We will jointly select an arbitrator who will conduct an arbitration under the rules of the American Arbitration Association. If for any reason we can't agree on an arbitrator within ___one month___ of the written demand for arbitration, ___Judge Marilyn Strauss of our local county court___ will select the arbitrator. By agreeing to arbitration, we each agree to give up the right to a jury trial.

   b. The costs of the arbitration will be split equally between the two of us. If either of us wishes to, she or he may bring an attorney to the hearing; however, each of us will be solely responsible for any attorneys' fees we incur.

   c. Each of us will provide the other with copies of all documents relevant to these disputes at least ___two weeks___ prior to the arbitration proceeding. At the same time, each of us will supply the other with a list of all witnesses who will be asked to testify at the arbitration hearing.

   d. The decision of the arbitrator will be binding, and either of us may enforce it through the local trial court if the other does not comply with its terms. If an attorney is needed to enforce the arbitration decision, the prevailing party will have the right to reimbursement of his or her attorney's fees incurred specifically for this purpose.

Eric Stall
Signature

March 20, 20xx
Date

Kate Palis
Signature

March 20, 20xx
Date

Lawyers and Lawsuits: Going to Court

If you can't even agree about setting up a mediation or arbitration procedure to settle your dispute or if one party is particularly aggressive, the courts may be your only resort. Litigation (an adversarial legal proceeding) is likely to be expensive, ugly, time-consuming, and very depressing, so you should only take this route if all else fails. But when nothing else works and there is a lot of money or property in dispute, going to court at least provides a way to resolve your conflicts.

TIP

Small claims court may be an option—if your suit involves a relatively small amount of money (generally, less than $7,500). For an overview of small claims court, see the "Small Claims Court and Lawsuits" section of Nolo's website at www.nolo.com. Nolo also publishes a complete book on the subject of bringing or defending a small claims court case, *Everybody's Guide to Small Claims Court*, by Ralph Warner. California residents can use *Everybody's Guide to Small Claims Court in California*, also by Ralph Warner (Nolo).

CAUTION

Avoid battles of principle. Oftentimes, one or both partners may be inclined to be very rigid, greedy, or vindictive in a breakup. Take our advice and avoid this tendency, no matter how much resentment you might have about past wrongs. Looking back at your breakup even a few years from now, you'll be very grateful if you can say, "We settled our disputes quickly and decently and got on with our lives." It follows that you should look out for any reasonable opportunity to make a deal and move on, even if this means you compromise a little more than you originally intended. If you are using an attorney who wants to win at any cost, find a more conciliatory attorney!

Typical Legal Claims in an Unmarried Dissolution

Here's a brief rundown of the types of claims commonly raised in court in an unmarried dissolution:

- **Breach of contract.** Was there an alleged contract (agreement) for a sharing of funds, debts, or assets written, oral, or implied? If so, which partner breached the contract?
- **Partition of real and personal property.** Who owns what real estate and personal property? How is it to be divided up or sold, and who is to receive what share of the proceeds?
- **Postseparation support.** Does either person claim that an oral or written agreement provides that the other owes him or her post-separation financial support? If so, how much, for how long, and what is the proof that an agreement for the payment of support exists?
- **Personal injury and financial compensation.** Does either partner have valid claims for personal injuries or financial harm, such as the destruction of a valuable possession, the wrongful withdrawal of money from a bank account, or an injury during a domestic violence episode?

Basic Rules for Going to Court

If, despite your best efforts at working out a reasonable compromise, you end up in court, here are a few basic guidelines:

- Find a good attorney experienced in unmarried dissolutions to represent you. Chapter 11 explains how.
- Try to evaluate how your ex is going to respond to the prospect of litigation. With some people the mere mention of going to court will bring them to the bargaining table, but with others it is likely to greatly increase tensions.
- Learn how the litigation process is likely to work to resolve your particular problems. If you are fighting over your house, find out whether there is a local protocol for appraising and dividing up real estate, and how it may affect the outcome. If your dispute concerns joint bank accounts or claims for postseparation support, research how the local courts deal with these issues (in many states, by law, alimony-type support is not ever awarded to unmarried partners). Try to evaluate how the litigation process will actually proceed for your particular case: Do you need to file any papers immediately?

(You might, especially if your name isn't on the title to a property you claim is part yours.) How much pretrial paperwork will there be; how will the trial be handled; will there be a jury? The more you know ahead of time, the better your decision making will be.

- Be honest about the difficulties of prevailing in a formal courthouse setting, especially if you never put your agreement in writing. Don't spend your limited resources on a legally weak claim.
- Make it clear to your lawyer—and frequently remind yourself—that while you are initiating litigation out of frustration or desperation, you will always remain open to compromise. Even after court papers are filed or a trial begins, it is not too late to put the litigation on hold and schedule a mediation session.

RESOURCE

What to do in court. If you're handling your case yourself without a lawyer, you'll probably need lots of help with basic issues, such as where to sit, when to stand, how to cross-examine hostile witnesses, and much more. By far the best book on the subject is *Represent Yourself in Court*, by Paul Bergman and Sara Berman (Nolo).

Solutions for Typical Property Division Problems

The following sections present an overview of legal rules that cover the types of property-related disputes that most frequently arise in unmarried dissolutions. Even though the basic issues unmarried people fight over (property ownership and support) are pretty much the same as those that arise in any divorce court, the law governing property division for unmarried couples differs in several important respects from the laws that control how married couples divorce.

If you have prepared a written living together or property agreement as we recommend in earlier chapters, many of the issues involving who owns what and how your property will be divided at separation should already be addressed.

Tenants: Who Gets the Rental?

For those of you who are renters, your home division process should be fairly simple. You will need to decide who is staying and who is moving on, how you are going to deal with your landlord, who gets the security deposit, and who will pay any debts that arise in the process. If you both plan to move out, be sure to give your landlord proper notice (typically 30 days for a month-to-month rental agreement).

What if you both want to keep the rental? Unless you had an agreement beforehand, generally there is no legal preference for who gets to keep the apartment. As discussed in more detail in Chapter 5, you need to act fairly and rationally (ideally, you should reach your agreement long before the time of separation).

If you lived in the place first, or are the only one who has signed the lease or rental agreement with the landlord and actually pays the monthly rent to the landlord, you probably have first claim on the apartment. If both of you have signed the lease or you both regularly pay rent, your rights to remain in the apartment are probably equal (unless you have a written agreement to the contrary), even if one of you got there first.

Try to talk about your situation, with an eye to allowing the person who genuinely needs the place the most to stay. Bend over backwards to be reasonable about the last month's rent and damage deposits. Sometimes it's fair to agree that the person staying will make a financial contribution to the departing partner's moving costs and perhaps even a portion of the new rent payment (especially if it is significantly higher). The security deposit should be returned to the partner who paid it, or split equally. Even if you end up paying a little more than you think is equitable, it will be well worth it if it helps keep the peace. We've found that the best compromises are made when both people feel they've gone more than halfway. Mediation may help resolve disputes over the rental, as it will give you a chance to reach a mutually satisfactory agreement that is not focused solely on the legal issues.

If both of you have signed the lease, you should jointly talk with the landlord and have the lease rewritten in the name of the remaining party alone. Be sure that the person moving out has a reasonable amount of time to leave, such as three or four weeks. Each person has the right to keep all his or her personal belongings, even if one person is behind in his or her share of the rent. Never lock up or toss out the other person's property.

> ![CAUTION icon] **CAUTION**
>
> **Don't deny your ex access to your shared home except in extreme circumstances.** If you're going to lock a person out, be ready to sign a police complaint, because it may come to that if your former partner uses force to try and get in. Except where a person has no legal right to live on the premises (in other words, the person hasn't signed a rental agreement or lease, hasn't been living with you long, and hasn't paid rent), locking a person out is illegal, and you can be sued for money damages if you try this tactic.

What if one person moves out without paying their share of the rent? As a general rule, each cotenant is 100% liable to the landlord, meaning that if one of you disappears in a huff, the other is on the legal hook for all the rent—but may be able to claim contribution from the other partner/owner. See "Cotenants' Legal Obligations to the Landlord" in Chapter 5 for more on the issue of tenants' "joint and several" liability for paying rent and complying with the lease.

Homeowners: Dividing the House

Life is more complex for separating couples who own a home. If the two of you didn't sign a joint house ownership agreement that sets forth your intentions in case of dissolution, you have two choices. You can either follow the legal procedures that apply in your state—typically this means the court will order the property to be sold, with the net proceeds (after paying mortgages, liens, and costs of sale) to be divided as the judge thinks is fair—or you can reach your own compromise settlement.

In order to sort out who gets what regarding your house, you will need to resolve a few basic issues.

Who Owns the House?

Your first possible conflict may be over who owns what percentage of your house or other real property. Especially if one of you believes he or she owns a larger share, or if only one partner is listed on the deed, this can be difficult if you haven't previously signed a house ownership agreement. Remember that in just about every state, having both names on the deed to the house creates a legal presumption that you are 50-50 owners, and anyone claiming a greater percentage has to prove the existence of an agreement saying so (often in writing). Merely paying more doesn't create an automatic right to a greater ownership share.

Fights frequently arise when your contributions to the property have been unequal. Often a partner who has contributed less financially (say, to the down payment) believes that he or she chipped in something else of equivalent value to the property, such as labor to fix up the house.

Or, they feel that as a "family" everything should be divided equally, regardless of financial contribution. Take into consideration whether either of you has made any significant extra monetary or labor contributions to the property (for example, one of you just paid $15,000 for a new roof, built a garage, or paid the entire mortgage payment for the last three months). If so, be ready to award that person appropriate additional compensation, most often in the form of a reimbursement rather than a greater share of the equity.

When trying to reach an agreement, put aside the most extreme arguments of either person, and acknowledge that there is merit to each side's more rational demands. If conflicts arise over house ownership, it's best to try the following approach to reach a fair settlement regarding these claims:

- Read the discussion on contracts for equal and unequal ownership of a house in Chapter 6 for ideas on how to adjust ownership fairly when one person contributes more to the down payment and the other makes other contributions (money or labor).
- One possibility is to reduce each partner's total contribution (down payments, mortgage payments, labor, improvements) to a dollar figure. By comparing the two figures, you can come up with what percentage of the house each of you owns. If you can't resolve disputes

over the value of your contributions, it often makes sense to get the help of a real estate professional, either an agent or an attorney.

• Narrow the financial gap between the two of your positions by compromising on other demands or making other financial concessions.

• Compare the benefit of splitting the difference to the cost of fighting over every last penny. Hopefully, looking at what will happen if you don't settle will encourage you to come to a compromise figure. If you still can't reach an agreement, convene a single mediation session where you limit your discussion to this one point of disagreement. In most instances you will reach a compromise by the end of the day. If you are still at odds, convene a single short arbitration session where you each present your side of the story, without hiring lawyers, and empower the arbitrator to resolve this financial dispute quickly.

If One Partner Will Sell to the Other

Next, you've got to decide whether you will jointly sell the house to a third party or whether one of you will buy out the other's interest. Usually, it is much easier and cheaper for both of you if one of you sells to the other (rather than selling it to a third party) because you avoid all the costs that accompany a market sale. So if either or both of you are interested in holding on to the real estate you own together, it makes sense to attempt to negotiate a mutually agreeable solution.

Assuming you haven't already agreed (prebreakup) that one person will have first dibs on buying out the other's share in the house, you may use a coin flip or some other simple mechanism to determine who stays and who goes. (These options are included in our house ownership contracts in Chapter 6.) Or, if both of you want to keep the house, you can conduct an informal "auction," where the partner who is willing to pay the most gets to keep the place. You can also use mediation or arbitration to resolve the conflict based on more subjective criteria. An arbitrator can be given the power to decide who should stay (after hearing whatever arguments you each make) and perhaps award the selling partner financial compensation for having to move.

If you can agree on who is going to buy the house but can't agree on a sale price, the best way to set the price is to get an appraisal from an experienced real estate appraiser familiar with the local market. If you can't agree on an appraiser, each of you can get your own appraisal and you can average the results. Or, you can get a less formal opinion from an experienced real estate broker—cheaper, but often less accurate.

Understand that most appraisals estimate the sale price, but do not take into account the cost of selling the property. If you have your jointly owned real estate appraised and then agree that one of you will buy out the other, you may want to reduce the price by the amount of the real estate commission that would be charged if you sold the place to a third party. In other words, even though you won't have to pay a commission when one of you sells to the other, the buying partner will need to do this eventually, so the buyout evaluation probably should reflect this.

In coming up with a buyout price, make sure, in addition to deducting the amount of the broker's commission, you also figure out and deduct the cost of any deferred maintenance that would have to be done if the place was put on the market. Next, of course, subtract the remaining mortgage amount to arrive at your combined "equity." Assuming this is a positive number, this is the sum that you should use to determine the buyout price (which will be 50% of that number if you own the property in equal shares).

> **EXAMPLE:** If the appraiser says your house is worth $400,000 and you still owe $220,000 on your loan, subtract $24,000 for the eventual 6% broker's commission, $15,000 for the necessary presale repairs, and $220,000 for the loan. The resulting amount ($141,000) is the equity which you will need to divide up; if you each own 50% of the place, the buying partner should pay the selling partner half that amount, or $70,500.

Find out from a local broker or attorney what the procedures are for doing an internal buyout, and make sure you take into account the costs of transfer. Some states or counties impose transfer taxes or recordation fees, and these will need to be allocated between the two of you. Often it's best to resolve this issue by agreeing to pay transfer costs and taxes 50-50. In addition, obtain the proper deeds and forms and, if necessary, have a professional help you fill them out. You may not need to use a title company or buy title insurance if your transfer is relatively straightforward and you aren't worried about the selling partner's ability to deliver title to his or her share free of any liens or judgments. If you are worried about possible liens, you will have to go through a title company and purchase title insurance—which can add more than $500 to the cost of transferring title. Either way, once the property has been deeded to one of you, this person will need to record the transfer deed with your local property recorder's office.

Finally, figure out your options regarding your mortgage. Quite often, the selling partner will agree to keep his or her name on the loan, at least for a year or two, in which case the buying partner would not need to obtain a new mortgage; of course, in this case the buying partner should give the selling partner written assurance that the mortgage will get paid each month, to help prevent the selling partner from ending up with a tarnished credit rating or facing a bank's demand for payment. If one partner applies to take his or her name off the loan, in some states and with some banks, the remaining partner can retain the existing loan in his or her own name even after a buyout. (With some loans the selling partner can even be absolved of any further liability.) But in other areas and situations, the buying partner may have to get a new loan. To present a financial statement strong enough to qualify for a new mortgage, the buying partner may need to defer making payments to the selling partner (or make very low payments) for a period of time. If this isn't acceptable to the selling partner, it may be possible for the buying partner to obtain a home equity loan in addition to the first mortgage.

Even if the buyout is amicable and all deed forms have been signed and recorded, be sure to write up a simple agreement stating what you've agreed to. This way you will have a document setting forth your entire agreement, in case a dispute arises later.

A sample Home Buyout Agreement you can tailor to your own situation is shown below.

 FORMS
The Nolo website includes a downloadable copy of the Home Buyout Agreement shown below. See the appendix for the link to this form.

Home Buyout Agreement (One Co-Owner Sells to the Other)

_____Bill Thomas_____ and _____Teresa Garcia_____ have agreed to settle the ownership of their house at_____4 Greenwood Road, Albany, New York_____, (hereafter property), as follows:

1. _____Bill_____ will purchase _____Teresa's_____ interest in the property by paying ~~him or~~ her $ _____42,000_____ , no later than _____April 1, 20xx_____ . Within _____three days_____ of this payment, _Teresa_ shall deliver to _Bill_ a signed and notarized quitclaim deed to the property. _Bill_ will handle the recordation of the deed and pay all costs of transfer.

2. _____Bill_____ agrees to purchase_____Teresa's_____ interest knowing that there are structural and roof problems in the property, and that there is a dispute with the neighbor over the use of the common driveway . _____Teresa_____ releases _Bill_ from these or any other claims arising out of the condition of the property or the title to the property.

3. _____Teresa_____ agrees to keep ~~his/~~her name on the current mortgage for at least _____one year_____ , by which time _Bill_ shall either obtain a new mortgage that does not involve _Teresa_ or sell the property.

4. _____Bill_____ will be responsible for any and all costs and obligations regarding the property, including all mortgage debt, as of _April 1, 20xx_ .

5. Either party may compel enforcement of this agreement by arbitration, at which the arbitrator may award attorneys' fees and costs to the prevailing party.

Bill Thomas
Signature

February 15, 20xx
Date

Teresa Garcia
Signature

February 15, 20xx
Date

> **SEE AN EXPERT**
>
> **Have your Home Buyout Agreement reviewed by a local broker or real estate attorney.** You'll want to make sure that any special rules covering internal buyouts are covered in your agreement.

If Both Partners Will Sell the Property to a Third Party

If neither of you wants the house, you will probably sell it on the market (most likely with a broker's help). Be sure to select a qualified broker who is sensitive to the fact that you are splitting up. The broker can handle the delicate arrangements of fixing up and showing the home, knowing that things may be tense between the two of you. But given that it's in both partners' interest to sell the property for the best possible price, try to work cooperatively.

Once you've sold the place, you still need to divide up the proceeds according to your respective percentages of ownership. Fortunately, a dispute about how much each of you owns need not slow up a sale. You can simply agree in advance to put all of the sales proceeds (or if appropriate, just the disputed portions of the sale proceeds) into a joint account requiring both signatures for anything to be withdrawn; include a proviso that the funds will not be disbursed until you jointly decide on the division and put your decision in writing. If you do not decide within some defined period of time how to divide the proceeds, you should agree that the dispute will be mediated and, if no agreement is reached in mediation, arbitrated.

If you can't resolve this dispute by negotiation or mediation, consider submitting it to binding arbitration. You can use a real estate broker (if the dispute is primarily about the value of each party's contribution) or an attorney (if the dispute is primarily legal) as your arbitrator.

However, if one partner is unusually obstinate, a court lawsuit might be required, so that there is a judge ready to issue orders to compel the difficult partner to behave.

TIP

Take advantage of capital gains tax breaks. If you sell your home, either to your partner or to a third party, you can probably shield $250,000 of your profits from capital gains tax. See "Check Out Legal and Tax Issues Before Transferring a Share of Your House" in Chapter 6 for details.

Dividing Other Real Estate

If you own other real estate, such as an investment property or a vacation home, you will need to go through the same process as with your primary residence. Decide whether either of you is going to buy out the other's share or whether you are going to sell the place to a third party. Then figure out the property's value and resolve any competing claims for reimbursement for extras. Once the dust settles, you may even be able to continue owning the property jointly as an investment. This is especially likely if you agree to hire a professional management company so you don't have to deal with each other over the details. But if you go this route, be sure to have a written management agreement for the property—you are business partners now, not lovers, so you need to act in a businesslike manner.

Foreclosure Divorce: Dealing With the Underwater House

We've all heard the horror stories about homeowners who owe more on their mortgage than the house is currently worth—either because they borrowed too much when values soared, or because they bought at the top of the market in an area where property values have tanked. While it's hard for anyone to deal with this sort of situation, it's particularly onerous when the owners are breaking up. We call this a "foreclosure divorce," where the couple is dealing with the failure of their relationship just as they are hit with a possible foreclosure of their home.

Part of what is so difficult in this situation is that you are faced with making some very tough decisions—choosing between a variety of undesirable options. You may each have different attitudes toward debt, legal obligations, and credit ratings, and you are likely to approach the process in very different ways. Some folks are eager to get things resolved immediately, whereas others procrastinate forever, hoping the dire situation will simply disappear.

Here are some tips for making your way through these very troubled waters:

1. **Start out by learning the hard facts about your situation.** Is your loan "recourse" or not (which means you are personally liable if the house is worth less than the total mortgage)? If you have more than one loan, learn the legal rules for each of your loans.

2. **Learn the tax rules for defaulting on a mortgage.** In some instances you can be taxed on the "imputed income" of not having to pay back your loan, especially if you borrowed money after you bought your house and didn't spend it on renovating the house. Every state has its own rules, and the IRS has its own set of rules, and they are changing constantly, so be careful here. You may not be able to find the answers online—it may require the advice of a tax expert.

3. **Figure out what it is costing to keep the house, compared with letting it go.** Sometimes the mortgage payments are so much higher than rental costs that it simply isn't worth keeping it, even if you think the values are going up.

4. **Once you evaluate these factors and have a clear sense of the options, each of you should decide what is in your personal best interest, and you should then talk about your different perspectives.** It is quite likely that you will have different positions, either because one of you already has rotten credit or has no choice financially, or because one of you has stronger feelings about the house or about handling your financial obligations.

5. **If you are going to try to negotiate a workout with a lender or undertake a short sale, designate one of you to handle the negotiations.** (A short sale is where you sell the property for less than the loan and the bank agrees to release the mortgage in exchange for avoiding having to deal with a foreclosure.) It just doesn't work to have two warring parties dealing with a financial or real estate institution.

6. **Your goal should be to find a solution that works best for both of you —or at least, causes the least amount of damage to either of you.** This is one area where talking to a real estate agent, mortgage broker, experienced lawyer, or mediator can be really helpful, as they may be able to think of creative solutions you haven't considered. If no solution emerges that is acceptable to both of you, you are in a tough bind: Most likely the more obstinate one is going to get his or her way—simply by not paying or not cooperating with the lender to work out any compromise solution.

Other Financial Assets and Liabilities

Joint bank accounts, stock accounts, and savings accounts also must be distributed when you separate. The same joint ownership rules that apply to real estate apply here—having both names on the account creates a legal presumption that it's owned 50-50, and whoever claims a larger share or is not named on the account normally has to prove an agreement (such as the ones in Chapter 4) stating otherwise. Once again, if disagreements arise, try to reach a compromise. But if you can't, consider mediating or, if necessary, submitting the dispute to binding arbitration. In the meantime, make sure you instruct the bank or stockbroker to hold all the funds pending a jointly signed release, to do away with worries that either party will abscond with all of the money.

> **SEE AN EXPERT**
>
> **See a financial consultant (in addition to your lawyer) if substantial assets are involved.** This is particularly important if you have no written agreement, you have lived together a long time, and the breakup is not amicable.

You will also need to make arrangements to allocate any joint debts. Your first task is to close all joint credit accounts immediately. Do this even if you have to act unilaterally (but, of course, inform your partner). Next, if possible, the two of you should promptly pay outstanding balances. (If you made an agreement to share assets and can't agree about who owes how much, one possibility is to divide your debts according to the same percentages as in your agreement.)

If either of you doesn't have the cash to pay his or her share of joint debts, consider having the richer one pay them up front, with the poorer one signing a promissory note promising to repay his or her ex the appropriate share of debt. (Chapter 6 includes a promissory note you can use for this purpose.) Be careful here, though, as the "creditor" partner can only collect if the "debtor" partner has the funds to pay the debt. If you don't pay off all joint debts, and the debtor partner doesn't come through, your bank will not forgive your obligation just because you had a private agreement that your partner would reimburse you later on. And even if both names aren't listed as debtors on a particular debt, if you had an agreement between you to share the debt you should honor that agreement and figure out how to allocate the debt. If one of you has taken on debts for funds that were for the other's benefit, and the "real" borrower can't pay back the loan, the legal debtor may have no choice but to pay the debt—or face the legal consequences.

Dividing a Small Business

If one or both of you have built up a small business during the course of your relationship, you may face a battle over who owns what share of it. If the business is considered a shared asset, or you can prove that there was an implied agreement between the two of you to share ownership, most courts will try to evaluate the current value of the business and determine the percentage interest of each partner. If only one partner is the true owner but the other one has contributed time or money to the business beyond what he or she has been compensated for, the courts may be willing to evaluate the situation based upon the reasonable value—called "quantum meruit"—of the nonowner's contribution. Unlike a married couple, you aren't entitled to a share of your partner's business unless you can prove that you had some kind of agreement regarding the business or performed lots of uncompensated work for it. If the business is valuable and you can't resolve your dispute, you may both need to consult lawyers experienced in small business matters.

Putting It All Together: Preparing a Settlement Agreement

Your final agreement should be a clearly written document covering all of the details of your separation. Be as specific and clear as possible and list each key provision (Who gets the car? The piano? The cat?) separately. A sample settlement agreement is shown below. You can use this as a model and substitute or incorporate clauses and sections from other agreements in this book.

Be sure you both date and sign your settlement agreement and each keep a copy. While not required legally, it's a good idea to have your signatures notarized, just in case there's a future need (in court or arbitration) to prove that the signatures on the agreement were not forged.

Your signed agreement is enforceable in court in the same way as is any other binding agreement.

 SEE AN EXPERT

As recommended many times throughout this book, have an attorney review your agreement, especially if children, a lot of money, or valuable property are involved. You also may need to consult with a tax advisor if a significant amount of money or real estate is involved.

Children: Custody, Visitation, and Support

The law can sometimes be very unfair to unmarried parents—both as it is written and as it is sometimes applied by prejudiced judges. Making matters even messier is the fact that although unmarried parents have far more rights than in the past, the law in many states is still in great flux if either adult is not a legal parent of the child.

But married or not, one thing never changes—when you split up, it's vital for your kids' current and future well-being that you try, try, try to reach a compromise about issues of custody, visitation, and support. Doing this in a constructive, humane way may be a great challenge. But, your ability to get along civilly—if not cheerfully—is the biggest gift you can give your children. Sometimes this can be accomplished

Sample Settlement Agreement

Arnie Woo and Alice Isaacs agree as follows:

1. In exchange for the promises described in this agreement dated April 10, 20xx, we agree to settle all our disputes arising out of our personal relationship and the co-ownership of our residence at 997 Pine Road, Boston, Massachusetts (hereafter residence), on the terms set forth in this Agreement.

2. Arnie shall purchase Alice's interest in our residence under a separate Home Buyout Agreement signed this same date.

3. Alice shall have sole ownership of the Audi automobile currently registered in her name, and Arnie shall have sole ownership of the Jeep Cherokee currently in both parties' names, with no equalization payment due from or to either party. Alice shall sign the required transfer document for the Jeep, which Arnie shall prepare. Arnie shall be solely responsible for all transfer costs and taxes for the Jeep Cherokee.

4. We have divided and distributed all items of shared or co-owned personal property, and any items left remaining in the residence as of the date of this agreement shall be the property of Arnie.

5. Any disputes arising out of this Agreement or out of our relationship shall be discussed in mediation, as follows:

   a. We will try to select a mediator jointly, and if no mediator is selected within two weeks of any demand for mediation, each one of us will nominate one friend, and the two of them shall select the mediator.

   b. We will meet no fewer than three times to mediate, in two-hour sessions, within one month of the selection of a mediator, with all costs of mediation split equally between us. The mediator will determine the time and place of each meeting.

   c. Until we reach an agreement, compromise offers or proposals presented by either of us will be confidential and, if mediation fails, will not be disclosed to anyone else or used in any subsequent arbitration or court proceeding.

   d. If we reach an agreement, it will be set out in writing and signed by both of us. If one of us fails to abide by it and an attorney is needed to enforce its terms in court, the prevailing party will have the right to reimbursement for his or her attorney's fees.

6. If, after we mediate on three occasions, no settlement is reached and we elect not to schedule any more mediation sessions, either of us may require arbitration by sending a written arbitration request to the other. If this occurs:

   a. We will jointly select an arbitrator who will conduct the arbitration under the rules of the American Arbitration Association. If for any reason we can't agree on an arbitrator within one month of the written demand for arbitration, Judge Marilyn Strauss of our local county court will select the arbitrator. By agreeing to arbitration, we each agree to give up the right to a jury trial.

   b. The costs of the arbitration will be split equally between the two of us. If either of us wishes to, she or he may bring an attorney to the hearing; however, each of us will be solely responsible for any attorneys' fees incurred.

   c. Each of us will provide the other with copies of all documents relevant to these disputes at least two weeks prior to the arbitration proceeding. At the same time, each of us will supply the other with a list of all witnesses who will be asked to testify at the arbitration hearing.

   d. The decision of the arbitrator will be binding, and either of us may enforce it through the local trial court if the other does not comply with its terms. If an attorney is needed to enforce the arbitration decision, the prevailing party will have the right to reimbursement of the attorney's fees incurred specifically for this purpose.

7. Contingent upon the implementation of the provisions of this agreement and the resolution of any disputes that arise in enforcing the terms of this Agreement, we agree to release each other from any and all claims arising out of or relating to our personal relationship, including any claim for financial compensation or property ownership.

Arnie Woo _____   _April 10, 20xx_
Signature   Date

Alice Isaacs _____   _April 10, 20xx_
Signature   Date

through open discussions between the two of you. In other situations it will require counseling, therapy, or mediation. No matter how scary or messy breaking up can sometimes be, as long as you are each determined to avoid a contested court battle and willing to put your egos aside in an effort to work together in the best interests of your child, you should be able to work out even the toughest parenting issues. One thing is sure— if you do, your children will thank you for it.

> **RELATED TOPICS**
> **The basics of the law regarding the children of unmarried couples are covered in Chapter 7, and Chapter 8 covers issues involving children from a prior relationship, including the impact of living together on custody of children from a prior marriage.** If you and your partner are arguing about your children, go back and reread these chapters for an overview of how the law generally regards your nonmarital family. While the discussion in Chapter 8 is focused on custody issues when a married couple separates, much of the general advice also applies to custody of children of an unmarried couple.

If you can't reach a compromise on the issues of custody (who has legal authority over the child and where does the child live), visitation (how often and under what conditions does the noncustodial parent spend time with the child), and child support (whether the noncustodial parent contributes anything to the costs of raising the child), you will have to submit your dispute to the court system.

While the specific rules for child custody and visitation differ from state to state, here is a general overview.

Your Rights Under the Law

Your rights vary depending on whether one or both of you are legal parents of the child.

If Both of You Are Legal Parents

If both of you are legal parents of the child—either because you are both biological parents, because you have jointly adopted your child, or because the nonbiological parent has been able to obtain a legally valid stepparent or second-parent adoption—your child-related disputes will normally be handled in the same way as if you were a divorcing married couple. Since you won't have a divorce action pending in family court, you will need to file a parentage or custody petition if you can't resolve everything by agreement. Even if you have reached an agreement, sometimes it makes good sense to open a parentage proceeding and file your agreement so that the court can enforce it quickly if either parent violates the terms.

You may be required to attend mediation sessions or submit to an investigative process with county personnel. After listening to a county social worker's report about each of your parenting abilities and home situations, the local family court judge will have great discretion to make child custody and visitation decisions. The legal standard the judge will always follow is the "best interests of the child."

In most states you can propose your own custody and visitation arrangements and you don't even have to formalize things with a court order. And even if you've been arguing in court for a while, you can still reach an agreement, and so long as the judge believes it to be sensible (and especially if you both agree to follow it), the court will often approve your proposal. But if the judge doesn't agree with your proposal, in some instances the judge can substitute a modified or even completely different arrangement.

Where Paternity Is an Issue

Sometimes there is a disagreement over whether the male partner is really the father of a child raised by an unmarried couple. If a paternity or parenthood statement has not been signed when a breakup seems imminent, do it right away. (Chapter 7 discusses this in detail and provides a form.) It's important to everyone's interests (most especially the father's) that this step be accomplished. If for any reason the father refuses to sign, this is a strong indication that he may not support his child, and the mother will want to seriously consider going to court to get a judgment of paternity and a child support order.

Custody. In many states the court will order that both legal parents retain legal custody (sometimes called joint, or shared, legal custody). This means each parent has equal authority over the key decisions in the child's life (such as education and medical care), as well as a legal obligation to care for and support the child. Physical custody (where the child lives) is typically shared, with the child spending some days or weeks with one parent and living with the other parent at other times. In other states the court will award both parents "joint legal custody," but stipulate that one parent will be the "primary physical custodian." In still other states, it is far more common for the court to award one parent "primary physical custody," while the other is given "reasonable rights of visitation." But no matter what the legal description, the usual practical result is that the parent who isn't the primary caretaker during the school week is granted liberal rights to spend weekends or other time with the child (called visitation) unless there is a strong reason why this would be detrimental to the child.

Visitation. Like custody, you and your former partner can make visitation arrangements voluntarily. However, if your efforts are frustrated by the actions of the other parent (or someone else with physical custody of the child), you will have to file a court action and request that a judge order visitation.

Support. In every state, both legal parents are required to support their children financially, regardless of whether they were married when the child was born. When it comes to supporting a child financially, if parental incomes are unequal—or if one parent is shouldering most of the costs of taking care of the child—the family law court will order the noncustodial parent to contribute a specified sum of money to the costs of child rearing (called child support), often by referring to published guidelines establishing minimum levels of support. The family law court will retain the right to modify this amount should parental incomes or the needs of the children change. Again, if you can work this out informally, or better yet, sign a settlement agreement, no court action is needed. But even if you reach a formal agreement, the court in most states retains jurisdiction for future support orders.

The amount of child support awarded will depend on how much each parent makes and spends on housing, health care, and other necessary child-related expenses, including dental bills and private school tuition. The monthly amount can vary widely, and each state has its own child support guidelines that are set by statute. We encourage you to learn what the court would likely order in your particular situation, so that you have an idea of where to start in the negotiation process. Most family law practitioners are familiar with the standard child support formulas in your area, and there's lots of information available online as well. You can use a search engine to look for child support calculators for your state and get a general idea of how much support is appropriate in your case.

If support isn't paid voluntarily, the parent with custody or someone acting on the child's behalf (such as the welfare department) can sue the noncustodial parent to obtain a court order setting the amount of child support the noncustodial parent must pay. If the noncustodial parent doesn't pay what he or she owes, but has the ability to do so, the district attorney can prosecute him or her under criminal laws.

For more details on legal requirements regarding child support, see Chapter 8.

If Only One of You Is the Legal Parent

Where only one parent is the legal parent (for example, you came along after your partner's child was born and did not adopt the child), the legal situation is very different. In most states, the nonlegal parent has few legal rights if the parties are unmarried, and in a few states, none at all. This is usually true even if the nonlegal parent has helped raise the child for many years and is a primary giver of care and emotional support.

In many states, the hard truth is that the nonlegal unmarried parent has no legal standing to seek custody, either partial or full. And, as if this isn't unfair enough, in some states the nonlegal parent doesn't even have the right to request court-ordered visitation privileges—no matter how emotionally close that parent had been to the child. A decision of the U.S. Supreme Court in 2000 (*Troxel v. Granville*, 530 U.S. 57 (2000)) denied grandparents the right to obtain legal visitation of their grandchildren over the mother's objection, and a similar outcome might result in a legal claim by a former partner.

Fortunately, an increasing number of states are beginning to recognize the right of nonlegal parents to visit the children they have helped raise; Ohio, Virginia, and Wyoming allow "any interested person" to bring an action for visitation, and Arizona allows visitation to persons who act as parents to a child. A few courts have even awarded custody to the nonlegal parent, especially where that person was the primary caregiver. And when the natural parent is unfit or deceased, it is more likely for courts to give the nonlegal parent a major child-rearing role (and sometimes to prefer the nonlegal parent to grandparents or other blood relatives).

Conversely, because the law does not fully recognize their relationship with the child, nonlegal parents rarely have any financial obligations to support their partner's children. And where a nonlegal parent offers to help support the children in exchange for visitation or custody rights, most courts say no.

In some states, second-parent adoption may be available even if you and your partner are not living together any more (but only if there isn't already a second parent, such as the legal parent's former partner). If the legal parent is willing to formalize the nonlegal parent's relationship with the child, consult a lawyer about whether a second-parent adoption is a possibility. If it is, you can incorporate a paragraph to the effect that you intend to complete a second-parent adoption into the parenting agreement shown below.

If you are being denied the right to continue actively participating in the life of a child you have helped raise, your first step should be to attempt to work with the legal parent to create a practical arrangement that meets the child's needs as well as yours. Failing this, you will need to consider whether it makes sense to attempt to achieve your goals by going to court. But before you do, you'll want to do the necessary legal research in your state or consult a lawyer to answer the following questions:

- Does your state allow you to present a claim for visitation or partial custody if you are not a legal parent? If so, what are the procedures you must follow? The technical term is likely to be "de facto" or "psychological" parent. And what legal standards does the court follow in deciding whether to grant your request?

- If no such procedures have been established in your state or if the law is hostile to unmarried couples, are you willing to be a "test case" and try to forge new law?

TIP

The legal parent should put the child's interests first. If you are the sole legal parent and you are facing a custody and visitation challenge from your former partner, make your children's emotional needs—not yours—the highest priority. If your children want to remain in close contact with your ex (who they may have lived with for many years), put their wishes before your own. Of course, if you truly believe that your former partner's interaction with your kids will be seriously harmful, by all means resist his or her claims for custody or visitation.

RESOURCE

The best resource on child custody and support. *Nolo's Essential Guide to Child Custody & Support*, by Emily Doskow, is a comprehensive guide on the subject—from choosing a custody plan to enforcing child support orders. It covers everything from types of custody and how child support is determined to custody trial procedures.

Parenting Agreements

Because unmarried couples don't get divorces, judges and lawyers aren't necessarily involved in the child-raising issues. Unmarried couples can make their own parenting agreements covering support, custody, and visitation issues, either on their own or with the help of a mediator or family law counselor. If it's possible, this is the best approach. Be mindful, however, that if the physical or financial well-being of your child is at risk, most courts will not consider themselves bound by your agreement, and may order modifications or additional obligations. Also, if court proceedings are likely, you're unclear about your rights, or there's conflict between you and the other parent over key issues involving your child, consult an attorney. One point to bear in mind—you can't agree by contract to be a legal parent when you aren't one already—that is something only a court can order.

Remember that each of your circumstances regarding jobs, residence, and relationships are likely to change, so it's a good idea to approach your agreement with a spirit of flexibility and openness. Also, no custody, support, or visitation agreement—even one ordered by a judge—is ever permanently binding. An amount of child support that seems fair and adequate today may not be enough tomorrow. Custody with one parent may work brilliantly for a year and then sour. Your agreement must be a living document, not a museum piece frozen under glass. It should be a statement of needs and expectations that lays a solid foundation for the changes and additions that will surely come.

Below are examples of two parenting agreements you can use as models to write your own:

- Parenting Agreement (Both Parents Are Legal Parents), and
- Parenting Agreement (Only One Parent Is a Legal Parent).

Be sure you both date and sign any agreement you reach and each keep a copy. It's a good idea to have your signed agreement notarized if you anticipate any future need (in court or arbitration) to prove that the signatures on the agreement are not forged.

CAUTION

Arbitration clauses may be unenforceable. In some states, you cannot make an agreement to arbitrate child custody. Check this out before including this provision in your agreement.

RESOURCE

How to prepare a parenting agreement. *Building a Parenting Agreement That Works: Child Custody Agreements Step by Step*, by Mimi Lyster Zemmelman (Nolo), is an excellent resource for preparing and negotiating a comprehensive parenting agreement covering custody and visitation. We highly recommend you read this when preparing your own agreement.

Sample Parenting Agreement (Both Parents Are Legal Parents)

Sam Matlock and Chris Woodling make this agreement because they have decided to stop living together, but wish to provide for the upbringing and support of their children, Natasha and Jason. Sam and Chris agree as follows:

1. Until Jason and Natasha are both in school, Chris will have primary responsibility for child care during the week and Sam shall pay child support to Chris in the amount of $800 per month per child.

2. Jason and Natasha will spend most weekends and at least one month during the summer with Sam; Sam will be available for babysitting at least two weekday nights.

3. All major decisions regarding Jason and Natasha's physical location, support, visitation, education, and the like will be made jointly by Sam and Chris; Jason and Natasha will be involved in the decision making to an extent consistent with their ages.

4. When both Natasha and Jason are in school, Chris intends to return to her career as a marketing consultant at least part time and Sam intends to return to school to finish his Ph.D. Sam and Chris contemplate that during this period, Chris will earn enough to support the children and Sam will take on a larger share of the child care duties.

5. Both Sam and Chris commit themselves to conduct their affairs without resorting to lawyers and courts, if possible. If communication becomes difficult, they promise to participate in joint counseling. If any issue becomes impossible to resolve, they will submit the dispute to binding arbitration. However, the parties acknowledge that the local family court will have jurisdiction over any child-related dispute. Should either party assert any legal claim, we will submit a copy of this agreement to the judge as guidance for resolving the dispute.

6. Any dispute arising out of this agreement will first be mediated by a mutually acceptable mediator, whose role will be to help the parties arrive at a solution. If good faith efforts to arrive at a solution with the help of a mediator prove to be fruitless, either party may make a written request to the other that the dispute be arbitrated or submitted to the local family court.

Sam Matlock
Signature

May 4, 20xx
Date

Chris Woodling
Signature

May 4, 20xx
Date

Sample Parenting Agreement (Only One Parent Is a Legal Parent)

This agreement is made on January 1, 20xx, between Edward Donato and Sarah Friedan of Cincinnati, Ohio, regarding the parenting of the minor child Brenda Sue Donato.

We agree as follows:

1. This agreement concerns the parenting of Brenda, who was adopted legally by Ed on July 15, 20xx, six months before he met Sarah. Because Brenda has been raised equally in our home for the last several years and is equally bonded to both of us, we intend that Brenda shall continue to be raised by both of us.

2. We agree to work cooperatively to share physical custody of Brenda, and we agree that it is in Brenda's best interests that we continue to do so for the foreseeable future.

3. We shall each contribute equally to the financial costs of raising Brenda.

4. We agree that each of us will either maintain our current residence or will live within twenty (20) miles of the other's current residence until such time as Brenda reaches the age of 18, and that if either of us changes our residence outside of this distance without the other person's written consent, the person moving will lose the right to have Brenda in his or her physical custody (but not the right to visit with her frequently).

5. We agree that Sarah shall have the same rights and obligations to Brenda as if she were her legal parent. Should any dispute arise between the parties, Ed shall not at any time assert that Sarah is not a parent of Brenda or that she has any lesser parental status than any other party, by virtue of the lack of legal parentage by Sarah.

6. In the event of any dispute between us regarding the custody, care, financial support, or upbringing of Brenda, we hereby agree that we will in good faith attend at least four mediation sessions, to be held weekly, with the cost of mediation to be shared equally by us.

7. We acknowledge that the District Court of the State of Ohio will have jurisdiction to resolve all matters regarding the enforcement of this agreement and the custody, visitation, and support of Brenda. However, Ed willingly agrees to allow the court to determine the custody, visitation, and/or support of Brenda without asserting as a defense Sarah's nonlegal parental

status. In any court proceeding, a copy of this agreement shall be submitted to the court as guidance for the court's decision.

8. If any attorneys' fees or costs are incurred by either of us in a court proceeding regarding the custody, visitation, or child support of Brenda, the court will have jurisdiction to award attorneys' fees and costs as provided by the relevant sections of this state's family code, even though the proceedings may be in a parentage or other action rather than in a dissolution or separation proceeding.

9. Sarah is hereby nominated by Ed as the guardian for the person and estate of Brenda, in the event that Ed becomes unable to care for Brenda, to serve without bond. If Sarah cannot serve as Brenda's guardian, then Ed's mother, Elaine Meritt, will be nominated to serve as guardian.

10. This agreement is the only agreement between us with respect to Brenda. It can only be changed if we both agree, and changes must be in writing. In the event that any part of this agreement is held to be invalid, the remainder of the agreement will be in full force and effect.

Edward Donato | _January 1, 20xx_
Signature | Date

Sarah Friedan | _January 1, 20xx_
Signature | Date

Lawyers and Legal Research

When to Hire a Lawyer.. 331

How to Find a Good Lawyer 332

What Kind of Lawyer Do You Need?.. 332

Getting Recommendations for a Lawyer 333

How to Evaluate Your Choices 335

Legal Fees 335

Although this book explains many of the legal issues faced by unmarried couples living together, here are some suggestions for those of you who wish to expand on what you learned here or get additional help from an expert.

The best ways to get more information are:

- **Legal research.** When you want more information on a specific legal issue, such as your state rules on common law marriage.

- **Do-it-yourself legal resources.** When you're ready to do a routine legal task such as prepare a simple will or child support modification, you may find good forms and instructions from the court, a book, software, or relevant website. We provide lots of recommendations throughout this book on resources that can help with different legal matters involving unmarried couples who live together.

- **Small claims court.** When your dispute with your former partner concerns a relatively small amount of money, as might be the case when you don't agree about how to divide a rental deposit. Depending on the state, you can normally sue in small claims court for an amount between $2,500–$10,000 without the need for a lawyer.

- **Legal advice.** When you want specific information from a lawyer or want a lawyer to review a form you've prepared, such as a living together contract or will.

- **Mediation.** When you and your partner (or former partner) are disputing who owns what, how to divide jointly owned property, or another issue, such as child custody, and you want help in attempting to work out a solution.

- **Legal representation.** When you want to explore the possibility of initiating a lawsuit, or you're defending a lawsuit and want a lawyer to represent you. For example, if you claim that you and the person you lived with had an oral contract to share property, but that person denies it, formal legal help may be necessary. You will also need to hire a lawyer if you are going through a contested child custody case or are adopting a child with your partner.

Which strategy is best depends on your personal circumstances, especially the complexity of your legal issue. A hybrid approach is best for many people: Educating yourself on the basics and then consulting a lawyer for the more complicated stuff.

When to Hire a Lawyer

As a general rule, you should consider hiring an attorney if the amount at stake is high enough to justify the legal fees or if there is something the lawyer can do for you that you can't do or choose not to do yourself. There are many reasons you might want a hire a lawyer:

- to review documents you've prepared using this book, such as your living together agreement
- to complete more complex forms than we've provided—for example, if you have complicated estate planning needs
- to check your state laws or court cases on a particular topic, such as adoptions or child custody
- to give you strategic advice on how to handle a particular legal problem—for example, a money-related dispute with an ex-partner
- to help you negotiate—perhaps if you and your ex are in the midst of a nasty breakup
- to assist you in an adoption
- to handle a real estate transaction
- to represent you (whether in a court or in a mediation session) in a breakup; when you need help obtaining rights to a child you helped raise; or if you believe your rights are being seriously violated or there's a lot of money at stake.

If you and your living together partner have only an oral contract to share all property, and your partner dies with no will or other estate plan, you'll likely need a lawyer to help you assert your claim that a portion of the property in your deceased partner's name actually belongs to you. Also, for almost any situation involving children—like adoption (other than stepparent adoption), or a fight to see a child you've been coraising—you will undoubtedly need a lawyer to represent you. You might also need representation if you've unsuccessfully tried every possibility to settle your breakup issues.

RESOURCE

If you do end up fighting in court, read *Represent Yourself in Court: How to Prepare & Try a Winning Case,* **by Paul Bergman and Sara J. Berman (Nolo).** This book will help you pursue your own lawsuit or can help you understand and monitor what your lawyer is doing.

> ### Before You Start Looking for a Lawyer
>
> To avoid the serious initial mistake of hiring the wrong lawyer, determine exactly what you need done. The best lawyer to review a document may be different from the best lawyer to mediate a dispute or represent you in court. Before you start your lawyer search, write down:
> - your goal—for example, buying a house together, reviewing a living together agreement, or mediating a property settlement with your ex-partner versus fighting it out in court
> - the kind of help you're seeking—full representation, legal coaching, or assistance with a particular task, and
> - how much time and money you can devote to achieving your goal.

How to Find a Good Lawyer

If you conclude that you need a lawyer, be aware that only a few lawyers know enough about the legal issues of living together to be worthy of serious consideration. Unfortunately, lawyers who don't know much about the law in this area (or who are even hostile to the idea of living together) can't always be trusted to decline this type of work. It's up to you to be sure any lawyer you consult has the skills and experience you need. Lawyers who specialize in marital law don't necessarily understand the law of cohabitation.

You might need to speak with several lawyers before finding one who is right for the job. Don't hire the first lawyer you pick out of the phone book —treat this like the important (and potentially expensive) decision it is.

What Kind of Lawyer Do You Need?

Like doctors, most lawyers specialize. Some handle divorces, some give tax advice, some work on corporate mergers, some do criminal defense, some do bankruptcies. And a few general practitioners still do a little of this and a little of that. But unless a lawyer has experience in your particular legal area of concern, keep looking.

A family law specialist is often a good place to start when dealing with living together issues. However, if your legal issue involves a breakup with your unmarried partner or a living together agreement, make sure the lawyer has the nonmarital law experience you need. If your legal issue involves a marital divorce, child custody, child support, or adoption, hire a lawyer who specializes in the specific area of family law you're looking for—which may be the same as that which applies to married couples. Bear in mind that a lawyer with deep experience in mediating child custody disputes may not have done many contested divorces when one ex-spouse is living with another person. It pays to work with a lawyer who has handled cases similar to yours.

Similarly, if you need help with estate planning or a real estate purchase or sale, find someone with legal expertise in that area. A family law expert is probably not the right person, since estate planning and real estate are considered their own specialties.

One of the main services a good lawyer can provide in these sorts of situations is counseling—not therapy, but rather, helping the two of you figure out what really is best for you, given all your practical, legal, and emotional concerns. You may think you need a co-ownership agreement, but maybe it's best if just one of you owns the house. You may have a desire to sue your former partner for alimony, but once you find out the rules in your state you may decide that negotiating for ownership of the car or the computer is more prudent. A good lawyer is not just a technical writer or interpreter of legal codes—he or she also will be able to guide you through the process to help you meet your long-term goals.

Getting Recommendations for a Lawyer

The best way to start looking for a lawyer is to get recommendations from sources you trust.

Lawyers and other legal professionals. If you know a lawyer who doesn't do the kind of work you need, you should still ask them for recommendations—that lawyer is very likely to know someone who specializes in whatever specific area you're looking for. Your business attorney may recommend a lawyer who can help you and your partner adopt a child together.

Friends, family, and social and professional networks. It can be very useful to canvass friends and acquaintances to get the names of lawyers they found helpful for a similar legal task or problem, such as another unmarried couple who have gone through a breakup or bought a house together. However, don't make a decision solely on the basis of someone else's recommendation. A lawyer who does well for one client, or has the time and energy to devote to one case, won't necessarily do as well on another case. Your friend's breakup may have been quite different from yours; her lawyer might have been great about working out all the financial details, while your main concern may be child custody. And different people have different responses to a lawyer's style and personality—so the bottom line is, you should meet with any attorney to make sure it's a good fit.

Lawyer directories. Many online lawyer directories, including Nolo's (www.nolo.com) can help you find an attorney. Other reputable directories include Justia's (www.justia.com) and the Martindale-Hubbell Legal Directory (www.martindale.com). Just be sure you are considering someone who has experience in nonmarital law.

Nolo's Lawyer Directory

To help consumers choose attorneys, Nolo's lawyer directory provides a detailed profile for each attorney listed. The profile contains information about the lawyer's experience, education, fees, and, perhaps most important, the lawyer's general philosophy of practicing law (information not typically available from other lawyer directories). Nolo has confirmed that attorneys have valid licenses and are in good standing with their bar associations. All attorneys have taken a pledge to communicate regularly with clients, provide an estimate of the time and cost involved, and provide a clear, fair written agreement that spells out how they will handle the legal matters and how clients will be charged. For more information, see www.nolo.com/lawyers.

How to Evaluate Your Choices

Once you have the names of some attorneys whose experience matches your needs and who look like they might possibly be a fit for you, it's time to do some checking before you whittle your list to the top two or three candidates.

Here are some ways to get started:

- Check the attorney's website and any other online resources to find out as much as you can about the lawyer's background, experience, attitude, and fees.
- Check with your state bar association (see www.abanet.org to find yours) to see whether the lawyer has been the subject of any disciplinary action.

Once you're ready to meet likely candidates, call to make an appointment. The lawyer or a member of the lawyer's staff will usually ask you questions about your issue. They may also ask who referred you and the names of other people involved in your case, in order to avoid conflicts of interest—for example, if you're in a dispute with your ex-partner, and the lawyer has represented your ex in the past, he or she won't be able to represent you now. If the lawyer is available and handles your type of legal matter, you can arrange a meeting at the lawyer's office. The lawyer may send you an intake form to complete before you come and might ask you to bring certain documents with you, such as financial statements or information about property you own, depending on your particular legal issue.

For advice on hiring and working with lawyers, including what to ask a prospective attorney, see www.nolo.com/lawyers/tips.html.

Legal Fees

Some lawyers don't charge for an initial meeting to discuss the possibility of representing a client, and some charge a relatively low flat fee, like $50 or $75, for a half hour consultation. However, most will charge their regular hourly rate for the first meeting to discuss the facts and law relating to your legal problem and the possibility of working together.

Generally, this fee should cover any time the lawyer spends before the meeting reviewing documents or researching the law and the time spent in meeting with you.

In family law matters, you're most likely to be charged an hourly rate. The rate depends on the attorney's location, experience, reputation, and type of legal work. For example, the rate for trial work is usually higher than for other work. If your lawyer works for a law firm (rather than on his or her own), other members of the firm will also charge hourly, often at different rates. For example, your lawyer might charge $250 per hour and bill a paralegal's time at $100 per hour and an associate's time at $200.

You should always sign a fee agreement with a lawyer. Many states require that lawyers enter into written agreements, often called retainer agreements or representation agreements, with clients to set out fees and other terms of the lawyer-client relationship. Whether or not your state requires one, get your fee agreement in writing.

Your written agreement should explain:

- the lawyer's fee, how it will be calculated, and whether there's any cap on the fee
- hourly fees of anyone else who might work on the case, such as legal assistants or investigators, and what that work might be
- how the lawyer's fees will be paid (for example, within 15 or 30 days of billing)
- who will pay for costs, such as court fees (in most cases, that will be you, the client)
- how often you will be billed
- how much detail the bill will include (an itemized monthly statement, listing the hours on each task, is standard), and
- whether you will need to pay a deposit in advance (often called a "retainer"), how much this will be, and how it will be used.

A written agreement will help prevent disputes about legal fees and clarify the relationship you expect to have with the attorney and the services the lawyer will provide. Some agreements state how each of you can end the agreement and explain how you expect to work together, such as any decisions the lawyer can make alone and which require your approval.

Doing Your Own Legal Research

If you want to do some legal research on your own, you can find most statutes (laws) and court decisions (cases) online, at no cost. To get started, check out the Laws and Legal Research section at nolo.com, www.nolo.com/legal-research. It explains how to do legal research and provides links to federal, state, and local laws.

Another site that will help with your legal research is www.law.cornell.edu (a site maintained by Cornell Law School), which has information and links on state, local, and federal laws as well as court cases.

You may also find useful information on your state's court websites. To find yours, check out the National Center for State Courts at www.ncsc.org.

If you need help finding something, go to the reference desk at your public library; many have good law collections. If your county maintains a law library that's open to the public (often in a courthouse, state-funded law school, or a state capital building), you can get help there, too, from law librarians.

RESOURCE

Legal research help. *Legal Research: How to Find and Understand the Law*, by Stephen Elias and the Editors of Nolo, gives easy step-by-step instructions on how to find legal information. It can help you navigate the law library and the Internet.

How to Use the Downloadable Forms on the Nolo Website

Editing RTFs 340
List of Forms Available on the Nolo Website 341

This book comes with eforms that you can access online at
www.nolo.com/back-of-book/LTK.html
You can open, edit, save, and print the RTF files provided by
this book using most word processing programs such as Microsoft *Word*,
Windows *WordPad*, and recent versions of *WordPerfect*.

Editing RTFs

Here are some general instructions about editing RTF forms in your
word processing program. Refer to the book's instructions and sample
agreements for help about what should go in each blank.

- **Underlines.** Underlines indicate where to enter information.
  After filling in the needed text, delete the underline. In most
  word processing programs you can do this by highlighting the
  underlined portion and typing CTRL-U.
- **Bracketed and italicized text.** Bracketed and italicized text indicates
  instructions. Be sure to remove all instructional text before you
  finalize your document.
- **Optional text.** Optional text gives you the choice to include or
  exclude text. Delete any optional text you don't want to use.
  Renumber numbered items, if necessary.
- **Alternative text.** Alternative text gives you the choice between two
  or more text options. Delete those options you don't want to use.
  Renumber numbered items, if necessary.
- **Signature lines.** Signature lines should appear on a page with at least
  some text from the document itself.

Every word processing program uses different commands to open,
format, save, and print documents, so refer to your software's help
documents for help using your program. Nolo cannot provide technical
support for questions about how to use your computer or your software.

> **CAUTION**
> **In accordance with U.S. copyright laws, the forms provided by this
> book are for your personal use only.**

List of Forms Available on the Nolo Website

Go to **www.nolo.com/back-of-book/LTK.html**

The following files are in rich text format (RTF):

Form Title	File Name
Agreement of Joint Intent Not to Have a Common Law Marriage	NoCommonLaw.rtf
Agreement to Keep Property Separate	PropertySeparate.rtf
Attachment A—Separately Owned Property	AttachmentA.rtf
Agreement to Share Property	ShareProperty.rtf
Attachment B—Jointly Owned Property	AttachmentB.rtf
Agreement for a Joint Purchase	JointPurchase.rtf
Agreement Covering Rented Living Space	RentedSpace.rtf
Letter Requesting Permission to Add a Roommate	AddRoommate.rtf
Contract for Equal Ownership of a House	EqualOwnership.rtf
Promissory Note	PromissoryNote.rtf
Contract for Unequal Ownership of a House	UnequalOwnership.rtf
Agreement for One Person to Move Into the Other's House and Become an Immediate Co-Owner	ImmediateCo-Owner.rtf
Agreement for One Person to Move Into the Other's House and Become a Co-Owner Gradually	GradualCo-Owner.rtf
Acknowledgment of Parenthood	Parenthood.rtf
Short-Term Agreement Regarding Separation and Housing	SeparationHousing.rtf
Agreement to Protect Property During a Breakup	ProtectProperty.rtf
Agreement to Mediate and Arbitrate	Mediate.rtf
Home Buyout Agreement	HomeBuyout.rtf

Index

A

Abandonment of child, defined, 216
Absent parent, 216
Acknowledgement of Paternity (sample), 211
Adjustable rate mortgage (ARM), 152–153
Adoption of children
  consultation with lawyers, 218
  fit parent status, 217–218
  by single-parents, 218–221
  state and federal laws on, 212–217
  by stepparents, 218–221
Adultery, 9, 229–230, 231
Advance Health Care Directive, 116
Affidavits, 263
Affordable Care Act, 112
Agents. *See* Durable power of attorney for finances; Durable power of attorney for health care
Agreement Covering a Joint Project (sample), 66–67
Agreement Covering Homemaker Services (sample), 69–70
Agreement Covering Rented Living Space (sample), 130–131
Agreement for a Joint Purchase (sample), 58–59
Agreement for Artists/Writers/Inventors (sample), 73–74
Agreement for One Person to Move Into the Other's House and Become a Co-Owner Gradually (sample), 200–203

Agreement for One Person to Move Into the Other's House and Become an Immediate Co-Owner (sample), 194–197
Agreement for People in School (sample), 76–77
Agreements, introduction to. *See* Living together agreements
Agreement to Keep Property Separate (sample), 45–46
Agreement to Mediate and Arbitrate (sample), 299–300
Agreement to Protect Property During a Breakup (sample), 288
Agreement to Share Property (sample), 52–53
Alabama
  common law marriage state, 15
Alaska
  marital status definition includes unmarried couples, 123
  prohibits employment discrimination based on marital status, 95
Alimony
  cohabitation and, 224, 241–243
  contracts for unmarried couples and, 21
  effect of fault-based divorce on, 230–231
  nonmarital dissolution and, 279–280
  seniors and cohabitation, 33
Alternative dispute resolution (ADR), 293–300

Alternatives to Marriage Project (website), 12

American Law Institute, 280

American Society of Home Inspectors (ASHI) (website), 160

Amortization calculators (website), 184

Annual percentage rate (APR), of loans, 156

Arbitration. *See* Formal arbitration

Arizona
  adopts Uniform Premarital Agreement Act, 31
  covenant divorce, 229–230
  recognizes unjust enrichment doctrine, 25
  visitation rights, 323

Arkansas
  adopts Uniform Premarital Agreement Act, 31
  alimony and cohabitation, 242
  child custody and cohabitation, 234
  covenant divorce, 229–230
  illegal to falsely represent yourself as married couple when not, 96
  prohibits employment discrimination based on marital status, 95

Artists/writers/inventors agreements, 71–75
  Agreement for Artists/Writers/Inventors sample, 73–74
  preparation of, 71–72, 75

Asset, defined, 40

Asset transfers. *See* Transfer of assets

Attorney-in-fact. *See* Durable power of attorney for finances; Durable power of attorney for health care

Attorneys. *See* Lawyers, consultation with

Automobile insurance, 63, 111

B

Bank accounts, 78, 84–85, 260–261, 262, 282, 314

Bankruptcy, 84

Beneficiaries
  for life insurance, 109–110
  naming for IRAs, 106
  naming for retirement plans, 105–106
  in property control trusts, 268–272
  transfer-on-death beneficiaries, 261

Best interests of the child, 231, 233–234, 238, 320, 324

Best interests of the pet, 288

Business formation, 67
  See also Small businesses

Business reasons, as justification for housing discrimination, 124

Buying and investing together
  keeping property separate, 90–91
  mix/commingling of property, 91
  property acquired after cohabitation, 90–91
  property acquired before cohabitation, 90
  sharing costs/not ownership, 91
  See also Home purchase/ownership

Buying homes. *See* Home purchase/ownership

Bystander rights, 119

C

California
  adopts Uniform Premarital Agreement Act, 31
  alimony and cohabitation, 242
  competing presumptions of fatherhood case, 215
  dual real estate agents, 145

house inspections, 159

implied contracts, 25, 85

marital status definition includes unmarried couples, 123

opposite-sex domestic partnership registration, for 62 or older, 10–11

paternity statements, 208–209, 210

prohibits discrimination against unrelated adults living together, 145

prohibits employment discrimination based on marital status, 95

prohibits religious belief as justification for discrimination against unmarried couples, 123

recognizes unjust enrichment doctrine, 25, 27

relocation and unemployment insurance, 113–114

workers' compensation death benefits, 113

California Supreme Court, *Marvin v. Marvin* (1976), 20–25

Capital gains, 102–103, 312

Caring Connections, 118

Car insurance, 63, 111

Car purchase agreements
joint ownership, 63–64
leases, 64
sole ownership, 63
state vehicle registration, 63

Child custody
best interests of the child, 231, 233–234, 238
Cooperative Custody Agreement sample, 237
court decision required for, 30
court-ordered evaluations for, 235
custody agreements, 236–238
joint custody, 232, 280

legal custody, 232

mediation for disputes, 235, 236, 238

physical custody, 232, 321

from prior marriage, impact of living together on, 231–232

separation of unmarried couples and, 280–281, 316, 319–324

trials for, 235, 238–239

Children. *See* Divorce and child custody, while living with someone else; Family and unmarried parents; Wills and estate planning

Child support
court orders for, 322
paternity statements and, 208
prior marriage divorce and, while living with someone else, 232, 239–241, 243
separation of unmarried couples and, 280–281, 316, 319–324
state laws on, 208, 213, 239–241
wage attachment for, 241

Child support calculators, 322

Child Support Enforcement Act, 239

Child visitation
prior marriage divorce and, while living with someone else, 233, 238–239
separation of unmarried couples and, 280–281, 316, 319–324
state laws on, 323
U.S. Supreme Court on, 323

City government
domestic partnership registrations, 10
domestic partnership registrations for employees, 11–13
health insurance for domestic partners, 111
prohibits discrimination against unrelated adults living together, 123

Civil unions. *See* Domestic partnerships

Closing costs, for home purchase, 160–161

COBRA (Consolidated Omnibus Budget Reconciliation Act), 112

Cohabitation
court decision on part-time, 23–24
historical definition, 9
legal history of, 20–25
varying state definitions of, 242
See also Living together agreements; Seniors and cohabitation

Colorado
common law marriage state, 15
competing presumptions of fatherhood case, 215

Common law marriage
criteria for, 14–15
intestate succession laws, 15
Joint Intent Not to Have a Common Law Marriage Agreement sample, 16, 98
joint tax returns, 14–15
same-sex marriage and, 14–15
sharing last names, 14, 98
Social Security, 104
state government and laws on, 14–17
state recognition of, 15–16
statutory law on, 13–14

Conflict resolution, post-separation, 289–300
Agreement to Mediate and Arbitrate sample, 299–300
formal arbitration, 297–300
informal negotiation via third parties, 294
mediation for disputes, 294–296
ten steps for, 289–293

Connecticut
adopts Uniform Premarital Agreement Act, 31

case on implied contracts and unjust enrichment, 27
estate tax, 266–267
prohibits employment discrimination based on marital status, 95

Consensual sexual activity, 8–9

Conservatorship proceedings, 117

Contract for Equal Ownership of a House (sample), 173–176

Contract law, 20, 22

Contracts. *See* Living together agreements

Cooperative Custody Agreement (sample), 237

Copyright, 71, 72

Cornell Law School (website), 337

Cotenants. *See* Leases and rental agreements

Counseling, prior to separation, 56

County government
domestic partnership registrations, 10
domestic partnership registrations for employees, 11–13
law libraries, 337
recording of agreements, 57
recording of home ownership contracts with, 171–172

Court costs, 37

Court orders
for alimony, 230, 241
for child custody disputes, 235
for child support, 322
compliance with, 239
for evictions, 125
for legal parent status, 324
mediation, 235
for name changes, 97, 98–99
paternity statements as equivalent to, 209, 212

Covenant divorce, 229–230

Creative work. *See* Artists/writers/inventors agreements

Credit. *See* Debt and credit

Credit agreements, 62

Credit cards, 62, 87–89, 282

Credit reports, 86–87

Credit scores, 149, 150

Custody. *See* Child custody

D

Death benefits, under workers' compensation, 112–113

Debt and credit, 83–94
  authorized users of credit cards, 89
  checking credit reports, 86–87
  discrimination by credit grantors, 92–94
  joint bank accounts, 84–85
  joint credit card accounts, 87–89
  partner's debts, 84
  post-separation, 314–315

Debt-to-income ratio, 149–150

Deed, defined, 161

Delaware
  adopts Uniform Premarital Agreement Act, 31
  estate tax, 266–267
  prohibits employment discrimination based on marital status, 95

Digital privacy, 284

Directives for health care decisions, 114–117

Discrimination
  against adoption by unmarried couples, 218
  based on religious beliefs, 123
  based on sexual orientation, 123
  by credit grantors, 92–94
  employment, 94–96

  legal remedies for, 94–96, 97
  in real estate negotiations, 144–145
  when renting together, 122–125
  when traveling together, 96–97

Disinheritance, 253

Dispute resolution. *See* Conflict resolution, post-separation; Formal arbitration; Lawyers, consultation with; Mediation

District of Columbia
  adopts Uniform Premarital Agreement Act, 31
  common law marriage state, 15
  estate tax, 266–267
  illegal to register in hotels under false name, 96
  living together agreements enforceable, 23
  opposite-sex domestic partnership registration, 10–11
  prohibits employment discrimination based on marital status, 95

Divorce and child custody, while living with someone else, 223–243
  abandonment of child, 216
  adultery claims, 229–230, 231
  best interests of the child, 231, 233–234, 238
  child custody evaluations, 235
  child support, 232, 239–241, 243
  child visitation, 233, 238–239
  Cooperative Custody Agreement sample, 237
  covenant marriage/divorce, 229–230
  custody agreements, 236–238
  division of marital property, 230
  grounds for divorce, state-by-state listing, 226–230
  impact on alimony, 230–231, 241–243

impact on child custody, 231–232

types of custody, 232

DNA tests, 213

Domestic partnerships

  defined, 10

  employer fringe benefits and, 11–13, 111–112

  as implied contract, 13

  property agreements, 49–50

  seniors and, 10–11

  Social Security and, 104

  state and local laws, 10–13, 91, 111

  surrogate medical decisions, 115–116

  welfare benefits and, 109

Domestic violence, 283

Down payments, for home purchase, 150–152, 155

Durable power of attorney for finances, 117–118

Durable power of attorney for health care, 116–117

E

Employer-based health insurance, 111–112

Employment discrimination

  based on marital status, 94

  federal law on, 96

  statutory law on, 94–95

Equal Credit Opportunity Act (ECOA), 92–93

Escrow and closing costs, for home purchase, 160–161

Estate plans

  impact of remarriage on, 32–33

  importance of for surviving partner, 246–247

  plan components, 247–249

  See also Wills and estate planning

Estate tax, 109, 264–268

Eviction, 129

Executors of wills, 257

Express contract, defined, 22

Ex-spouses. *See* Divorce and child custody, while living with someone else

F

Fair Credit Reporting Act (FCRA), 86

Fair Housing Acts, 123

False names, 96

Family and unmarried parents, 205–222

  abandonment laws, defined, 216

  Acknowledgement of Paternity sample, 211

  birth certificates, 207–210

  child adoption, 217–221

  establishment of paternity, 208–212, 221

  inheritance rights of children, 222

  legal obligations of parents, 206

  legitimacy of children born within, 212–217

  naming the baby, 207

  public/private benefits for children, 221

  See also Separation of unmarried couples

Family counseling, 232

Family law attorneys. *See* Lawyers, consultation with

Fault-based divorce, 225–226

  See also Divorce and child custody, while living with someone else

Federal Housing Authority (FHA), 150–151, 155

Federal National Mortgage Association (Fannie Mae), 153

Federal taxes. *See* Taxation

Federal Trade Commission, 93

Final arrangements. *See* Funerals and final arrangements

Financial aid for college-age children, 32
Financial decisions
    authorization for, 114–117
    durable power of attorney for, 117–118
Financing and mortgages, for home
    purchase, 148–157
    comparison of lenders, 156–157
    down payments, 150–152, 155
    government loans, 150–151, 155–156
    househunting online, 148
    loan preapproval vs. prequalification,
        157
    mortgage information online, 154
    sources of loans/mortgages, 153–154
    types of mortgages, 152–153
First-time home buyer programs, 154
Fixed rate mortgages, 152–153
Florida
    adopts Uniform Premarital Agreement
        Act, 31
    prohibits employment discrimination
        based on marital status, 95
    recognizes unjust enrichment doctrine,
        25
Foreclosure divorce, 312–314
Formal arbitration
    Agreement to Mediate and Arbitrate
        sample, 299–300
    clauses in agreements, 42, 50
    pre-trial agreement points, 297–298
    See also Mediation
Forms
    downloadable via Nolo website, 341
    editing RTFs, 340
    See also specific sample forms by title
Fornication, historical definition, 9
Fringe benefits
    eligibility for, 12
    employee domestic partner benefits,
        11–13

same-sex marriage and, 13
    as taxable compensation, 12
FSBO (for sale by owner), 147, 148
Funerals and final arrangements, 272–273

G
Gays. See Same-sex couples
Georgia
    criteria for common law marriage, 15
    restrictions on contract rights for
        unmarried couples, 24
Gift tax, 67, 71, 79, 85, 198, 262, 264–268
Government loans, for home purchase,
    150–151, 155–156

H
Hawaii
    adopts Uniform Premarital Agreement
        Act, 31
    estate tax, 266–267
    opposite-sex domestic partnership
        registration, 10–11
    prohibits employment discrimination
        based on marital status, 95
Health care directives, 115–117
Health insurance, 111–112
Holographic wills, 254
Home Buyout Agreement (One Co-
    Owner Sells to the Other) (sample), 310
Homemaker services agreements, 67–71
    Agreement Covering Homemaker
        Services sample, 69–70
    preparation of, 67–68
    Social Security and, 104
Homeowners' insurance, 110
Home purchase/ownership, 141–204
    Agreement for One Person to Move
        Into the Other's House and Become
        a Co-Owner Gradually sample,
        200–203

Agreement for One Person to Move Into the Other's House and Become an Immediate Co-Owner sample, 194–197

changing title, 168–169, 199

Contract for Equal Ownership of a House sample, 173–176

Contract for Unequal Ownership of a House sample, 188–191

contracts for co-ownership, 170–172

equal ownership contracts, 172–186

escrow and closing costs, 160–161

foreclosure divorce, 312–314

FSBO (for sale by owner), 147

house inspections, 159–160

joint tenancy title, 164–167

joint tenancy with right of survivorship, 56

move in/immediate co-owner agreements, 192–199

move in/phased co-owner agreements, 199–204

post-separation division of, 305–314

Promissory Note (Loan Repayable in Installments With Interest) sample, 183

real estate agents and, 145–147

real estate offers, 158–159

reference to in living together agreements, 50

seller discrimination based on marital status, 144–145

sole owner title, 162–164

taking title, 161–168

tenants in common title, 167–168

timing of planned marriage and, 162

unequal ownership contracts, 187–192

See also Financing and mortgages, for home purchase

Hotel registrations, 96, 97

Househunting online, 148

See also Home purchase/ownership

House inspections, for home purchase, 159–160

Housing discrimination, 122–125, 144–145

Housing Discrimination Hotline, 124

Housing rights law, 123–124

Human Rights Campaign, 111

I

Idaho

adopts Uniform Premarital Agreement Act, 31

criteria for common law marriage, 15

Illegitimacy. *See* Legitimate/illegitimate child distinction

Illinois

adopts Uniform Premarital Agreement Act, 31

alimony and cohabitation, 242

estate tax, 266–267

opposite-sex domestic partnership registration, 10–11

prohibits employment discrimination based on marital status, 95

restrictions on contract rights for unmarried couples, 24, 42

Immoral behavior, use of term, 125

Implied contracts, 13, 19, 23–27, 85, 251

Incapacity. *See* Financial decisions; Medical decisions, authorization for

Income taxes, 99–103

claiming children as dependents, 102, 104

claiming partner as dependent, 101–102

homemaker services and, 67, 71, 104

home sales and capital gains exclusion, 102–103, 312

joint returns in common law marriage, 14–15

Social Security and, 101

tax rates and standard deduction, 100

Indiana

adopts Uniform Premarital Agreement Act, 31

case on implied contracts and unjust enrichment, 27

competing presumptions of fatherhood case, 215

Individuals with disabilities, 116–117

Inheritance. *See* Estate plans; Wills and estate planning

Inheritance laws, 32–33, 247–248

Inheritance tax, 266–267

Injury, and loss of consortium, 119

Insurance

for home purchase, 151

impacts on unmarried couples, 109–114

life insurance, 109–110, 262–263, 268

private mortgage insurance, 151

property inventories for, 49

Intellectual property law, 71

Inter vivos trusts, 259–260

Intestate succession laws, 15, 63, 247

Inventors. *See* Artists/writers/inventors agreements

Investments. *See* Buying and investing together

Iowa

adopts Uniform Premarital Agreement Act, 31

common law marriage state, 15

inheritance tax, 266–267

IRA (Individual Retirement Account)

beneficiary designation, 106

distribution of, 107

rollovers, 107–108

IRS (Internal Revenue Service). *See* Taxation

J

Job change/relocation agreements, 79

Joint custody, 232, 280

Joint Intent Not to Have a Common Law Marriage Agreement (sample), 16, 98

Jointly and severally liable, use of term, 126–127, 129, 131

Jointly Owned Property attachment (sample), 54

Joint ownership agreements, 49

Joint project agreements

Agreement Covering a Joint Project sample, 66–67

legal advice for businesses, 67

preparation of, 65

Joint purchase agreements. *See* Shared ownership of joint purchase agreements

Joint Purchase Agreement When Only One Partner Is the Legal Borrower (sample), 60–61

Joint tax returns, and common law marriage, 14–15

Joint tenancy

car purchase agreements, 63

home ownership, 56, 164–167

right of survivorship and, 261–262

Justia (website), 334

K

Kansas

adopts Uniform Premarital Agreement Act, 31

common law marriage state, 15

Kentucky

criteria for common law marriage, 15

inheritance tax, 266–267

L

Landlords. *See* Leases and rental agreements
Last names, sharing of
change of name by court order, 98–99
change of name by usage, 98
in common law marriage, 14, 98
legal impacts, 97–98
Lawyer Directory (website), 43, 334
Lawyers, consultation with, 329–337
business formation, 67
child adoption, 218
hiring of, 331–335
home purchase/ownership, 161, 171, 198
intellectual property rights, 72
lawsuits and court actions, 301–303
legal fees, 335–336
marital dissolution, 294
modification of agreements, 55
not required for written agreements, 25
property control trusts, 268
remarriage by seniors, 33
review of living agreements with assets, 38, 42
review of premarital agreements, 31
trustworthy recommendations of, 333–334
when registered and relocating from recognition to nonrecognition state, 11
while married/separated from another person, 41–42
wills and estate planning, 253
Leased cars, 64
Leases and rental agreements, 121–139
Agreement Covering Rented Living Space sample, 130–131
communication with landlords, 124–125
as cotenants, 126–129
discrimination based on marital status, 122–125
housing rights law, 123–124
landlord objections to move ins, 132, 135–137
Letter Requesting Permission to Add a Roommate sample, 137
move in rental increases, 136
post-separation, 304–305
requesting landlord's permission, 135–136
security deposits, 136–139
small claims court, 127–128
Tenant's Notice of Intent to Move Out and Substitute New Tenant sample, 133–134
as tenants/subtenants, 129–132
Legal fees, 37, 335–336
Legal issues, overview, 7–34
common law marriage, 14–17
domestic partners, 10–14
issues for seniors, 32–33
living together contracts, 17–25
marriage impact on prior agreements, 28–32
sex relationships, 8–9
written living together agreements, 25–32
Legal research, 337
See also Lawyers, consultation with
Legitimate/illegitimate child distinction, 215, 221
Lesbians. *See* Same-sex couples
Letter Requesting Permission to Add a Roommate (sample), 137
Life beneficiaries. *See* Property control trusts
Life insurance, 109–110, 262–263, 268
Living together agreements, 35–79
overview, 17–25, 39–42

differ from marriage contracts, 22

downloadable forms via Nolo website, 341

enforceability after marriage, 28–32, 43

exclusion of nonmonetary issues, 18–19, 41

importance of written agreements, 25–32, 37–39, 278

initialing of changes, 51

invalidity if based on sexual services, 23, 28, 41

Joint Intent Not to Have a Common Law Marriage Agreement sample, 16, 98

legal history of, 20–25

modification of, 55

periodic review of, 55

premarital agre
ements and, 28–32, 43

property division at death clauses, 56

terminology to avoid, 28

while married/separated from another person, 41–42

See also Separation of unmarried couples; *specific types of agreements*

Living trusts, 259–260

Living wills, 116

Loans, 72, 75, 91

See also Financing and mortgages, for home purchase

Loss of consortium lawsuits, 119

Louisiana

child visitation, 239

covenant divorce, 229–230

nonadoption of Uniform Transfers on Death Security Registration Act, 261

restrictions on contract rights for unmarried couples, 24

Lover, use of term, 28

M

Maine

adopts Uniform Premarital Agreement Act, 31

competing presumptions of fatherhood case, 215

estate tax, 266–267

illegal to register in hotels under false name, 96

Maintenance support. *See* Alimony

Marriage equivalent registrations, 10–11, 91

Married couples

enforceability of living together agreements upon marriage, 28–32, 43

state-imposed contract and, 17–18

state rental laws and, 123

tax breaks for, 265–266

travel discounts for, 96–97

See also Divorce and child custody, while living with someone else

Martindale-Hubbell Legal Directory (website), 334

Marvin v. Marvin (California Supreme Court/1976), 20–25

Maryland

estate tax, 266–267

inheritance tax, 266–267

marital status protection vs. single people, 123

prohibits employment discrimination based on marital status, 95

tenant restrictions, 145

workers' compensation death benefits, 112–113

Massachusetts

estate tax, 266–267

marital status definition includes unmarried couples, 123

prohibits employment discrimination based on marital status, 95

prohibits religious belief as justification for discrimination against unmarried couples, 123

relocation and unemployment insurance, 113

Mediation

Agreement to Mediate and Arbitrate sample, 299–300

for child custody disputes, 235, 236, 238

clauses in agreements, 38, 42, 129

court orders for, 235

post-separation, 294–296, 299–300, 304

See also Formal arbitration; Lawyers, consultation with

Medicaid, 114

Medical decisions, authorization for, 114–117

Medical expenses

liability for partner's, 114

seniors and cohabitation, 33

Meretricious consideration, 20, 28

Michigan

cohabitation case, 95

prohibits discrimination against unrelated adults living together, 145

prohibits employment discrimination based on marital status, 95

prohibits religious belief as justification for discrimination against unmarried couples, 123

Minnesota

estate tax, 266–267

marital status protection vs. single people, 123

prohibits employment discrimination based on marital status, 95

written requirement for living together agreements, 23

Missouri

eviction of unmarried couples, 145

Modification of agreements, 55

Montana

adopts Uniform Premarital Agreement Act, 31

common law marriage state, 15

prohibits employment discrimination based on marital status, 95

Mortgages. *See* Financing and mortgages, for home purchase

Multiple Listings Service (MLS), 148

N

Names. *See* False names; Last names, sharing of

National Association of Homebuilders (website), 148

National Association of Realtors (website), 148

National Center for Health Statistics (website), 207

National Center for State Courts (website), 337

National Child Support Enforcement Association, 240

National Coalition Against Domestic Violence, 283

National Domestic Violence Hotline, 283

National Gay and Lesbian Task Force (NGLTF) (website), 9

Nebraska

adopts Uniform Premarital Agreement Act, 31

inheritance tax, 266–267

prohibits employment discrimination based on marital status, 95

Nevada
  adopts Uniform Premarital Agreement
    Act, 31
  opposite-sex domestic partnership
    registration, 10–11
  workers' compensation death benefits,
    113
New Hampshire
  criteria for common law marriage, 15
  prohibits employment discrimination
    based on marital status, 95
New Jersey
  adopts Uniform Premarital Agreement
    Act, 31
  case on implied contracts and unjust
    enrichment, 27
  estate tax, 266–267
  inheritance tax, 266–267
  marital status definition includes
    unmarried couples, 123
  opposite-sex domestic partnership
    registration, for 62 or older, 10–11
  prohibits employment discrimination
    based on marital status, 95
  prohibits religious belief as justification
    for discrimination against unmarried
    couples, 123
New Mexico
  adopts Uniform Premarital Agreement
    Act, 31
  loss of consortium, 119
  prohibits employment discrimination
    based on marital status, 95
New York State
  alimony and cohabitation, 242
  estate tax, 266–267
  marital status protection vs. single
    people, 123
  nonrecognition of implied contracts, 23

  prohibits discrimination against
    unrelated adults living together, 145
  prohibits employment discrimination
    based on marital status, 95
  rejects unjust enrichment doctrine, 25
No-fault divorce, 225, 227–229, 230
  See also Divorce and child custody,
    while living with someone else
Nonmarital agreements. *See* Living
  together agreements
Nonmarital dissolution. *See* Separation of
  unmarried couples
Nontaxable gifts, 267
North Carolina
  adopts Uniform Premarital Agreement
    Act, 31
  case on implied contracts and unjust
    enrichment, 27
  employment discrimination case, 94
  illegal to falsely represent yourself as
    married couple when not, 96
North Dakota
  prohibits employment discrimination
    based on marital status, 95
Notarization
  of home ownership contracts, 171–172
  of paternity statements, 212
  for premarital agreements, 31
  for written agreements, 25, 57
Nursing home expenses
  liability for partner's, 114
  seniors and cohabitation, 33

O

Ohio
  criteria for common law marriage, 15
  visitation rights, 323
Oklahoma
  common law marriage state, 15

Online resources
  househunting online, 148
  legal research, 337
  mortgage information, 154
  See also Websites
Oral agreements, 19, 26, 48, 251, 331
Oregon
  adopts Uniform Premarital Agreement
    Act, 31
  case on implied contracts and unjust
    enrichment, 26
  estate tax, 266–267
  prohibits employment discrimination
    based on marital status, 95
  workers' compensation death benefits,
    113

P

Palimony, use of term, 21
Parental rights. *See* Adoption of children;
  Family and unmarried parents; Paternity;
  Separation of unmarried couples
Parenting Agreement (Both Parents Are
  Legal Parents) (sample), 326
Parenting Agreement (Only One Parent
  Is a Legal Parents) (sample), 327–328
Partner, use of term, 3
Part-time cohabitation, 23–24
Patent law, 71
Paternity
  Acknowledgement of Paternity sample,
    211
  child support and, 208
  establishment of, 208–212, 221
  notarization of, 212
  state laws on, 208–212
  statements as equivalent to court
    orders, 209, 212
  U.S. Supreme Court on, 210, 213, 222

Patriot Act, 98
Payable-on death (POD) bank accounts,
  260–261
Pennsylvania
  cohabitation case, 95
  criteria for common law marriage, 15
  inheritance tax, 266–267
Pensions
  impact of remarriage on, 32
  survivor benefits, 106
  See also Retirement plans
Permanent restraining order, 283
Personal agreements, 41
Personal property
  annual updates of lists, 51
  defined, 40
  inclusion of listing in property
    agreements, 47, 48–49, 51
  Jointly Owned Property attachment
    sample, 54
Pets, during separation, 288
Physical abuse, 283
Physical custody, 232, 321
POSSLQ (Person of the Opposite Sex
  Sharing Living Quarters), 3
Premarital agreements, 28–32, 43
Prenuptial agreements, 29
Private mortgage insurance (PMI), 151
Probate, avoidance of, 106, 258–263
Promissory Note (Loan Repayable in
  Installments With Interest) (sample),
  183
Promissory notes, 63, 72, 75, 91,
  182–185, 192, 315
Property, defined, 40
Property agreements, 43–57
  Agreement to Keep Property Separate
    sample, 45–46

Agreement to Share Property sample, 52–53

inclusion of domestic partnership issues, 49–50

ownership of personal property, 44–49

retention of printed copies, 51

Separately Owned Property attachment sample, 47

sharing of property, 50–51

Property control trusts, 268–272

Property division at death clauses, 56

Property ownership

domestic partnership and, 13

premarital agreements and, 29

written contracts for, 13

See also Buying and investing together; Home purchase/ownership; Separation of unmarried couples; Wills and estate planning

Property Ownership Agreement (sample), 250

Property title. *See* Home purchase/ownership; Titles to property

Prostitution. *See* Meretricious consideration

Public benefits, 108–109, 208, 221, 256

Q

Quantum meruit, defined, 315

Quicken (software), 177

Quicken WillMaker Plus (software), 254, 255, 273

R

Real estate agents, 145–147

Real property, defined, 40

Recognition states, 11

Religious belief, as justification for treatment of unmarried couples, 123

Relocation agreements. *See* Job change/relocation agreements

Remarriage, issues for seniors, 32–33

Rental agreements. *See* Leases and rental agreements

Rent control, 136

Renters' insurance, 110

Representation agreements, 336

Retainer agreements, 336

Retirement plans, 105–108

beneficiary designation, 105–106

rollovers, 107–108

transfer-on-death beneficiaries, 261

wills and, 106

Revocable living trusts, 259–260

Rhode Island

adopts Uniform Premarital Agreement Act, 31

common law marriage state, 15

estate tax, 266–267

Rollovers, in retirement plans, 107–108

S

Safe deposit boxes, 172

Same-sex couples

housing rights law and, 123

tracking of sex laws, 9

U.S. Supreme Court on state sex laws, 8–9

Same-sex marriage, 10

common law marriage and, 14–15

fringe benefits and, 13, 112

Second-parent adoptions, 218–221, 323

Securities, 261

Security deposits, for rentals, 136–139

Seniors and cohabitation

alimony, 33

domestic partnerships, 10–11

estate planning, 32–33

increase in, 1, 3–4, 32

keeping things separate approach, 78

living together agreements, 19

medical and nursing home expenses, 33, 114

Social Security and pensions, 32

Separately Owned Property attachment (sample), 47

Separation of unmarried couples, 18, 275–328

   agreement to counseling before, 56

   Agreement to Mediate and Arbitrate sample, 299–300

   Agreement to Protect Property During a Breakup sample, 288

   child custody/visitation/support compromise, 280–281, 316, 319–324

   civil court and, 279

   closure of joint bank/credit accounts, 89

   dealing with domestic violence, 283

   division of financial assets/liabilities, 314–315

   division of home ownership, 305–312

   division of investment property, 312

   division of lease/rental property, 303–305

   division of small businesses, 315

   foreclosure divorce, 312–314

   Home Buyout Agreement (One Co-Owner Sells to the Other) sample, 310

   immediate tasks, 282, 284–289

   legal court claims, 301–303

   length of as grounds for divorce, state-by-state listing, 227–228, 229

   Marvin case, 20–25

   Parenting Agreement (Both Parents Are Legal Parents) sample, 326

Parenting Agreement (Only One Parent Is a Legal Parents) sample, 327–328

parenting agreements, 324–328

prebreakup tasks, 281–282

preparation of final settlement agreement, 316

property rights, distinguished from married couples, 278–280

provision for in property agreements, 44

Settlement Agreement sample, 317–318

Short-Term Agreement Regarding Separation and Housing sample, 286–287

steps for resolving conflicts, post-separation, 289–293

tax implications, 292

Settlement Agreement (sample), 317–318

Sex laws, 8–9

Sexual orientation, and housing rights law, 123

Sexual services, and contract invalidity, 23, 28, 41

Shared ownership of joint purchase agreements, 57–65

   Agreement for a Joint Purchase sample, 58–59

   car purchases, 63–64

   Joint Purchase Agreement When Only One Partner Is the Legal Borrower sample, 60–61

   preparation of, 57, 62

   Title Slip sample, 65

   transfer of property ownership, 64–65

Short-Term Agreement Regarding Separation and Housing (sample), 286–287

Single-parent adoption, 218

Small businesses, 67, 315

Small claims court, 127–128, 139, 296, 301, 330
Small estates procedures, 263
Social attitudes, 24, 231, 234
Social Security
  cohabitation and, 103–105
  from former marriage, 104
  homemaker services and, 104
  impacts on unmarried couples, 103–105
  income taxes and, 101
  remarriage before age 60 and, 32
  state-registered domestic partners and, 104
  taxes, 71, 103–105
  website, 105
Sodomy, historical definition, 9
Sole ownership
  car purchase agreements, 63
  home insurance coverage, 110
  home purchase, 162–164
Sound mind, defined, 116–117
South Carolina
  common law marriage state, 15
  workers' compensation death benefits, 113
South Dakota
  adopts Uniform Premarital Agreement Act, 31
Special needs trust, 256
Spousal support. *See* Alimony
Spouse, use of term, 88
Springing power of attorney, 117
State government and laws
  alimony and cohabitation, 242–243
  arbitration clauses, 325
  Bureau of Vital Statistics, 207
  child adoption, 218
  child support, 208, 213, 239–241
  common law marriage, 14–17
  discrimination based on marital status, 123
  distinction between legitimate/illegitimate children, 215, 216–217, 221
  domestic partnership registrations, 10–13, 91
  employee domestic partner benefits, 11–12
  estate tax, 266–267
  grounds for divorce, state-by-state listing, 227–229
  health care directives, 115–116
  health insurance for domestic partners, 111
  inheritance rights, 32–33, 247–248
  intestate succession, 15, 63, 247
  living together agreements enforceable, 23
  name change by court order, 99
  no-fault/fault-based divorce, 225
  oral agreements, 48
  paternity statements, 210–212
  premarital agreement laws, 29–30, 43
  retirement plans and probate, 106
  Uniform Parentage Act, 212–217
  Uniform Transfers on Death Security Registration Act, 261
  vehicle ownership, 64
  visitation rights, 323
  welfare benefits, 108–109
  wills and estate planning, 254
  workers' compensation death benefits, 112–113
  wrongful death, 119
  See also specific states
State taxes. *See* Taxation
Stay-at-home partners. *See* Homemaker services agreements

Stepparent adoptions, 218–221

Stock accounts, 314

Student/educational expense agreements, 75–78
  Agreement for People in School sample, 76–77
  preparation of, 75, 78

Student loans, 75

Subtenants. *See* Leases and rental agreements

Successor trustees. *See* Property control trusts

Supplementary trusts, 256

Surrogate medical decisions. *See* Medical decisions, authorization for

T

Tax advisors, consultation with
  asset transfers, 51
  selling share of co-owned house, 198
  separation and splitting of assets, 314
  tax-saving trusts, 268

Taxation
  domestic partner benefits as taxable, 12
  estate tax, 109, 264–268
  gift tax, 67, 71, 79, 85, 198, 262, 264–268
  impact of remarriage on, 32
  income tax, 14–15, 67, 71, 99–103, 104, 312
  inheritance tax, 266–267
  mortgage defaults, 313
  portability rule, 266
  separation and splitting of assets, 292
  Social Security, 71, 103–105
  state inheritance tax, 266–267
  transfer of assets, 85

Temporary restraining order (TRO), 283

Tenancy in common, in car purchase agreements, 63

Tenant's Notice of Intent to Move Out and Substitute New Tenant (sample), 133–134

Tenants/subtenants. *See* Leases and rental agreements

Tennessee
  alimony and cohabitation, 242

Texas
  adopts Uniform Premarital Agreement Act, 31
  cohabitation case, 95
  common law marriage state, 15
  nonadoption of Uniform Transfers on Death Security Registration Act, 261
  written requirement for living together agreements, 23

Time off agreements, 72, 75

Title Slip (sample), 65

Title slips, 65, 249

Titles to property
  names matched to agreements, 50
  property ownership agreements and, 43–44, 249
  Title Slip sample, 65
  See also Home purchase/ownership

Transfer of assets
  to avoid probate, 258–263
  property ownership, 64–65
  tax obligations, 51, 85
  Title Slip sample, 65

Transfer-on-death beneficiaries for assets, 261

Traveling and discrimination, 96–97

Trials, for child custody, 235, 238–239

Trusts
  to avoid probate, 258–260
  consultation with tax advisors, 268
  for minor children, 256
  property control trusts, 268–272
  purpose of, 253

U

Unemployment insurance, 113–114
Unequal bargaining power, 42
Uniform Parentage Act, 212–217
Uniform Premarital Agreement Act (state law), 29–31
Uniform Transfers on Death Security Registration Act, 261
Uniform Transfers to Minors Act (UTMA), 256
Unjust enrichment doctrine, 24–27
Unmarried dissolution. *See* Separation of unmarried couples
Unspoken agreement. *See* Implied contracts
U.S. Department of Health and Human Services, 208
U.S. Department of Housing and Urban Development (HUD), 124, 144, 155
U.S. Department of Veterans Affairs (VA), 150–151, 155–156
U.S. Supreme Court
  on establishment of paternity, 210, 213, 222
  on housing discrimination, 145
  on state distinction between legitimate/illegitimate children, 215, 221
  on state sex laws, 8–9
  on visitation rights, 322
Utah
  adopts Uniform Premarital Agreement Act, 31
  common law marriage state, 15

V

Vermont
  estate tax, 266–267
Violent behavior, 283

Virginia
  adopts Uniform Premarital Agreement Act, 31
  employment discrimination case, 94
  prohibits employment discrimination based on marital status, 95
  visitation rights, 323
Visitation rights. *See* Child visitation

W

Wage attachment, for child support, 241
Washington State
  estate tax, 266–267
  marital community property law applicable to unmarried couples, 22
  nonmarital dissolution, 278
  opposite-sex domestic partnership registration, for 62 or older, 10–11
  prohibits employment discrimination based on marital status, 95
Websites
  Alternatives to Marriage Project, 12
  American Society of Home Inspectors (ASHI), 160
  Caring Connections, 118
  credit reports, 86
  credit scoring, 149
  domestic violence and family law, 283
  Federal Reserve Board, 94
  Federal Trade Commission, 93, 94
  FHA loan programs, 155
  FSBO (for sale by owner) homes, 148
  Human Rights Campaign, 111
  intestate succession laws, 247
  Justia, 334
  legal research, 337
  Martindale-Hubbell Legal Directory, 334
  mortgage amortization calculators, 184

mortgage rates, 154

multilender shopping sites, 154

National Center for Health Statistics, 207

National Center for State Courts, 337

National Child Support Enforcement Association, 240

National Gay and Lesbian Task Force (NGLTF), 9

Nolo's Lawyer Directory, 43, 334

real estate calculators, 150

Realtor.com, 148

Redfin.com, 148

small claims court, 296

Social Security Administration, 105

state consumer protection agencies, 124

state estate tax, 266

U.S. Department of Housing and Urban Development (HUD), 124

VA loan programs, 156

wills and estate planning, 254

Zillow.com, 148

Welfare benefits, 108–109, 208

Wills and estate planning, 245–273

avoidance of probate, 258–263

being of sound mind, 252–254

changing or revoking wills, 257–258

common law marriage and, 15

disinheritance, 253

function of wills, 252

funerals and final arrangements, 272–273

inheritance of cars, 63

naming executors, 257

preparation of basic will, 254–258

property control trusts, 268–272

property division at death clauses, 56

property inventories, 249

Property Ownership Agreement sample, 250

provisions for minor children, 222, 254–256

retirement plans, 106

See also Estate tax; Gift tax

Wisconsin

adopts Uniform Premarital Agreement Act, 31

case on implied contracts and unjust enrichment, 26

marital status protections vs. for single people, 123

prohibits employment discrimination based on marital status, 95

Workers' compensation, 15, 112–113

Writers. *See* Artists/writers/inventors agreements

Written agreements. *See* Living together agreements; *specific types of agreements*

Wrongful death lawsuits, 119

Wyoming

visitation rights, 323

⚖ **NOLO** *Online Legal Forms*

Nolo offers a large library of legal solutions and forms, created by Nolo's in-house legal staff. These reliable documents can be prepared in minutes.

Create a Document

- **Incorporation.** Incorporate your business in any state.
- **LLC Formations.** Gain asset protection and pass-through tax status in any state.
- **Wills.** Nolo has helped people make over 2 million wills. Is it time to make or revise yours?
- **Living Trust (avoid probate).** Plan now to save your family the cost, delays, and hassle of probate.
- **Trademark.** Protect the name of your business or product.
- **Provisional Patent.** Preserve your rights under patent law and claim "patent pending" status.

Download a Legal Form

Nolo.com has hundreds of top quality legal forms available for download—bills of sale, promissory notes, nondisclosure agreements, LLC operating agreements, corporate minutes, commercial lease and sublease, motor vehicle bill of sale, consignment agreements and many more.

Review Your Documents

Many lawyers in Nolo's consumer-friendly lawyer directory will review Nolo documents for a very reasonable fee. Check their detailed profiles at **Nolo.com/lawyers**.

Nolo's Bestselling Books

Making It Legal
A Guide to Same-Sex Marriage, Domestic Partnerships & Civil Unions
$29.99

A Legal Guide for Lesbian & Gay Couples
$34.99

The Legal Answer Book for Families
$24.99

Prenuptial Agreements
How to Write a Fair & Lasting Contract
$34.99

Neighbor Law
Fences, Trees, Boundaries & Noise
$29.99

Every Nolo title is available in print and for download at Nolo.com.

⚖ NOLO *Save 15%* off your next order

Register your Nolo purchase, and we'll send you a
coupon for 15% off your next Nolo.com order!

Nolo.com/customer-support/productregistration

On Nolo.com you'll also find:

Books & Software

Nolo publishes hundreds of great books and software programs for consumers and
business owners. Order a copy, or download an ebook version instantly, at Nolo.com.

Online Legal Documents

You can quickly and easily make a will or living trust, form an LLC or corporation, apply
for a trademark or provisional patent, or make hundreds of other forms—online.

Free Legal Information

Thousands of articles answer common questions about everyday legal issues
including wills, bankruptcy, small business formation, divorce, patents,
employment, and much more.

Plain-English Legal Dictionary

Stumped by jargon? Look it up in America's most up-to-date source for
definitions of legal terms, free at nolo.com.

Lawyer Directory

Nolo's consumer-friendly lawyer directory provides in-depth profiles of lawyers all
over America. You'll find all the information you need to choose the right lawyer.

LTK16